FIGHT LIKE A GIRL

FIGHT LIKE A GIRL

How to Be a Fearless Feminist

SECOND EDITION

Megan Seely

NEW YORK UNIVERSITY PRESS • *New York*

NEW YORK UNIVERSITY PRESS
New York
www.nyupress.org
© 2019 by New York University
All rights reserved

References to Internet websites (URLs) were accurate at the time of writing. Neither the author nor New York University Press is responsible for URLs that may have expired or changed since the manuscript was prepared.

Library of Congress Cataloging-in-Publication Data
Names: Seely, Megan, author.
Title: Fight like a girl : how to be a fearless feminist / Megan Seely.
Description: Second Edition. | New York : New York University Press, [2019] |
Revised edition of the author's Fight like a girl, c2007. |
Includes bibliographical references and index.
Identifiers: LCCN 2018044169| ISBN 9781479877317 (cl : alk. paper) |
ISBN 9781479810109 (pb : alk. paper)
Subjects: LCSH: Feminism. | Women's rights.
Classification: LCC HQ1236 .S37 2019 | DDC 305.42—dc23
LC record available at https://lccn.loc.gov/2018044169

New York University Press books are printed on acid-free paper, and their binding materials are chosen for strength and durability. We strive to use environmentally responsible suppliers and materials to the greatest extent possible in publishing our books.
Manufactured in the United States of America
10 9 8 7 6 5 4 3 2 1
Also available as an ebook

Dedicated to those who fight for justice

And to my mom, Elaine, and my daughters, Molly and Lola

CONTENTS

PREFACE

How I Became a Teenage Activist

For the most part, I grew up in the small town of Aromas, California, a largely agricultural area. Early in high school, I was introduced to the United Farm Workers movement and the work of activists like Cesar Chavez and Delores Huerta. In 1987, when I was fourteen, my friends and I joined Chavez's hunger strike during the grape boycott.[1] I had to answer a lot of questions about not eating grapes, particularly after I passed out in the pool during swim practice. But once I learned about the dangers of using pesticides on foods and about the plight of most farm workers, I had to act.[2] I believed that if people only knew of the working and living conditions of the people who provide our nation's food, then something would change.

During the time of my hunger strike, I made a grocery trip with my mother. I entered the store and saw grapes in the produce section. I asked to see the managing grocer. I wanted to know where the grapes had come from and to educate the grocer about the plight of the farm workers. It took a bit of persuading, but finally someone came out to speak to me. I told him about the working and living conditions, the pesticides, the harassment, and the discrimination. Quite a crowd of shoppers had formed, unnoticed by me. I vividly remember catching a look in his eyes and realizing that not only was he not interested in what I was saying but he was irritated, and, to my surprise, I realized that I was the source of his irritation. How could he not care? I was in disbelief. I was frustrated. I was upset. But, more than anything, I was outraged. He was saying something, but I could barely make sense of it through my cloud of confusion. He wanted me to leave. I was causing a disturbance. So I did the only thing that I could think of. I grabbed a bunch of grapes and raised them above my head. Shaking them in my fists, and in the deepest, most serious fourteen-year-old voice I could muster, I yelled, "These grapes have blood on them!" I slammed the grapes against the floor. Only then did I notice the crowd. I spun around and marched out of the store. I wasn't sure where I was headed, but I had to move. A few minutes later, my mom was at my side, saying it would be a long time until we would or could go back to that store. I wasn't sure if she was speaking in support of me or out of embarrassment because of what I had just done. I didn't care.

It wasn't until years later that I found out that the grocer had tried to make my mother pay for the grapes. Not only did she refuse, but she left her shopping cart in the middle of the produce section and left the store. We never shopped there again.

My early stages of activism were so filled with passion and outrage that I was often unsure of what to do with myself. I was angry a lot and embraced the saying "If you're not outraged, you're not paying attention." Many people told me that I overwhelmed them, that I turned people off to what I was saying because I yelled. I never thought that I yelled; I thought I spoke with passion. These responses were hard to understand because I thought I had a message people needed to hear, quite frankly, whether they thought so or not. I was learning so much, and my awareness of the issues was growing, perhaps faster than my diplomatic skills. I was searching for my voice and a way to use it effectively.

Around this time, my mother began to find her voice—or at least a new one. At forty-one, she became a re-entry student at the University of California, Santa Cruz, and took classes with, and later became a teacher's assistant to, Bettina Aptheker, a women's studies instructor and a long-time activist. And, while the experience and transformation was hers, as her daughter, I was deeply affected. I would often beg my mother to take me to class with her. I had grown up in a predominately female family, one that supported strong women, but I had not been widely exposed to the political nature of being female in a male-dominated society. I grew up on a ranch with two sisters where there were no boys to do the "boys' work" and with a father who had no sons and who didn't see that as a deficiency. I grew up being told that I could do anything that I put my mind to and that my voice mattered. This, as I began to learn in Aptheker's class, was not the norm. I sat in huge lecture halls, and, while I learned about women's empowerment and many political victories, I also began to learn about violence, oppression, racism, sexism, and homophobia. And, again, I was outraged.

Four years later, when I left my mother's college for my own, I looked around for the feminist community, and I found NOW, the National Organization for Women. I began a relationship that would change the course of my life. Not in my wildest dreams did I ever imagine that, a few years later, at age twenty-eight, I would become California NOW's youngest president, leading the largest statewide feminist organization in the country at that time. I soon found myself a part of an active, vocal, and diverse group of young women and men who considered ourselves third-wave feminists. We were (and are) in a unique position of working alongside many second-wave feminists, those who came of age in the 1960s and 1970s. I am indebted to the people who mentored and guided me, women who fought similar battles before me, who had an understanding of the "big picture," and who could guide me to more effective ways of using my voice. At the same time, I believe that those of us who consider ourselves "third wavers" have something unique to offer. As a result of the efforts of our foremothers, we came of age with many of the rights and advantages that they did not have. We didn't have to fight for the right to be educated or to have a career; we could choose to obtain a safe and legal abortion, if we wanted one; we did not have to fight these struggles because the women and men who came before us already had. With these battles already waged, many of us were all the stronger, which in turn informed our experience with feminism. As third wavers joined with second wavers, we were charged with building intergenerational partnerships in which we incorporate the knowledge and experience of the women who came before us and the knowledge and experience of women who were coming of age.

For many of us the language of "third wave" gave us a position in a movement at a time when emerging young voices were not always recognized. Since writing the first edition of this book, much has changed. I am no longer with NOW and those who called ourselves "third wavers" no longer see ourselves as "young feminists." Instead, we have witnessed younger and younger people take up feminism in many diverse ways. As they enter the movement, they add new perspectives and experiences to an already rich history. The integration of new voices and varied definitions serve to expand and further our movement in critical ways.

One of the most significant aspects of the women's movement is that it gives validity to women's voices and to women's experiences. Throughout history, women have fought against the notion that they have little or nothing to contribute to politics or society. They have fought to have their voices heard, their experiences recognized, and their leadership respected. But, even within the context of the women's movement, our voices have sometimes been misrepresented. For example, in the 1960s, when middle-class white women like Betty Friedan began to talk about the frustration of being relegated to the home and their desire to be in the paid labor force, they represented only one part of women's experiences. At the same time, women of color and poor women who had long been in the paid labor force were working without fair wages, safe work environments, or recourse for rampant sexual harassment. All of these women represented the struggles that became part of the women's movement. Who got the attention, which stories were told, and which women were recognized as leaders became a political choice both within and outside the movement that created an image of feminism that did not fully recognize all its contributors. This continues to be an issue with feminism today. There is room for us all in this movement, and indeed it is essential that all voices are honored as we continue our work for social justice. I point this out not to be politically correct or to unnecessarily chastise but rather to suggest that we must embrace the experiences, perspectives, and leadership of all peoples if this movement is to continue to move forward and effect positive change. That's the kind of movement that I envision and that I hope to give voice to here.

In my work within organizations, as well as within my teaching, I have been called on to address criticism and explain the relevance both of feminism and of the feminist movement. I recognize that many see feminism as unnecessary, or too radical, or not radical enough. Many see feminism as only about white women, or lesbians, or strictly about abortion rights. While this criticism is somewhat deserved and organizations, efforts, and the academy should be answerable to their history and current-day practices, feminism does represent women of color, poor women, young women, women with disabilities, mothers, working women, lesbians, transwomen—all women. But the media, and those who actively oppose feminism, have created a campaign against our movement. From the 1998 *Time* magazine cover claiming that feminism is dead to the radio talk shows of Laura Schlesinger and Rush Limbaugh to the writings of conservative women like Christine Hoff Sommers and Anne Coulter, the so-called horrors of feminism have been force-fed to a new generation. This media hype has had a lasting imprint on the women's movement and continues to divert attention from the true goals of feminism—ending discrimination against all women and girls, securing our safety, protecting our health, ensuring equal opportunities, and respecting our gender and sexual identities.

I first wrote this book after many conversations about the relevance of feminism and after answering seemingly endless questions about young women in the movement. Questions came from active feminists, media interviews, friends, and family, all wanting to know, where are the young people in feminism today? Do they care? Are they active? Are they apathetic? I wrote this book because I see a great deal of activism among young people, but also a generation that doesn't feel that this movement belongs to them or that there is a seat at the table for their ideas and leadership. On the other hand, I see a generation of women who benefit from the gains of the feminist movement, who align themselves with the tenets of feminism but reject the term and any association with the movement. It is an interesting phenomenon that these empowered young women have little, if any, understanding of the fight that was necessary to win their rights and little connection to the fight that must continue to protect and advance rights for all women. Like the generations before, young women must be able to draw on their experiences, critique their political, social, and economic environments, and create a plan of action for instituting change. Activists today enter into a movement that has a great deal of history, and as a result are confronted with the challenge of making a place within feminism to call their own.

UPDATES FOR THE NEW EDITION

This book focuses on the voices of my generation, and those of today. I share my experiences as someone who is involved in the movement, is a self-proclaimed feminist, and has a great passion for teaching (and learning). I discuss my thoughts and my fears for the world we live in today. Beyond my voice, you will hear from women, men, trans and gender non-conforming individuals who have volunteered their opinions and views on social justice issues and the meaning of feminism in their lives.

This book is a rebuttal to the message that feminism is dead and that young people are apathetic. It is a call to action. Dispelling the myths of feminism and detailing what is at stake for women and girls today, I outline the steps for taking action toward political, social, and economic equity for all. Exploring the issues of body image and self-acceptance, education and empowerment, health and sexuality, political representation, economic justice, and violence, this book looks at the challenges that women and girls face, while emphasizing the strength that we, both independently and collectively, embody. Additionally, I delve into the politics of the feminist movement from both inside and outside the movement, exploring the history and current realities. With an emphasis on young women, I discuss what the movement and activism mean to youth today. I look at how and where we encounter feminist ideas and activism—including how we employ a critical, intersectional analysis, how we address the challenges to building multi-identity bridges and how to forge meaningful intergenerational partnerships.

Perhaps more importantly, I want the book to be used, not just read. I have included a variety of resources to aid in taking action, including "Fabulous Feminist Web Resources," with lists of websites that offer more information and an organizational community; various issue-specific timelines to aid the reader in a better understanding of the breadth of activism and social change; "Spotlight" sections that are designed to give the reader more information about a specific issue, campaign, or activist; and sections that suggest actions that call for varying degrees of involvement—Getting Started, The Next Step, and Getting Out There. But this book is far from an exhaustive list of perspective, information, or activism. My hope is that you will use this as a reference and begin to build your own set of books, resources, and organizations you can work with and to develop your own activist strategies. For the fight for justice belongs to us all. We must educate ourselves, empower one another, and unite under a common vision of creating a just society.

I write this book with this vision, looking critically at the issues that impact our lives, putting women at the center, and defining issues from the perspectives of those most affected. My focus is on self-exploration, self-discovery, and self-definition. I believe that we must speak up for what we believe in, work to end discrimination and oppression, question that which already is, and envision what is still to come. Women and girls must be shown that they are valuable, strong, beautiful, and capable. I believe in the assertion that we are entitled to equal rights—including the right to be respected in our homes and workplaces and in our choices. I believe we must learn our history so that we know the contributions of our foremothers. I believe in the safety, health, education, economic security, independence, and free will of all. In this book, I want to reclaim the idea of fighting like a girl—a phrase that is usually meant to suggest that those who fight like girls, as opposed to fighting like boys or men, don't really know how to fight and that their struggle is not real, not intense, not legitimate—just hair pulling and nail scratching. I don't agree with that characterization at all. I know how to fight, and I know plenty of women whose struggles are all too real, all too harrowing, all too dangerous. I'm here to say that not only can we fight like girls; we can win.

THE "F-WORD"

An Introduction

FEMINIST.
Bitch.
Fat.
Ugly.
Dyke.
Man hater.
Bra burner.
Hairy.
Butch.
Loud.
Militant.
Radical.
Angry.

These are some of the negative words that regularly surface when I ask people what comes to mind when they hear the word "feminist." But, for me, "independence," "strength," and "equity" come to mind when I think of feminism. After fifty-plus years of the modern feminist movement, many people have negative ideas about feminism. Ironically, many of these same people reap the benefits of feminism in their own lives. From Title IX[1] and educational equity to political representation, women in the United States have greater social, political, and economic equality today than their mothers experienced a generation ago. First and foremost, feminism simply means that women are the equals of men. A feminist is someone who supports this principle. Study after study tells us that the majority of people in the United States agree with this, but fewer and fewer want to identify with feminism. "Feminism" has thus become a bad word, the "f-word."

Fem·i·nism *n.* **1.** a doctrine advocating social, political, and economic rights for women equal to those of men. **2.** a movement for the attainment of such rights. (Definitions, unless otherwise noted, come from *Random House Webster's College Dictionary*.)

I come to feminism from a different view, a view that suggests that feminism is about equality and also equity, empowerment, strength, self-definition, and self-determination. It is an assertion that all women and girls can have not just equality in their lives but also quality of life—in the United States and around the globe. Feminism is about advocacy, activism, standing up, and speaking out. It is about fighting for social justice. And it is about working toward a solution to the continued discrimination and violence we as women face in the world—rape, sexual harassment, trafficking, police violence, sexual assault, and domestic violence. Feminism is about eradicating not just sexism but also racism, ageism, ableism,[2] sizism,[3] homophobia, and transphobia. Most of all, feminism does not have a static definition but encompasses and encourages many types of feminisms. So why do some turn away from feminism today?

THE MYTHS ABOUT FEMINISM

Many myths surround the term "feminism." The word has been distorted, diluted, misrepresented, stolen. So let's take a moment to break a few of these myths down.

Do All Feminists Hate Men?

No. It's more complicated than that. Take my friend "Jane." When Jane was five, the boys in her school wouldn't let her play on the big playground. She wanted to climb and pretend to be a firefighter like the boys did, but they teased her and pushed her off the jungle gym every time she tried to participate. When she was seven, she wanted to play football, but there was only a boys' team in her town. She was not allowed to play. When she was in high school, she was frequently

> The word "feminist" has a lot of negative stereotypes, for example the term "feminazi" and the fact that feminists are depicted as fat, angry, bitter, butch lesbians who hate men & probably couldn't get one if they tried. Christina, 21, Korean-Irish American, heterosexual, California

frustrated that the boys' athletic teams had more resources—better equipment, new uniforms, and better practice times—than did the girls' teams. These inequities have long been a source of frustration for Jane. Does this mean that Jane hates all men? No. Does she realize that there have been times in her life when her gender has caused her to be discriminated against? Yes. This awareness is disturbing and makes her apt to speak up about her experiences, but it doesn't make her hate men. Jane is now married (to a man), a successful attorney, and a mother. She is also a feminist. She continues to confront gender inequity, but, like most women, over time, she has learned that what we are up against is not just men—individually or collectively—but a system that values men over women, a system that promotes men over women, and a system that allows and, some would argue, encourages the violation of women. This system is called patriarchy. Patriarchy—the rule of the father—is at the root of a society that exalts men and the male experience—often at the cost of women and women's experience. Many young women don't want to talk about patriarchy—it is too boring, too political, and too 1970s. But, like it or not, we must name the system that orders our society if we have any hope of changing that system.

Patriarchy sets a tone for society—a tone that allows for the devaluing of women and our experiences and encourages the interpretation

Pa·tri·arch·y *n.* 1. a. a form of social organization in which the father is the head of the family, clan, or tribe and descent is reckoned in the male line. b. a society based on this social organization. 2. a. an institution or organization in which power is held by and transferred through males. b. the principles or philosophy upon which control by male authority is based.

of society through male eyes. Patriarchy allows for the overall—covert and overt—privileging of men and their experiences. As a set of spoken and unspoken rules or codes, patriarchy permeates the world's religions, political systems, and sociocultural structures, which allows for, and supports, the power of men. This explains everything from why for more than 235 years there have been only male presidents in America, to why most Fortune 500 companies are led by men, to why male movie stars often get top billing and are, by default, paid more than women. Patriarchy is also a system that creates, requires, and reinforces strict gender roles, putting men into a rigid box of allowable behavior and denying the validity of varied gender expressions and identities. As a system, it's important to understand that patriarchy is also connected to race, class, and sexual orientation. That is, if patriarchy were a pyramid, sitting at the top would be straight, white, rich men. And they would most likely be smiling, because they have had it made for a long time. Women, depending on their race, class, and sexuality, are usually not at the top—yes, there's Hillary and Oprah—but they are the exception and not the rule.

Instead, we live in a time when self-empowerment is sold to women and girls as packaged, magazine-cover "beauty" and when "acceptance" is often defined through male attention. As a result, we have women raised in an environment where far too many quietly question their strength, their value, their contribution, and their voice even as they, at times, project a public image of control. Women often embrace a belief that the sexes are treated equally, while accepting the notion that women are on display, and in existence, for male use and pleasure. American society teaches girls that their value and success are tied to their appearance and convince them to embrace this concept as their own self-definition. Playing into the patriarchy, girls dismiss feminism, all the while claiming equality as their right. The "I'm not a feminist but . . ." generation has persisted, denying feminism but embracing its rewards. And thus, in combination with the ongoing attack on feminism, the myths about the feminist movement thrive.

Are All Feminists "Bra Burners"?

The idea of "bra burning" is still commonly associated with the women's movement, although bra burnings never happened, at least not as many were led to believe. In 1968, feminists protested the Miss America pageant and, as Ruth Rosen writes in *The World Split Open*, "into a large 'Freedom Trash Can,' they threw 'instruments of

I don't look like a feminist. I do my hair, wear light make-up, and don't preach anti-men. Kathryn, 32, white, queer, Michigan

torture'—girdles, curlers, false eyelashes, cosmetics of all kinds, wigs, issues of both *Cosmopolitan* and *Playboy*, and, yes, bras."[4] At the request of city fire officials, the trash can was not lit on fire. The *New York Times* quickly began referring to the event as "bra burning." And, as Rosen writes, "by then, the media, all by itself, had ignited what would prove to be the most tenacious media myth about the women's movement— that women 'libbers' burned their bras as a way of protesting their status in American society."[5] The irony is that a vast number of the world's women do not wear bras, and I dare say that many American women have forgone the experience. But the world has not fallen apart, at least not yet, and when and if it does, I venture to argue that women and their bras will not be at the center of its demise. But, even today, girls and women equate feminism with bra burning and fear an association with such a "radical" movement.

But Aren't Feminists Fat, Ugly, and Hairy?

In the tradition of Rush Limbaugh, who called feminists "femi-nazis" and said that "feminism was established to allow unattractive women easier access to the mainstream," this is classic name calling. Most recently, we saw Donald Trump argue that Carly Fiorina, his then-opponent in the Republican primary, was not attractive enough to be president, saying, "Look at that face! Would anyone vote for that?" We might as well be on the playgrounds of elementary school or the quads of high school. The goal of this type of name-calling is to attack a woman's self-esteem, to have control over her actions, and to knock her down. If being a feminist means being fat, ugly, and hairy—traits women fear most in a culture that sets a limited definition for women's acceptable beauty—then it is no wonder that many women don't want to be labeled as such. In this sense, Limbaugh and his conservative friends, including women like Christine Hoff Sommers and Anne Coulter, have successfully stolen this word. As Bono once said, we're stealing it back.

From the early stories of "bra burners," the media and our society continue to marginalize women and their intellect, convincing many that our issues are individual, rather than structural and political. The attempt is to convince us that relationships, exercise, weight loss, clothing, and, of course, make-up are the critical issues of our lives. Make-up per se is not the issue. In fact, many women who consider themselves part of today's feminist movement are embracing their lip gloss and demanding equality in spite of it—or maybe because of it! The problem is that society places a higher value on women's appearance than on anything else, including the fight for our social, political, and economic equality. As a result, our energies are diverted, we question, or deny, our worth, and patriarchy lives on.

In 2001, when I was first elected president of the California National Organization for Women (NOW), I was asked to do numerous interviews. Much attention was paid to the fact that I was the youngest woman ever elected president of California NOW, and reporters had great interest in why someone in her twenties would embrace not only

NOW but feminism. Perhaps not surprisingly, what most reporters questioned me about was whether a feminist can wear make-up. I had been prepared to talk about economic justice, health care, reproductive freedom, LGBTIQ+ issues, and violence against women, but they wanted to talk make-up. The more important question is whether this emphasis helps women to identify with feminism. Or does it dilute the perception of its importance?

I gave my little sister a book called Feminism Is for Everyone by bell hooks and she told me she couldn't read it because she likes men. Allison, 21, white, pansexual, Colorado

The issues of make-up, or other popular magazine cover topics like relationships and weight loss, certainly should not replace or overshadow our opinions about policy, economics, or politics. Nor should it refute the importance of feminism and a feminist analysis of society.

LGBTQQIAP2S: *Lesbian, Gay, Bisexual, Transgender, Queer, Questioning, Intersex, Asexual, Pansexual, Two Spirit (2S). Sometimes another A is added for Ally. As this alphabet grows with the goal of being inclusive, often LGBTIQ+ is used to summarize.*
Transgender: *is a broad term that can be used to describe people whose gender identity is different from the gender they were thought to be when they were born. "Trans" is often used as shorthand for transgender. Some transgender people identify as neither a man nor a woman, or as a combination of male and female, and may use terms like non-binary or genderqueer to describe their gender identity. Those who are non-binary often prefer to be referred to as "they" and "them."* **(National Center for Transgender Equality)**
Intersex: *a general term used for a variety of conditions in which a person is born with a reproductive or sexual anatomy that doesn't seem to fit the typical definitions of female or male. Intersex is a socially constructed category that reflects real biological variation.* **(Intersex Society of North America)**
Asexual: *having a lack of (or low level of) sexual attraction to others and/or a lack of interest or desire for sex or sexual partners.* **(Social Justice Advocate's Handbook)**
Pansexual: *a person who experiences sexual, romantic, physical, and/or spiritual attraction for members of all gender identities/expressions.* **(Social Justice Advocate's Handbook)**
Two Spirit: *a sacred term used by Native/First-Nation peoples to represent individuals with a blend of feminine and masculine traits. Used by Native/First-Nation "LGBT communities in order to honor their heritage and provide an alternative to the Western labels of gay, lesbian, or transgender."* **(National Congress of American Indians)**

Are All Feminists Dykes and Butch?

Let's face it, society is uncomfortable with women's sexualities. Perhaps nothing is more frightening to men, and to some women, than a woman whose sexuality is defined outside the context of straight men. Moreover, when women are butch—strong, tough, and unfeminine—they are also threatening because they are seen as not needing male help. If women can take care of themselves and each other—physically and sexually—then what do they need men for? The irony is that we have a culture obsessed with lesbianism—well, faux lesbianism, at least. Sexual pairing of women is common in male-centered porn and advertising. Of course, these women are not there for the enjoyment of other women— but for men, they are the ultimate male fantasy. Calling all feminists lesbians, dykes, or butch is to equate women with these notions of being unfeminine and sexually independent from men. This negative labeling reinforces a narrow definition of woman and femaleness. It is true that many feminists are lesbian, dyke, and/or butch. It is also true that many are not. The more important and disturbing point is the widespread belief of this myth and the acceptance of the notion that homosexuality is an accusation. Homophobia is the problem, not feminism.

Is Feminism Needed Any More?

As I previously mentioned, we are often confronted with the sentiment "I'm not a feminist but . . ." Many believe today that feminism is no longer necessary, that equality has been achieved and that any hardship women encounter must be the result of their own actions. I suppose that this is an understandable reaction, given the feminist message that women can do anything. In other words, if women believe this message but have difficulty in achieving their dreams, then it must be their failure. The myths that surround feminism play into this feeling of failure and discourage women from aligning themselves with feminism. This makes it much more difficult to recognize that discrimination against women is real and that often gender serves as the source of the barrier, rather than personal "failures." Making feminism the enemy redirects our attention away from that which serves to hold us back. Instead, we need to be able to celebrate our successes and be proud of ourselves even while appreciating that feminism helped open the way to our opportunities. I have known many women friends who are talented and who work very hard in their careers but who have faced challenges because of their gender. My sister, an audiologist who works with people with hearing difficulties, frequently confronts the assumption that since she has had children and is married, her career is no longer important or has become secondary to that of her husband and colleagues. She has confronted a lack of support with regard to her childcare needs, lack of flexibility with her schedule, barriers to advancement, and attitudes of resentment from colleagues. She is a strong feminist and fortunately recognizes that her work situation is the result of gender bias and discrimination. She also recognizes that solutions to this work-life integration lie in feminist tenets. It is feminism that asserts that we need better support for the multiple family models that exist today—stay-at-home moms or dads, moms in the workplace, dual-parent-earner households, single parents, and all the many combinations we create that constitute family. We still need the support of feminism in our lives and in achieving our many goals.

Aren't All Feminists Angry?

A few years ago, I was invited to speak in a classroom at San Francisco City College. The discussion was great—we covered topics from health care and reproductive rights to pay equity and the glass ceiling. And then . . . the inevitable. From the back of the room, a young man raised his hand and said something to the effect that he understands all the "stuff" we were talking about but just can't get over the "fact" that most feminists he meets are so angry—"Not you, Ms. Seely," he quickly added. I asked him, and the class, why, given all that we had been discussing, they thought that feminists get an angry label? I guess this young man could see where I was headed, and he blurted out, "Well, I can understand the anger, but why are they so bitchy?" Here we have it—feminists are "angry bitches." Why is it that a woman who gets angry is immediately called a bitch? Why, when people are speaking of angry women, are these two terms synonymous? A man may put his fist through a wall, and, while we may think him foolish, we rarely demean his character. But we are extremely uncomfortable with women's anger. Are people afraid that if women get angry enough, they might revolt? Indeed, our collective anger might cause a stir—to say the least. But, instead, we women learn to control ourselves, not speak out of turn, keep our voices and our heads low, and ask for qualifiers for our speech.

Of course I'm a feminist—everyone should be, if they believe that all people are equal. Cassie, 19, Caucasian, straight, California

But my question is, why *aren't* we angry? All of us—female, male, gender non-binary alike? And why aren't we speaking up and acting out? I believe that the stereotypes I have described were assigned to feminists because of fear—fear of women collectively speaking out and standing up to the gross inequities and atrocities we face daily and globally. Years ago, Robin Morgan said that sisterhood is global, and it is timely to remember this and that collective sisterhood is even more powerful. What would the world look like if we said "no more"? No more to violence, no more to inequity, no more to lack of representation. What if women stood together, joined forces, and understood the common thread of oppression we collectively face? What if we realized our power? What if?

We live in a culture where women are not safe in their homes, workplaces, or schools, or on the street, where someone is sexually assaulted every ninety-eight seconds in the United States,[6] where one in four women suffer severe physical violence by an intimate partner,[7] and where one in four women experience sexual harassment on the job[8] and 48 percent of girls in grades 7 through 12 report experiencing sexual harassment at school.[9] Women are stalked, intimidated, humiliated, and violated in both their everyday lives and their "make-believe lives" of entertainment—on television, in movies, and in video games.

Less than 24 percent of the members of Congress are women.[10] Women hold a mere 4 percent of S&P 500 CEO positions and only 19.4 percent of all S&P 500 board seats,[11] and are far less likely than men to hold leadership positions in unions, despite their growing participation in union-based labor.[12] Women still experience pay inequity based on both gender *and* race. According to the National Women's Law Center, women earned on average 80 percent of what white men made in 2016.[13] When race is considered, these statistics change dramatically; African American women earn 61 percent, Latina women 53 percent, Native Hawaiian and Pacific Islander women 62 percent, and Native American women 58 percent of what white men made in 2016. The figure for Asian American women is estimated to be the highest, at 85 percent, which still isn't parity and is also a bit misleading, as the experience for women under this broad classification is greatly varied.[14]

Women have to fundraise with benefits, walks, runs, and the like to raise money for health research and services because our issues are disproportionately ignored by the National Institute of Health and other research arms. Women's reproductive health choices are consistently up for debate, with the male-dominated Congress and state legislatures blocking funding and resources and, although abortion has been legal for more than forty years, women still travel extended distances, suffer shame and blame, walk through dangerous picket lines, and put themselves at risk—not because of the abortion itself, which is ten times safer than childbirth[15] and even safer than a tonsillectomy[16]—but because of anti-choice extremists who believe that picketing, violence, and fire bombing are "pro-life" acts. And, yes, this makes me angry.

If all this were not enough, in the year 2016, we elected a man with no experience whatsoever to the highest political position in the land. And we did so following an outrageously racist and misogynistic campaign where Donald Trump threatened to build a wall to keep out Mexicans, encouraged the denial of civil liberties to anyone assumed to be Muslim, made fun of people with disabilities, called women too ugly to harass, called Hillary Rodham Clinton a "nasty woman" in the middle of a candidate debate, and was recorded boasting about his own acts of sexual assault. Since his election, the Southern Poverty Law Center reports daily of increased acts of violence against Muslims, people of color, and women. And, yes, this makes me angry.

We still have no constitutional amendment securing rights on the basis of sex—or sexual orientation, gender identity, or gender expression, for that matter. To the contrary, efforts to pass an ERA (Equal Rights Amendment) are dismissed as passé. Those most dedicated to its passage are often very resistant to expanding the ERA to include LGBTIQ+ peoples, so if passed, even though it will be a significant gain, the ERA will immediately fall short.

With violence in our lives, pay inequity and a lack of equal representation at work, challenges in balancing family demands without adequate support or accommodation, inadequate access to and research on women's health issues, and politics that define our rights without our being fully represented in the decision-making process, women continue to fight for equality and equity. We have made many gains, but we are not there yet. Better, yes; equal, no. Perhaps more disturbing than all these realities is that so many people today believe that women are equal—that it's all good, no worries. Well, there are worries, and perhaps the first and most significant worry is that people—particularly women—continue to believe that equality exists even in the face of so much evidence to the contrary.

Why am I a part of the feminist movement? Because my anger is legitimate. And because I believe that passivity is exactly what the radical conservative right wants from us so that it can continue to violate our rights and limit our resources. I also believe that anger is useful when we channel that energy into creating positive social change and improving lives. I believe that women are fierce—we are leaders, role models, and visionaries. I believe that we deserve more; we deserve better. I am a part of the feminist movement because I want girls to learn our history, to know our strength, to appreciate the gains made, and to pick up the fight. I am part of this movement because women have no secure future without feminism. I benefited from the work of feminists before me, and I will continue that work until all women everywhere enjoy a life of true social, political, and economic equality. And I am a part of this movement because, when the next generation of children ask me what I did to help, I want to be able to tell them that I did do something, that I thought of them in my actions and fought for their safety, their health, and their right to equal opportunity.

So what about these myths and labels? There's no question that the backlash that writers like Susan Faludi have written about is real. But there is also no question that women and girls are at risk. I believe that it is more important to counter these attacks on feminism with the truth of our lives. The biggest truth is that feminism, in its true definition, is supported by a majority of people. Ask women to tell their stories. Talk to your mothers and grandmothers. Learn our history—particularly the history that has been left out of our school books. Tell your story. One of the greatest gains of the feminist movement was that it recognized the legitimacy of women's voices. Use yours. Stand up. Speak out. And speak often.

WOMEN HAVE THE FEMINIST MOVEMENT TO THANK IF . . .

You vote.

You read.

You wear pants, skirts cut above your ankle, short-sleeved shirts, or any clothing that shows your skin.

You travel without a male chaperone or you drive a car.

You use, or have ever used, birth control. Or your birth control is covered by your insurance company or by state or federal funds.

You have had, or anyone you know has had, a safe and legal abortion.

You have given birth at home, developed a birth plan that was utilized during your hospital birth, your partner was present for the delivery; you have adopted a child, or you have chosen not to have children.

You own property or have credit cards or a bank account in your name.

You participate in sports.

You have run for and/or held elected office, worked on the campaign of a woman who was running for office, or voted for a woman candidate.

You have a job in the paid labor force or actively choose to stay home in the unpaid labor force to raise children.

You go to college.

You are studying religion or have become a member of the clergy.

You are openly lesbian, living with a partner; you share domestic partnership; or you were married as part of a same-sex couple.

You choose to marry, to keep your last name, to build an egalitarian marriage, or to cohabitate or remain single; you have the right to divorce.

You marry whom you want to.

You leave an abusive husband or report a rape or sexual harassment—you have legal recourse for violence against you.

Wearing corsets is a choice, not a mandate, as is wearing make-up, a bra, or high heels.

You serve in the armed forces and receive veteran's benefits.

You decide to cook or become a chef.

You pierce or tattoo any part of your body.

You climb trees, run, jump, do somersaults, or skin your knees.

SPOTLIGHT ON FEMINISM

Sometimes I feel like my whole life has been a process of coming into feminism and being a feminist. Mandy, 27, white, queer, New York

Women want equal rights . . . who wouldn't be for that besides people who are threatened by a strong willed woman who doesn't need to depend on a man? Katrina, 22, African American, lesbian, Virginia

I think that I've always been a "feminist," even before I knew it or knew what the term meant. Morgan, 27, white, heterosexual, California

It would be foolish for me to NOT identify as a feminist since the educational, social and career opportunities that I enjoy are a direct result of past feminist struggles. Mingzhao, 21, Chinese American, heterosexual, California

As a feminist, I am often teased. People have called me a "femi-Nazi," a term I abhor and, as a Jew, find repulsive. Amy, 23, Washington, DC

Personally I love the word and am proud to identify as a feminist. The word has been stolen from us and we need to reclaim it, redefine it for our generation and what's going on in our world now. Katherine, 23, Caucasian, bisexual, Florida

I am a feminist because I never liked hearing camp counselors ask for "big strong boys" to help set up the bonfire and "nice young ladies" to set out the picnic. I am a feminist because I got sick of reading textbooks written by white/heterosexual/able-bodied/middle-class men about themselves, and the god-like role they had played in shaping the whole human history. I am a feminist because I am scared to think that men can pass laws that limit my reproduc-

tive freedom. I am a feminist because I believe in compassion for all living things, and damn a world that says might makes right. Elspeth, 22, bisexual, Michigan

It was with extreme trepidation that I decided to become a self-declared feminist. I was very familiar with the implications of such a declaration in terms of how society would perceive me . . . In reality, I had always been a feminist because I have always believed in the equality of men and women. Marina, 21, Cuban, California

There's no, "I'm a feminist but . . ." for me. I'm a feminist. Period. Cynthia, 33, white, heterosexual, Massachusetts

1

FIGHT LIKE A GIRL

In my work as an activist and teacher, I hear people ask, "What can I do?" One of the main goals of this book is to answer that question. Activism can often seem out of reach, but in truth the best part of activism is that anyone can do it. Activism can easily be incorporated into our daily lives—from the conversations we have with friends to where we decide to shop. Activism is individual, but it is also collective. The action we take impacts those around us directly and indirectly. Whether small and individual or large and in a group, the steps we take to change the world connect us with others. True equity and respect have not yet been achieved; activism is still necessary. Sharing our realities to educate one another on the challenges that persist is an important step to politicizing our lives and recognizing that the issues we face are shared by others. Sometimes the largest hurdle to activism is finding commonalities with one another so that we share the common goal of ending all discrimination and creating a world where we are not only treated but also regarded as equal. Beyond this hurdle, we learn that all of our voices are valid, that activism takes many forms, and that activism can be incorporated into every aspect of our lives.

Young adults today are confronted with the challenge of how to strike a balance between personal desires and social responsibilities. We have inherited a sense of equality that leads us to believe that the fight for justice is complete. We are told that feminism and social change are no longer necessary. Unfortunately, the emphasis on individuality, along with the misconception that equity has already been achieved, leads to the failure to fully appreciate the necessity of activism and feminism.

Let there be no mistake—equity and equality are not yet enjoyed by all, and feminism is not dead. Indeed, we have achieved many rights and made many gains, but we are not there yet. The fight for true political, social, and economic justice continues. And, while we often enjoy the benefits of a fight for equality that many today were not required to undertake, we must realize that this equality is not universal, equity has not been achieved, and that it is this generation that must take up the fight. This movement belongs to us all. We each have a stake; we all can contribute. All voices, experiences, perspectives, and visions can be incorporated and represented, for we all benefit from shared and practiced equity. We can raise our voices to speak against injustice at every level—individually and institutionally. We can elect people to office at every level of government who will honor and protect us all. We need to make sure that women are represented in leadership in every social institution within our global society—so that women are represented in any and all decision-making bodies. Women must have control over their bodies, sexualities, choices, and lives. Women must be safe at each and every turn—no exception. We can join together, work together, protect and support one another. We can be individuals who also find a common ground from which to speak collectively. We can share our stories, lead by example, and be activists in our daily lives. This is what it means to fight like a girl.

> *It is terrifying how many gains have been undone or have come under serious attack in just the last two years. It serves as a powerful reminder of how much work remains to be done.* Jen, 30, white, heterosexual, Colorado

---

Grass roots *n.* 1. ordinary citizens, esp. as contrasted with the leadership or elite. 2. the people inhabiting these areas, esp. as a political, social, or economic group. 3. the origin or basis of something.

Ac·tiv·ism *n.* the practice of vigorous action or involvement as a means of achieving political or other goals, as by demonstrations, protests, etc.— ac·tiv·ist, *n., adj.*

HOW TO FIGHT LIKE A GIRL

No act is too small; you may never know the full extent of your impact. Activism is contagious. While you may be one person, your voice and actions can touch others, whose voices and actions can touch still others, and so forth until we experience change. This is how activism works. This is how Title IX was achieved, how sexual harassment was recognized, how laws are passed and policies created. Social change begins on a small level with a small group of people who envision a new way. But before we get too far, let's get right to it. Here are some actions you can take:

- Talk to friends, family, students, and/or co-workers about political or social issues that concern you. Gather information to share with them from organizations, websites, books, or classes.
- Make a phone call to an elected official, advertising sponsor, business, or school to let them know how you feel about their policies, practices, or products.
- Write a letter to the editor of your local newspaper in response to an article about women, gender, race, health care, politics, or any issue that interests you.
- Set up a table to give out information in your community or on your campus. You may need to get permission from your campus or community business, or check into using a free-speech area. Make sure that you position yourself in front of the table to hand out materials and answer questions—don't hide behind the table; be accessible. Let the table hold your materials, not you! One variation to a table is sidewalk chalking. When I was in college, we did a sidewalk chalking where we wrote meeting and event information on the sidewalk in front of the student union and main buildings—requires less people power and still gets your message out!
- Host a consciousness raising group—bring together friends, family, or colleagues to discuss an important issue.

- Organize a house party to educate and mobilize your friends to vote or to support a feminist candidate running for office. Invite people to come over to discuss an upcoming election—have each participant research a different issue and bring the information to the group. Make it a potluck, or meet over coffee.
- Work on a voter registration campaign; register people in your community to vote in the next election.
- Offer to watch the children of someone you know so that the person can go to the polls and vote.
- Give testimony at your local city hall or before the state legislature or Congress.
- Organize a human billboard action—gather some friends to line a main street in your town with signs that have a message, each sign carrying a portion of the message: for example, "Honk . . . if you . . . support . . . equity."
- Organize a candlelight vigil to raise awareness about an issue or to commemorate an important event/date. After a series of clinic bombings in northern California, I participated in a candlelight vigil that served a dual purpose—the vigil raised awareness about violence directed toward our reproductive health care providers and also provided some much-needed protection for a specific health center. We surrounded the building in shifts and camped out to protect the health center from attack that night.
- Organize a speak out, like the Take Back the Night rallies where women have the opportunity to speak about their experiences with violence in a safe and supportive environment. This can be done with any issue.
- Organize an informational picket—make signs, bring together a bunch of people, and walk back and forth in front of a business, courthouse, or legislature, sharing information with people passing by.
- Utilize social media—Twitter, Instagram, Snapchat, Reddit, and other effective sources—to share news stories, promote events, and comment on the political issues of the day. You can also create a social media campaign. For example, a student of mine created a campaign a few years ago where she posted a photo of herself holding up a sign that read "I'm a Feminist Because . . ." with her response. She created

this from a classroom discussion about a generation or more of young folks who claim the benefits of feminism and yet reject the name, the "I'm not a feminist but . . ." folks. She created a Facebook page, invited others to join her, and soon gained the attention of *Ms.* Magazine and the Feminist Majority who worked with her to attach her campaign to their already long-standing "This is What a Feminist Looks Like" project.

- Boycott—a boycott is the withholding of financial support (e.g., by refusing to buy a particular product) as a form of protest against the policies or practices of a business, institution, or organization. There are many legal guidelines for a boycott, so make sure to get legal advice before calling for one.
- Plan a girlcott or a "boycott" related to a specifically woman-centered cause. Sometimes, a "girlcott" is defined as bringing resources into an organization, business, or institution to support their efforts—in other words, the opposite of a boycott.
- Organize street theater. Dress up and act out your concerns in a public venue. During the 2000 elections, I was one of nine people who dressed up as the Supreme Court justices and then held a press conference about what we saw as a threat to the Court.
- Organize a benefit—for example, a walk-a-thon, a concert, a comedy night, an art show.
- Organize a rally—small, medium, or large. Have people come together in a central location to hear speakers and receive information about a given event.
- Organize a march—small, medium, or large. Have people gather in one place, hear speakers, and then move in an organized fashion to another location. People carry signs with political messages and/or shout chants to raise awareness about an important issue. Notably, in April 2004, the feminist movement hosted the March for Women's Lives in Washington, D.C., to emphasize the critical issues that women are facing today. The march has been called the largest march in U.S. history, with approximately 1.15 million participants![1] In 2017, in cities across the country,

people of all genders joined together to create a nationwide, even global, Women's March, protesting the presidency of Donald Trump. In 2018, following the Parkland school shooting, high school students across the country organized individual marches in their cities and towns to collectively stand against gun violence in schools.

The possibilities for action are endless; I've provided just a few ideas that I've used and taught. Be inclusive. Talk to organizations, talk to friends, and come up with your own ideas. Look for allies and partners. Don't let taking action overwhelm you; start at the level you are comfortable. Throughout this book, I offer suggestions for actions you can take related to the issues discussed in the book. Again, this list is not exhaustive. Be creative. Have fun.

Regardless of the type of action you plan, there are a few guidelines that always apply:

Don't try to do it all on your own. Involve others—delegate responsibility.

Develop a realistic timeline and follow it.

Check your W's—who, what, where, when, why. Make sure to answer these questions whenever planning. Be clear on the details.

Imagine all the things that could go wrong, and plan for contingencies in advance.

Develop a media strategy from the beginning.

Fundraise and recruit new people to help with future actions.

HOW TO BE AN ALLY

Social justice begins when we stop "othering" experiences. Prejudice and discrimination affects us all. While we may experience these uniquely and individually, the responsibility of true equity is a collaborative effort. As such, there are times when the activism we need to engage in does not directly relate to our own experience. I encourage you not to shy away from this opportunity.

Learning to be an effective ally is a skill. You have to work at being an ally; it is an ongoing process. I'll talk more about this throughout the book, but a few general guidelines include:

- Listen. First and foremost, be a good listener. An active listener. This requires you to avoid making assumptions and withhold judgment. Being an ally means honoring all voices, and making space for everyone to speak.
- Be open. Know that you don't know everything; your experience is not everyone's experience. Being an ally is recognizing that you always have something to learn.
- Take responsibility. Educate yourself. You don't have to have been directly involved in a specific discrimination to work to be a part of the solution.
- Own your privilege. Most everyone has privilege in some form or another. Some have more than others. Own it. Recognize it. Work to find ways to use that privilege for social justice.
- Take action, but not always leadership. I've always loved the saying "if you are not part of the solution, you are part of the problem." Just because you don't think you have directly caused an injustice doesn't mean you don't have responsibility to end it. Recognizing how your privilege contributes and benefits from inequity is part of the process to doing social justice work. Being a good ally means being willing to step back and follow the leadership of others, particularly those who have direct experience with the topic at hand.

STEPS TO TAKING ACTION

Activism is critically important, and it should be fun. Participants, observers, and the press all respond better to something that is creative and fun. You don't have to do activism on your own; invite others to join. Share the planning and the responsibilities. Look for creative funding to support the event—remember, there are many useful donations besides just money. Don't be afraid to ask. Many grocery stores and shops are happy to support your work, and they can donate supplies, food, drinks, advertising, or prizes. Where possible, start with locally owned businesses that share your ideology. When asking a company, make sure that it is a company with which you want to be associated. For example, given Walmart's consistent opposition to unionizing and its track record of treating women workers unfairly, I don't want to be connected to the store in any way. I particularly don't want to give it recognition for donating to my event. Many activists are also having great success fundraising online with Kickstarter, Go Fund Me, and social media sites.

The following are twelve steps to help you in taking action.[2] I include these steps to give you the full range of assistance for the largest event you can take. Note, however, that not everyone will plan a major event. Depending on the size and extent of your action, you may not need all twelve steps. Remember, activism has many levels; start where you are comfortable and build from there.

1. *Define the issue that you want to raise awareness on.* Does the problem concern Reproductive Justice, motherhood, economic justice, police brutality, ending violence against women, the environment, the media, or young feminist issues, or something else?

2. *Work with other activists, and dialogue the issue to clarify the feminist analysis of the problem and the solution.* Keep in mind everyone's perspective, and be inclusive: How does this issue affect young women, women of color, lesbians, mothers, disabled women, older women, or transwomen?

3. *Decide what action to take.* Should you picket, create street theater, host a speak-out or a candlelight vigil, organize a mass rally, create a social media campaign, or present testimony to your local government on the issue? What action would best address the issue you want to raise awareness on?

4. *Decide where to hold the action.* Is it in a virtual space or an actual physical site? If in a virtual space, plan your message, be clear, use multiple platforms (i.e., Twitter, Facebook, Instagram), and con-

nect with a wide audience who will share your message. If working in a physical space, try to make the place of the action symbolic of the issue you want to raise. If the issue concerns the courts, demonstrate at the courthouse. Scout the location to anticipate any needs or problems with the site. Check to see if you need permits or insurance. Make sure you check to see

Without young voices demanding an open, informed, and fair dialogue, the moneyed status quo will always prevail.
Kemble, 26, male, California

that the date you choose does not conflict with holidays or other community events that will diminish your success. And make sure the site is accessible to people with disabilities and to public transportation. Is there childcare or activities for children?

5. *Decide whom to invite to speak on the issue on which you want to raise awareness.* Make sure you represent the community affected by the issue, as well as a good spectrum of supporters. Don't have too many speakers, and don't let the speeches go on too long; two to five minutes is a good amount of time. If you have a main speaker, you can give that person a bit more time. Get someone to provide sign language for your action. Invite entertainers like musicians or poets, if you can. Make sure you have the appropriate equipment needed—for example, a microphone, a sound system.

6. *Make it a visual action.* Brainstorm on slogans for posters and signs. Think about what props you could bring or create. Also, think about what you all will wear—are there costumes that would relate to your topic and create a point of interest? The goal is to stand out!

7. *Create a great name for the event that is clever and media savvy.* Create a meme or a hashtag. For example, #BlackLivesMatter, #MeToo, and #BringBackOurGirls all became powerful hashtags to unify people across the globe. Write up chants to use at the action or songs to sing. Get a bull horn(s), and assign someone to lead the chants!

8. *Write a press release and mail, e-mail, or tweet it to the appropriate staff person at all your local media.* Contact newspapers, radio, tele-

vision/cable stations, and any Internet sites that would be appropriate. Work on your short statements to the media, called sound
bites. They are usually fifteen- to thirty-second statements that the
press will use to represent your action for broadcast. I'll talk more
about how to handle the press later in this chapter.

9. *Plan to set up a table or tables for information, and have sign-up sheets
   for future meetings or actions.* Collect email addresses and/or social
   media links to stay in touch with interested people. Always table at
   your own events—it is a great way to get more information out about
   your activism. Assign a person or two to attend to the table while the
   event is going on. Choose someone who can answer basic questions—
   why are you having the event? What is the goal of the event? When is
   the next event or meeting? How can someone get involved?

10. *Think about everything that needs to be done* from the start to the
    finish of your action and assign activists to those tasks. We call that
    logistics! Write it down. Create a checklist.

11. *Make sure you have some fundraising at every action.* As a good
    friend of mine always says, "The movement won't move without
    money." Donations = actions! Create a Kickstarter campaign. Have
    a donation jar, or make pledge envelopes for people to take home
    so they can send in a contribution. Have someone get up and make
    a pitch for the participants to give donations. Sometimes it can be
    very intimidating to ask for money, but, remember, you are not
    asking for yourself; you are asking for the movement.

12. *Once the action is over, have a meeting to debrief on how it went.*
    Be open, and listen to everyone's feedback. Follow up on any final
    details—such as returning anything you borrowed or paying out-
    standing bills. And always make sure you thank everyone involved.

WORKING WITH THE MEDIA

My first opportunity to deal with the media was in college. My college
chapter of NOW was hosting a Take Back the Night event. The lead

organizer on the event quit about two days before the event, and I was left to organize speakers, lead chants, and handle the media. Before I knew it, there was a camera from a local news station in my face, and I had become the "spokesperson" for the event, my campus, and my NOW chapter. I was overwhelmed, and I can't even remember what I said. I learned how to give a media interview the hard way. Fortunately, I knew the significance of the event and could articulate our goals. In the end, the march was successful, and we received good press. But giving an interview to the media can be intimidating and a bit tricky. Sometimes you give a good interview, and sometimes the coverage you later see barely resembles the interview you gave! I certainly have had both experiences.

> I'm just not into the whole "girly power," "girls rule," "girls kick ass thing." I'm more concerned with achieving equality rather than denying inequality even exists. Kara, 20, heterosexual, Virginia

Activists need media skills. We need to understand and use social media politically. We need to know how to do an interview, talk in sound bites, tweet effective messages, and hold the attention of our viewers if we are to get our message across and make an impact on the lives of women and girls. We also need to consider the best outlet to getting our message to our intended audience. If it is a campus action, how do your fellow students access information? School paper? Social media site? School radio station? If it is a local or national issue, you may need to look at traditional news media in addition to the social media you may normally use. While people are diversifying the means with which they access news and while, for many younger activists, social media is a comfort zone, the majority of our population still turn to television and print media for news information.[3] We must be a part of that—if for no other reason than that feminism puts women at the center of the story, making us the subject of news rather than the objects of it. It's the difference between having a voice and being told what to do.

There are two types of media coverage—media coverage you pay for and media coverage you earn. Media coverage you pay for is airtime or ad space that you have purchased. The reality is that purchasing media coverage is often cost prohibitive and limiting for activists, since an average ad can cost $50,000 and even more during peak times. Media outlets are also controlled by a select few who decide what is to be aired or published. If the ad is not favorable to the owners, the likelihood that the ad will be published or aired is minimal. In 2013, a similar situation occurred in Washington, D.C., when two sports radio stations refused to run a previously scheduled "Change the Mascot" ad by Oneida Indian Nation. CBS Radio Washington's senior vice president, Steve Swenson, essentially argued that the ad would not be beneficial to listeners as the station had already entertained the conversation about mascot naming.[4] Yet, Oneida Indian Nation, along with Native Americans and allies throughout the country continue to challenge racist native imagery used for sport. Social media campaigns, particularly in this case, have proven essential. #ProudtoBe, #NotYourMascot, and #ChangeTheMascot have been effective hashtags to create recognition and community for activists fighting against racist native imagery, in sports as well as in other cultural venues, i.e., Halloween.

Unpaid media attention is often a goal of activists because it can be much more accessible to the average activist. Your success rate is dependent upon how media savvy you are and how effective you are in getting the media's attention. Whether writing public service announcements (PSAs), writing letters to the editor, giving an interview, or inviting the press to cover an event, you have to catch the media's attention. You need to create a message or event that is enticing enough to get the press not only to show up, but also to publish or air your efforts. In the appendix, I have included some guidelines to help you create and earn effective media attention.

It is important to note that we have to hold media accountable. Being critically aware of how a story is told, which perspectives are included, and how bias is checked are essential issues all activists should keep in mind. As we have seen with the Arab Spring, Occupy Wall Street, Black Lives Matter, Standing Rock, and Dakota Pipeline protests, and many other on-the-ground activist movements throughout history, putting activists at the center of the story gives voice to those most impacted and changes the narrative of important events. This allows the public a more thorough understanding of the issue at hand. These are also examples of how social media, YouTube, and the like can serve as vital tools for getting the truth out to the masses, and eventually forcing the mainstream media to pay attention.

The media, in all its forms, are a powerful resource for gathering and delivering information. Activists need to know how to use the media to get their messages across to the public and to influence policy. We also need to hold media accountable for what is told and how stories are presented. After all, as activists, our goal is to create effective social change. Activism is a vital method for creating awareness and changing perceptions. This will not happen unless people are aware of our efforts.

ACTIVISM IN DAILY LIFE

So often when activism or social change is discussed, we hear only of the BIG movements—we hear of marches on Washington, Supreme Court decisions, legislative changes. Indeed, these are examples of critically important activism. When we primarily focus on mass movements, however, we fail to tell the story of the importance of individual and daily actions that also make change.

I think that this part of the story is key for two reasons. One, no mass action ever took place that didn't first begin with an individual, or a small group of individuals. Those whom we hold on the social justice pedestal started off as unknown individuals who decided to take a stand. They likely did not set out to become famous, or even with the knowledge that they would inspire millions for generations to come. The second reason that I think it is important to look at individual and daily activism is that otherwise it becomes too easy to separate ourselves from taking action. If we believe that we have to be the next Rosa Parks, Delores Huerta, or Mother Teresa, then we will never act. If we think the only activism that counts is a mass march on Washington, then we will never act. It is understandable to become overwhelmed by the injustice we see in our society and around the globe. It is understandable that we may feel hopeless, and even despondent, from time to time. While I think that it is important to recognize these emotions, I also think that it is important to find ways daily that we are a part of moving toward a just world. No matter how bad we think things are, they only get worse with inaction.

Constrains on time are a real struggle. Many of us are balancing work, school, and family obligations. Adding civic engagement to that list can feel impossible. I talk to many folks who feel guilty that they missed an organizing meeting, or didn't attend the latest community rally. I have felt this same guilt. It is important to be realistic about what you can take on, and what is too much. When deciding what activism to involve yourself with, consider your financial situation, time constraints, and political priorities. While I think it is important to push beyond your comfort zone, I believe it is also important to create an environment where you are more likely to show up and take action. Make activism doable in your life. One way to achieve this is to consider the ways in which you can take action in your daily life.

You can incorporate activism into your daily life. Opportunities are everywhere. No act is too small. Each day I look for ways to be active. I believe that going to acupuncture and utilizing alternative health care is a political act. I believe that texts and phone calls to my sisters and my friends about current events are activism. Discussions with my partner about household chores or how we raise our daughters are political. Where I buy my clothes, my books, my food, are all choices that support my beliefs. The classes I teach, the curriculum I author, the events I plan are activism. I write letters to legislators, I post important stories and actions on social media, I work phone banks for important ballot measures, I work to get feminist candidates elected to office, I work in coalition with other progressives, I vote, I speak out against injustice,

I may run for office someday. I live my life as an activist. I live my life politically. We can all do this. We all have it in ourselves; titles don't make us leaders. It is our actions that mean something and impact our community. It is our voices that inspire. And our commitment to justice that makes a difference.

THE IMPORTANCE OF SELF-CARE

When I was first coming into my activism, I don't recall much training, or even discussion, about self-care. Though it is not a new concept, I must confess that I continue to struggle to embrace the practice. I keep a quote from Audre Lorde, who once wrote, "Caring for myself is not self-indulgence, it is self-preservation, and that is an act of political warfare." I find that this inspires and motivates me, because activist burn-out is real, and when the stakes are high, as they are often are, it can be difficult to convince oneself to take a break. But taking time to rest and recharge is extremely important to the longevity of any movement. Lately, I have noticed critique of self-care, arguing that it is elitist and pampered. Perhaps some of this criticism is warranted, and I do think it is important to be mindful not to perpetuate the very cycles of oppression that we are trying to fight. In other words, one's self-care should not come at the expense of another's freedom. That said, I think that there are many ways to engage in self-care that are beneficial. Self-care doesn't have to cost much—or even anything. Self-care is individualized—there is no one-fits-all method. What recharges you? Is it getting out in nature? Is it a movie or some music that you can get lost in? Is it a good laugh—the kind that comes from deep in your belly? Is it therapy? Acupuncture? A long talk with a friend? The idea of self-care is to do something for yourself, alone or with others, that fills you up. Whether you are just embarking on activism or you are a long-time veteran activist, I encourage you to integrate a regular practice of self-care and support others in doing so as well.

WHAT DO YOU THINK ARE THE GREATEST GAINS OF THE FEMINIST MOVEMENT?

The greatest gain made by the feminist movement is the equal rights we women get and people get to hear our voices. Xuo, 20, Mien

We have more control over our own bodies, we are more self-sufficient, and in many ways feminism is 'in the water.' Elizabeth, 22, white, bisexual, Michigan

To let everyone know that you have a voice, mind and spirit and that you are fully capable of doing anything and everything a man can do. MaLinda, 25, Hispanic/Native American

Freedom to vote and be heard. . . . Mireya, 30, Mexican, heterosexual, California

Credit in our own name. Veronica, 28, Latina, Illinois

Freeing up women's roles and allowing them greater access to professional lives and thereby forever changing the basic structure of the patriarchal nuclear family. Ruby, 30, white, transgender queer, Ohio

The biggest achievement of the feminist movement, in my opinion, is simply getting people to realize how prevalent discrimination against women was and remains. Karen, 29, white, straight, Queens, New York

Economic freedom and reproductive choice. Tanya, 23, Chinese-American, Minnesota

An acknowledgement of the vast problem of violence against women in the world. Crystal, 25, Caucasian, Virginia

Definitely, the Roe v. Wade *Supreme Court decision. That has to be the greatest gain by far.* Ben, 32, Asian, Republican, heterosexual, California

When the movement suddenly realized—on a number of occasions—that it still had its own "isms" it needed to confront. Class issues. Race issues. Sexual orientation issues. Only upon those realization did any changes begin. Kyle, 33, transsexual FTM, Irish Canadian

. . . female world leaders . . . our own powerful women in government and business . . . Nicole, 20, hetero, Maine

Education for girls. Marianna, 26, white Caucasian, California

The awakening of multiple generations and the empowering of my fellow women. Claire, 20, mixed—white, Mexi, Indian, hetero w/live-in boyfriend, California

My reality, and every opportunity I have ever had, are a direct result of the feminist movement. It's hard for me to pinpoint the greatest gain of all because I have trouble imagining what life was like before. Hannah, 22, Caucasian, heterosexual, Washington, D.C., metro area

Little girls can be who they want to be. And get paid equally for the same job—like with the women who play soccer. Lola, 6 ½, California, author's daughter

The best thing about the feminist movement is that women and girls in the future will have rights because women and girls fought in the past for them. Molly, 10, California, author's daughter

GREAT FEMINIST FILMS

9 to 5 (1980)

The Abortion Ship (2003)

Action for Justice: Making a Difference for Women and Girls (2002)

The Adventures of Priscilla, Queen of the Desert (1994)

Amélie (2001)

Antonia's Line (1995)

Battle of the Sexes (2017)

Beloved (1998)

Boys Don't Cry (1999)

Boys on the Side (1995)

A Brand New You (2014)

Carol (2015)

Citizen Ruth (1996)

The Color Purple (1985)

Como Agua Para Chocolate/Like Water for Chocolate (1992)

The Contender (2000)

The Danish Girl (2015)

Drunktown's Finest (2014)

Eat Drink Man Woman (1994)

Erin Brockovich (2000)

Frida (2002)

Fried Green Tomatoes (1991)

From the Back Alleys to the Supreme Court and Beyond (Dorothy Fadiman's trilogy, 1999)

Ghostbusters: Answer the Call (2016)

G.I. Jane (1997)

Girl, Interrupted (1999)

A Girl Like Me: The Gwen Araujo Story (2006)

Go Fish (1994)

Guyland (2015)

He Named Me Malala (2015)

The Hours (2002)

How to Make An American Quilt (1995)

The Hunting Ground (2015)

If These Walls Could Talk (I and II) (1996 and 2000)

I'm the One that I Want (Margaret Cho, 2000)

Iron Jawed Angels (2004)

The Joy Luck Club (1993)

Killing Us Softly 3 (2000)

Lady Bird (2017)

A League of Their Own (1992)

The Magdalene Sisters (2002)

The Mask You Live In (2015)

Million Dollar Baby (2004)

Miss Representation (2011)

Mi Vida Loca (1993)

Muriel's Wedding (1994)

North Country (2005)

Off the Straight and Narrow (1999) and *Further off the Straight and Narrow* (2006)

Paris is Burning (1990)

Passion for Justice: 21st Century Feminism (2002)

Playing Unfair (2002)

Poetic Justice (1993)

Prey for Rock & Roll (2003)

The Purity Myth (2011)

Rachel's Daughter (1998)

Raise the Red Lantern (1991)

Real Women Have Curves (2002)

Set It Off (1996)

Shakespeare in Love (1998)

Small Justice (2002)

Spy (2015)

Suffragette (2015)

Tangerine (2015)

Tea with Mussolini (1999)

Thelma & Louise (1991)

Tough Guise 2 (2013)

Transamerica (2005)

The Vagina Monologues (2002)

Vera Drake (2004)

Votes for Women (1996)

Whale Rider (2002)

What Happened, Miss Simone? (2015)

Yentl (1983)

2

CATCH A WAVE

I was an exchange student in Sweden during my junior year of high school. At my school at home, junior year included a class on U.S. politics and history. So while living in Sweden was great and I could take corresponding literature, math, and sciences classes, learning about American political history wasn't so simple. My parents and teachers decided that I would take a correspondence class to make up this work, but when they gave me my textbook, my mother discovered a problem. There were virtually no references to women. She suggested to my school a textbook change but met a great deal of resistance. Most disturbing, she read their resistance as rooted in an undervaluing of women's history and the belief that a knowledge of women's contributions was unnecessary in studying American history. While she lost the battle with the school, she instituted her own curriculum for me that I was required to complete in a correspondence course with her. Yes, more homework for me, but work that was well worth it. We also did a bit of subversive activism—we added our own commentary in the margins of all the textbooks that my school sent, hoping that whoever got the textbooks after me would learn about women's history, too. That year, I learned a great deal about American political history. I learned the valuable lesson that claiming women's place in society has always been a fight. I also learned that women's history is American history and that our contributions help to shape the world we live in today.

The feminist movement has a rich history—a history full of struggle, sacrifice, justice, resistance, and many victories. But, unfortunately, feminist activism is often left out of our textbooks, the halls of our educational institutions, and, as a result, far too often, our consciousness. Far too many move forward without a complete understanding of the past—without a full accounting of the struggles both within and outside the movement. We talk of the future with little emphasis on the present. But if we are to create a future, we need to build upon the past. And to do so, we must know, respect, and understand our history.

Fortunately, there is a commitment today to reclaiming the past contributions and stories of women and to teaching women's *herstory* to the current and future generations—so as not to lose this heritage. Great writers like bell hooks, Ruth Rosen, and Estelle Freedman have chronicled this history. From the women who fought for more than seventy years to win the right to vote to the women who work today to further advance women's quest for equality, American women have a tremendous tradition of fighting for justice. I have included a chronology of these women, their efforts, and the history of American feminism. I believe that we need to know our history to understand the present and in order to plan for the future. Women's history is American history. Knowing this, knowing what women have done in the past, can empower women today. I include the following chronology as both information and inspiration.

> *The greatest gain in the movement was when women noticed that they had power, both as a group and individuals.* Andrea, 22, white, straight, Washington state

CHRONOLOGY OF THE U.S. FEMINIST MOVEMENT

March 31, 1776—Abigail Adams writes her now-famous "Remember the ladies" letter to her husband, John Adams, asking him to "remember the ladies" and not to "put such unlimited power into the hands of the Husbands."

1790—Judith Sargent Stevens Murray publishes *On the Equality of the Sexes*, advocating that women and men should have equal education.

1792—Mary Wollstonecraft publishes *Vindication of the Rights of Woman*, advocating equal opportunity for women.

1821—Troy Female Seminary is started in New York by Emma Hart Willard, the first endowed school for girls.

1832—The Female Anti-Slavery Society of Salem, Massachusetts, is founded.

1833—Oberlin College, in Ohio, becomes the first co-educational college in the United States.

1837—Mount Holyoke College is founded by Mary Lyons, in Massachusetts, the United States' first four-year college for women.

1839—Mississippi is the first state to pass a Married Women's Property Act, allowing married white women to own property in their own name.

1848—The Lowell Female Labor Reform Association is organized by female textile workers in Massachusetts. The first women's rights convention in the United States is held in Seneca Falls, New York. Married white women are allowed to own property in the United States.

1850—"Bloomers" cause controversy in the United States as Amelia Jenks Bloomer introduces knee-length pantaloons as women's clothing.

1851—Sojourner Truth, a former slave, delivers her famous "Ain't I a Woman" speech at Akron, Ohio's women's rights convention.

1865—The Thirteenth Amendment is passed, ending official slavery in the United States. Dr. Mary Edwards Walker becomes the first woman to receive the Medal of Honor for her service in the Civil War; she was the first woman surgeon in the Union Army and an abolitionist and suffragist. She was also a dress reformer, frequently challenging traditional female clothing. She was harassed, assaulted, and even arrested for wearing men's clothing.

1866—Elizabeth Cady Stanton and Susan B. Anthony organize the American Equal Rights Association, an organization that worked for universal suffrage.

1868—The Fourteenth Amendment, defining "citizens" and "voters" as male, is ratified.

1869—Elizabeth Cady Stanton and Susan B. Anthony form the National Woman Suffrage Association, while Lucy Stone, Henry Blackwell, and Julia Ward Howe found the more conservative American Woman Suffrage Association.

1872—Victoria Woodhull becomes the first woman to campaign for the U.S. presidency.

1873—Myra Bradwell, an attorney from Illinois, sues in the U.S. Supreme Court for the right to practice law. Her case is rejected by the Court because she is married.

1878—A Woman Suffrage Amendment is introduced in the U.S. Congress. This amendment eventually becomes the Nineteenth Amendment, which, in 1919, wins women the right to vote.

1883—Sarah Winnemucca publishes *Life Among the Paiutes: Their Wrongs and Claims*, an autobiography detailing the treatment of Indians by European Americans.

1890—The National Woman Suffrage Association and the American Woman Suffrage Association join together under the leadership of Elizabeth Cady Stanton, forming the National American Woman Suffrage Association. Matilda Joslyn Gage forms the more radical Woman's National Liberal Union.

1892—A nationwide antilynching campaign is launched by Ida B. Wells after the murder of three black businessmen in Tennessee.

1893—The National Council of Jewish Women is founded by Hannah Greenbaum Soloman. Colorado becomes the first state in the U.S. to allow women the right to vote. Matilda Joslyn Gage publishes *Women, Church, and State*, in which she discusses equity between the sexes among the Iroquois.

1895—Elizabeth Cady Stanton publishes *The Woman's Bible*, criticizing churches for their narrow definition of women's roles within the church.

1895–1899—Rosa Sonnenschein publishes *The American Jewess*, the first Jewish women's magazine.

1896—The National Association of Colored Women is founded by Fanny Jackson Coppin, Charlotte Forten Grimké, Frances E. W. Harper, Josephine St. Pierre Ruffin, Mary Church Terrell, Harriet Tubman, Margaret Murray Washington, Frances Ellen Watkins, and Ida B. Wells-Barnett.

1903—The Women's Trade Union League of New York is formed, later becoming the forerunner of the International Ladies' Garment Workers' Union.

1911—Opposition to women's suffrage formalizes with the creation of the National Association Opposed to Women's Suffrage.

1913—Alice Paul and Lucy Burns organize the Congressional Union, which becomes the National Women's Party in 1916. Using more radical means, such as hunger strikes and White House pickets, they work to publicize the importance of women's suffrage.

1915—The Women's Peace Party is formed.

1916—Jeannette Rankin of Montana becomes the first woman to serve in the U.S. House of Representatives.

1919—The Nineteenth Amendment passes in Congress and moves to the states for ratification.

August 26, 1920—The Nineteenth Amendment is ratified by the necessary three-quarters of the states on August 18 and is officially added to the Constitution on August 26. The National American Woman Suffrage Association closes but becomes the foundation for the League of Women Voters.

1921—Margaret Sanger founds the American Birth Control League, later to become Planned Parenthood.

1923—The National Women's Party introduces the Equal Rights Amendment, proposed to eliminate gender discrimination. The Equal Rights Amendment still has not been ratified.

1932—Amelia Earhart is the first woman to fly solo across the Atlantic. Frances Perkins is the first woman to hold a Cabinet position, when Franklin D. Roosevelt appoints her as the Secretary of Labor.

1933—Katharine Hepburn wins her first Oscar for her performance in *Morning Glory*. Hepburn goes on to win three more Academy Awards, making her the winner of more Oscar awards for performance than any other actor.

1935—Mary McLeod Bethune organizes the National Council of Negro Women.

1936—Birth control is no longer classified as "obscene" following the modification of a federal law prohibiting the dissemination of birth control information through the mail.

1943—The Equal Pay Act is introduced in Congress.

1955—Rosa Parks refuses to give up her seat on a bus in Montgomery, Alabama, which leads to the Montgomery Bus Boycotts. Del Martin and Phyllis Lyon found the first U.S. lesbian rights group, Daughters of Bilitis.

1960—The birth control pill is approved by the U.S. Food and Drug Administration (FDA).

1961—Eleanor Roosevelt is appointed by President Kennedy as the chair of the first President's Commission on the Status of Women. Pat Maginnis founds the Society for Humane Abortion in California.

1962—Delores Huerta helps to found the United Farm Workers. Fannie Lou Hamer, a Mississippi sharecropper, is beaten and jailed for leading efforts to register neighbors to vote. She co-founds the Mississippi Freedom Democratic Party.

1963—The Equal Pay Act passes Congress, prohibiting sex discrimination in pay. Betty Friedan publishes *The Feminine Mystique*. The Commission on the Status of Women reveals widespread sex discrimination against women in employment and under the law in its first report, *The American Woman*.

1964—The Civil Rights Act passes, Title VII of which includes a clause prohibiting discrimination on the basis of sex. Casey Hayden and Mary King address sexual inequality within the civil rights movement. The Homosexual League of New York / The League for Sexual Freedom stages its first protest in New York City.

1965—The U.S. Supreme Court decision *Griswold v. Connecticut* permits the use of birth control devices by married couples on the basis of a constitutional right to privacy. President Lyndon B. Johnson signs Executive Order 11246 requiring companies that do business with the government to utilize affirmative action in hiring minorities.

1966—Out of frustration at the Equal Employment Opportunity Commission's lack of enforcement of the Civil Rights Act of 1964, the National Organization for Women (NOW) is created. NOW then petitions the EEOC to end sex-segregated employment ads.

1967—Affirmative action is extended to women. The Chicago Women's Liberation Group is founded. New York Radical Women forms. NOW adopts a Bill of Rights for women. Alicia Escalante begins the East Los Angeles Welfare Rights Organization (she later founds the Chicano National Welfare Rights Organization). Johnnie Tillmon, Etta Horn, and Beulah Sanders start the National Welfare Rights Organization to educate women about negotiating the welfare system.

1968—Shirley Chisholm is the first African American woman elected to Congress. Women's Liberation, New York Radical Women, and New York NOW protest the "Miss America" pageant in Atlantic City. The National Domestic Workers Union is formed.

1969—Cornell University in New York offers the first women's studies course. The Boston Women's Health Collective begins publishing its pamphlet *Our Bodies, Ourselves* (later published as a book in 1973 and still widely referred to for woman-centered health information). The National Abortion Rights Action League (now NARAL Pro-Choice America) is formed. Redstockings, a radical feminist activist organization combating derogatory and discriminatory attitudes about women, is formed. The first full women's studies program is established, at San Diego State University. The Stonewall Riots occur in New York City, protesting discrimination against the gay community.

1970—Pat Mainardi proposes "wages for housework," bringing awareness to the unpaid work of women. The North American Indian Women's Association is formed. Bella Abzug is elected to Congress. Maggie Kuhn creates the Gray Panthers to address older women's rights. Hawaii, Alaska, and New York are the first states to liberalize abortion laws. Barbara Seaman, who published *The Doctors' Case against the Pill* in 1969, disrupts a Senate subcommittee's hearing on the birth control pill, arguing that women are being used as "guinea pigs." The Lavender Menace Action is one of the first actions fighting for the rights of lesbians. The Gay Liberation Front Women is formed.

1971—The Feminist Women's Health Center is founded by Carol Downer and Lorraine Rothman in Los Angeles, California. The National Women's Political Caucus is formed to encourage and support more women to run for office. The National Press Club allows women members.

1972—Title IX is passed by Congress to enforce sex equality in education. *Ms.* magazine is launched. (*Ms.* first appeared as an insert in *New York* magazine in 1971.) Charlotte Bunch, Rita Mae Brown, and Joan E. Biren found *The Furies*, a collective lesbian newspaper. Margo St. James starts COYOTE (Call Off Your Old Tired Ethics) in San Francisco to improve working conditions of sex workers. The Equal Pay Act of 1963 is expanded to include administrative, executive, and professional employees. Juanita Kreps becomes the first woman director of the New York Stock Exchange (she is later appointed as the first woman Secretary of Commerce). The first U.S. battered women's shelters open in California and Minnesota. *Free to Be . . . You and Me* is published, providing an entire generation with nonsexist, multiracial songs, poems, and stories for kids. The Older Women's Liberation holds its first conference in New York City. Sally Priesand becomes the first ordained woman rabbi.

1973—*Roe v. Wade* is decided in the U.S. Supreme Court, legalizing abortion in the first trimester. Helen Reddy wins a Grammy for her song "I Am Woman." The National Black Feminist Organization is formed.

Billie Jean King defeats Bobby Riggs in the much-publicized "battle of the sexes" tennis match. The U.S. Supreme Court rules against sexually segregated classified employment ads. The AFL-CIO nationally endorses the ERA.

1974—The Equal Credit Opportunity Act is passed in Congress, allowing married women credit in their own names. Helen Thomas is the first woman reporter to be named a White House reporter for UPI. Girls are allowed to play in Little League. Domestic workers are covered by the minimum wage law. The National Women's Football League is formed. The first All-American Girls' Basketball Conference is held. The Coalition of Labor Union Women (CLUW) is formed.

1975—The United Nations sponsors the First International Conference on Women, held in Mexico City. For the first time, under Title IV-D of the Social Security Act established by Congress, federal employee wages can be garnished to pay child support and alimony.

1976—The United Nations Decade for Women begins. The National Alliance of Black Feminists organizes in Chicago. The Organization of Pan Asian American Women is founded. Barbara Jordan is the first African American and the first woman to give the keynote address at the Democratic National Convention. NASA begins accepting women for astronaut training. Joan Nestle and Deborah Edel found the Lesbian Herstory Archives—the largest and oldest of its kind in the world. Sarah Caldwell becomes the first woman to conduct at New York's Metropolitan Opera House. *Lilith Magazine* is founded. Nebraska enacts the first marital rape law—setting a precedent that it is illegal for a husband to rape his wife. Military service academies begin to admit women. In August, the Michigan Womyn's Music Festival kicks off, creating a womyn-only space featuring feminist artists. The festival was controversial until its end in 2015, receiving much criticism for trans-exclusion.

1977—The National Association of Cuban-American Women is founded. The National Coalition Against Domestic Violence is founded.

1978—The Pregnancy Discrimination Act passes Congress, prohibiting job discrimination against women who are pregnant. Women Against Pornography is formed in New York City. The group later sponsors the first Take Back the Night march and rally protesting violence against women.

1981—Sandra Day O'Connor is the first woman appointed to the U.S. Supreme Court.

1983—Sally Ride is the first American woman in space. Byllye Avery founds the National Black Women's Health Project, now the Black Women's Health Imperative. The anthology *Shadow on a Tightrope: Writings by Women on Fat Oppression* is published by Lisa Schoenfielder and Barb Wieser.

1984—Geraldine Ferraro runs as the Democratic Party's vice-presidential candidate, with the presidential candidate Walter Mondale.

1985—Emily's List is started. The group gives campaign donations to Democratic, pro-choice candidates (EMILY stands for Early Money Is Like Yeast). Wilma Mankiller becomes the first woman chief of the Cherokee Nation of Oklahoma.

1987—The Feminist Majority is founded by Eleanor Smeal, past president of NOW. Congress designates March as "Women's History Month." Sandy Stone publishes "The Empire Strikes Back: A Posttransexual Manifesto," a powerful transfeminist response to the 1979 article "The Transsexual Empire" by Janice Raymond, which blames trans people for perpetuating the gender binary.

1989—Reverend Barbara C. Harris becomes the first woman consecrated as a bishop in the Episcopal Church. Kate Bornstein co-produces *Hidden: A Gender*, a theater production challenging the gender binary.

1990—Congress passes the Americans with Disabilities Act. Dr. Antonia Novello becomes the first woman and the first Latino to serve as U.S. Surgeon General. Considered the vanguard of the riot grrl movement, radical feminist punk band Bikini Kill forms.

1991—Anita Hill bravely testifies at the Senate Supreme Court Confirmation Hearings about sexual harassment by her former employer and then-nominee to the U.S. Supreme Court, Clarence Thomas, setting off a national conversation about sexual harassment in the workplace. The U.S. Senate overturns the "gag rule," which barred federally funded family planning clinics from discussing abortion as an option. Sharon Pratt Dixon becomes mayor of Washington, D.C., and as such becomes the first African American woman to serve as mayor of a major U.S. city. Susan Faludi publishes *Backlash*, detailing the attacks on the women's movement throughout the 1980s and introduces a whole new generation to the importance of feminism. *Thelma & Louise* is released in theaters.

1992—Rebecca Walker and Shannon Liss create the Third Wave Direct Action Corporation to address the issues of a new wave of feminists. The Third Wave Direct Action Corporation later becomes the Third Wave Foundation. An estimated 750,000 people converge on Washington, D.C., for the Pro-Choice March. More women are elected to political office than any time in U.S. history, prompting some to name 1992 "the year of the woman" in U.S. politics. Carol Moseley-Braun (D-IL) is the first African American woman elected to the U.S. Senate (she later runs for president, in 2004). The Supreme Court reaffirms a woman's right to abortion in *Planned Parenthood of Southeastern Pennsylvania v. Casey*. Mae Jemison becomes the first African American woman astronaut.

1993—Congress passes the Family and Medical Leave Act. *Bust* magazine is published. The Center for Young Women's Development is founded in San Francisco, California. Ruth Bader Ginsburg is appointed to the U.S. Supreme Court.

1994—Congress passes and President Clinton signs the Freedom to Access Clinic Entrances Act, making it illegal to obstruct the entrances to abortion clinics. Congress passes the Violence Against Women Act, providing services and funding for victims of rape and domestic violence.

1995—The United Nations Fourth World Conference on Women is held, in Beijing, China. Shannon Faulkner becomes the first woman to be admitted to the Citadel, the formerly all-male South Carolina military college.

1996—Rape is officially recognized as a weapon of war and as a human rights violation, thus as a war crime. The Feminist Expo is held in Washington, D.C. Hosted by the Feminist Majority and sponsored by nearly 300 organizations, it brings thousands of feminists together to create a feminist vision for the future. Andi Zeisler and Lisa Jervis found *Bitch* magazine. The U.S. Women's National Soccer Team wins the first-ever Olympic gold medal for women's soccer, at the Atlanta Olympic Games.

1997—Madeline Albright becomes the first woman to serve as the U.S. Secretary of State, making her the highest-ranking woman in the history of the U.S. government. Sarah McLachlan kicks off Lilith Fair, with a full lineup of women musicians. The Women's National Basketball Association (WNBA) is formed. The Lusty Lady, in San Francisco, unionizes, taking an important and historic step toward sex workers' rights. (For more information on sex workers' unionization efforts, see Julia Query and Vicki Funari's film *Live Nude Girls Unite.*)

1998—Congress passes the Violence Against Women Act II, extending funding to sexual assault programs. Eve Ensler hosts *The Vagina Monologues* in New York, launching the V-Day campaign to end violence against women.

1999—Carly Fiorina becomes the president, CEO, and, in 2000, chairperson of Hewlett-Packard, becoming the first woman to hold all three positions in a Fortune 500 company. Lieutenant Colonel Eileen Collins is the first woman astronaut to command a space shuttle mission. Nancy Ruth Mace becomes the first woman to graduate from the Citadel, the formerly all-male military school in South Carolina. Dot Nelson-Turnier founds the National Organization of Lesbians of Size Everywhere.

2000—The Second Feminist Expo is held, in Baltimore, Maryland. Jennifer Baumgardner and Amy Richards publish *Manifesta: Young Women, Feminism and the Future*. Hillary Rodham Clinton is elected to the U.S. Senate to represent the state of New York, making her the first U.S. First Lady ever to hold public office. Beijing +5, "Women 2000: Gender Equality, Development and Peace for the Twenty-first Century," takes place in New York. The World March for Women is held in Washington, D.C., and in New York City. Emi Koyama publishes "The Transfeminist Manifesto."

2002—Nancy Pelosi becomes House Minority Leader, making her the highest-ranking woman in the U.S. House of Representatives and the first woman to lead a major political party in the U.S. Congress. The California State Legislature passes SB 1301, codifying *Roe v. Wade* language into state law, further securing abortion rights in California.

2003—The Fat Feminist conference is hosted in San Francisco, California.

2004—An estimated 1.15 million people march on Washington, D.C., for the "March for Women's Lives"—the largest march (of any kind!) in U.S. history. Susan Hockfield becomes the first woman president of the Massachusetts Institute of Technology (MIT). Massachusetts becomes the first U.S. state to legalize same-sex marriage.

2005—Condoleezza Rice becomes the first African American woman to serve as U.S. Secretary of State.

2007—Nancy Pelosi becomes the first woman Speaker of the House.

2009—The Lily Ledbetter Fair Pay Act is signed into law by President Obama. Sonya Sotomayer becomes the first Latina to serve as U.S. Supreme Court justice.

2011—Activists gather in Zuccotti Park in New York City to protest social and economic inequality and the Occupy movement is born.

2012—Alicia Garza, Opal Tometi, and Patrisse Cullors create Black Lives Matter to challenge anti-black racism and the intersection of black lives with gender, trans and queer, immigrant, incarceration, and (dis)abled rights.

2013—The Violence Against Women Act (VAWA) is reauthorized to include Native American women, immigrants, and LGBT peoples.

2015—As a result of a U.S. Supreme Court ruling, same-sex marriage becomes legal in the United States. The African American Policy Forum (AAPF) publishes a report and coins the hashtag #SayHerName to raise awareness of anti-black violence and police brutality specifically targeted at African American women.

2016—Women are now able to serve any job in the U.S. armed forces. Hillary Rodham Clinton wins the popular vote in the U.S. presidential election but does not win the electoral college, falling just short of becoming the first woman president of the United States.

2017—Millions turn out, across the globe, to join the Women's March, protesting the election of Donald Trump. First coined in 2006 by Tarana Burke, the #MeToo hashtag goes viral, calling attention to sexual assault, resulting in the firing of a number of high-profile men in media.

2018—The second year of the Women's March happens in cities around the globe. A record number of women register as candidates for elected office. Activists stage hunger strikes and take to the streets in protest of President Trump's zero-tolerance immigration policy, not the least of which included separating children from their families.

THE "WAVES" OF A MOVEMENT

The American women's movement is often discussed in terms of "waves," but it is important to understand that the presumed boundaries of these waves can be misleading. For example, these waves are not entirely separate from one another, but rather blend into one other. There is no true stopping point where one wave ends before another begins. Rather, the triumphs and the setbacks of one wave become the starting ground for the succeeding waves, passing from one generation to the next. Each wave of the feminist movement builds upon efforts of previous generations. Suffrage and the right to vote, a gain made in the first wave, which most scholars designated as occurring in the late 1800s through the early 1900s, became an accepted reality for women of the next generation, who then began to work on additional issues of access, representation, and equality. The second wave, which most designate as beginning in the 1960s, emphasized the importance of personal politics. Under its classic banner "the personal is political," the second wave led the charge for abortion rights, child care, recognition of unpaid labor, access to health care, and equal pay for equal work. While many of these battles have not yet been won, the fight continues. Subsequently, along with the gains of the first and second waves, the challenges also carry over. Significant criticism of the first and second waves—such as concerns about racism, generational tensions, and relevance of issues—continues to be central to the dialogue about the women's movement. This dialog passed onto the next generation, the third wave, which gained momentum in the 1990s. The third wave was challenged to look critically at our collective past and to build a more diverse, inclusive, and integrated movement.

> *A second-wave feminist professor told me that the Third Wave does not exist. I was like, thanks for denying me my identity.* Sally, 25, Caucasian, bisexual, Colorado

> The American feminist movement is often seen as occurring in waves. The *first wave* was characterized by the fight for suffrage and the right to vote for women. The *second wave* was characterized by the concept of "personal politics" and the fight for full recognition of women in society. And the *third wave* is characterized by multicultural, inclusive feminism.

Arguments, both within and outside the movement, focus on a debate about whether or not we should even look at the American women's movement in terms of waves. Questions have arisen about the risk of isolating and pigeon-holing generations of women's-rights activists and thus diluting the strength of the movement. There are also questions about those who don't generationally fit into the waves as commonly defined, such as those who were born in the mid- and late 1960s, who are too young to have been at the center of second-wave activism but who are too old to be included with the activists of the third wave. They are often stuck between the experiences and consciousness of the second and third waves and find themselves not belonging to either group. Active in the movement, they often express frustration at being ignored in the dialogue of intergenerational feminism. Further challenging is the question of how to

The greatest achievement made by the feminist movement is to collectively raise the consciousness of women regarding the inequalities of their social condition. Ilun, 23, Taiwanese-American, asexual, New York City

categorize the ever-present youth who enter the scene of feminism and the feminist movement, starting feminist clubs at high school, doing activism on campus, and engaging in a national dialogue via community organizing and social media presence—are these the fourth wave, or have we seen too many waves to count? On the other hand, it has been argued that looking at the women's movement in this country in terms of waves can help to organize, understand, and build upon efforts of the past. Whether or not you believe in the "waves" of this movement, there is no question that the contributions of people who took, and continue to take, action to improve the lives of women and girls is valid and critically important.

The classification of a wave as a wave may seem to be less critical as it once was. With feminist efforts reaching far into a variety of movements, colleges, communities, high schools, and even in elementary schools, it is evident that determining when and where a wave begins and ends is less significant in today's activism. Women's Studies programs often continue to utilize the wave metaphor, but likely more as a categorization of periods of time, and not necessarily as an indication of today's feminism. It is with this intention that I organize the following discussion.

SUFFRAGE AND THE FIRST WAVE OF FEMINISM

The first wave of the women's movement is characterized as the suffrage movement and occurred primarily during the 1800s and early 1900s.

Originating in the abolition movement to end slavery, women began working toward winning the right to vote. Hosting the first American women's rights convention, in Seneca Falls, New York, in 1848, women came together to create the Declaration of Sentiments, a document that asserted true gender equality. Women won suffrage in 1919 with the passage of the Nineteenth Amendment, and the final state approval necessary for the ratification of the amendment came on August 26, 1920—recognized today as Women's Equality Day.

Winning the right to vote is a cornerstone to the women's movement because it gave women political power through representation for the first time in modern history. The 2004 HBO film *Iron Jawed Angels* introduced a new generation to Alice Paul, Lucy Burns, and the fight for women's suffrage. Recalling the challenges, pickets, arrests, and hunger strikes, the film gives today's generation a more realistic look at the intense struggle endured by the suffragists. Often we underestimate the sacrifices and struggles that women endure for their freedom. *Iron Jawed Angels* leaves us with a graphic memory of Alice Paul being force-fed during her hunger strike in prison and an understanding that the right to vote was not readily granted to women. Indeed, the fight for suffrage lasted for more than seventy years. Many who began the struggle—Susan B. Anthony, Elizabeth Cady Stanton, and Sojourner Truth, for example—did not live to see their life's work achieved. But their legacy lives on. The fight for suffrage began a modern movement to change the regard in which women were held. It challenged the way in which women were treated and the resources to which they had access. However, while the women's movement was touted as a movement for all women, in fact race divisions within the movement were strong. These divisions have long been glossed over by historians, the media, and the movement itself, undervaluing the importance and truth of this history. We need to examine the racism that permeated the first wave in order to understand its ongoing influence in the movement. If we are to strengthen the feminist movement today, then we need to fully recognize and understand the contributions of all while learning from the mistakes of the past.

The fact is that women of color, like Ida B. Wells, were instrumental to suffrage and to the consciousness that women's rights must include all women. Wells protested the "back of the bus" politic of the women's movement by refusing to march at the back of the 1913 suffrage parade, as was the plan for delegations of women of color. Further, in response to segregated and exclusionary suffrage groups, Wells established Chicago's Alpha Suffrage Club, perhaps the first suffrage group for black women. White Christian feminist groups of the time refused to join anti-lynching campaigns, address anti-Semitism, or fight discriminatory immigration policies. With few exceptions, divisions among activist women began as women of color looked to create new venues to recognize and address issues ignored by "mainstream" women's organizations. Women of color have been forced to fight for their place in history and for their inclusion on the movement's agenda. Tragically, this fight continues today.

In addition to the challenge of racism within the U.S.-based women's movement, American women were largely unaware of feminist activity that was occurring in other regions of the world. At the time of the Seneca Falls convention, women throughout Europe, Asia, and Latin America were arguing for gender equality.[1] Suffrage, education, political representation, property rights, labor rights, and pay equity were all central issues for women activists in Japan, Germany, England, France, Mexico, and other nations. Women around the globe contributed significantly to the structure of their home country's gender dynamic. They also contributed to a wider understanding of globalization and imperialism and their impact on the status of women worldwide.

While the first wave of feminism left us with intense racial divisions and little understanding of women of the world, the suffragists made a critical contribution to American women's liberation and set into motion a movement that continues to change the lives of women for the better. With the right to vote, we have a voice in our democracy and a better opportunity to impact the system.

PERSONAL POLITICS AND THE SECOND WAVE
OF FEMINISM

The second wave of the women's movement was characterized by economic and personal power. Beginning in the early 1960s, the second wave took on the issues of advancement for women in the workplace (e.g., pay equity, the glass ceiling, sexual harassment); recognition of women's labor in the home; contraceptive equity and legality and access to reproductive health care; constitutional equality; women's safety; and political participation among women, from voting activity to holding elective office. Fortunately, there has been no noted end to the second wave, as this generation's activists are still vigorously working to end discrimination against women.

Perhaps one of the most important gains of the second wave was to identify a sexism so pervasive that it could no longer be ignored. By identifying sexism, in the courts to the household, the second wave taught us the importance of ending discrimination, not just on a political level, but also on a deeply personal one. Coining the phrase "the personal is political, the political is personal," the second wave of the women's movement championed the fight to bring recognition to women's lives, arguing that our collective experience is a legitimate part of the American experience. With this recognition came consciousness-raising groups, speak-outs, marches, rallies, demonstrations, feminist publishing houses and publications, research, women's studies programs at colleges and universities, court battles, and legislative efforts to bring women closer to parity with men. The second wave is noted for its great victories, such as Title IX, which instituted a vision of gender equity in education. Title IX made sexual harassment in school illegal and outlined the goal of a fair and level playing field in sports and in the overall pursuit of academic excellence. Additionally, the second wave championed important court wins for women's health and reproductive rights, most notably *Griswold v. Connecticut* (1965), in which the U.S. Supreme Court invalidated a Connecticut statute that prohibited the use of contraceptives by married persons; *Eisenstadt v. Baird* (1972), in which the Court extended the right to privacy to include both married and non-married persons with regard to reproductive health decisions; and *Roe v. Wade* (1973), in which the Court legalized abortion in the first trimester. Indeed, the second wave championed the issues that impact women's lives—including the right to be safe from violence at work, on the street, and in our homes; the right to equitable pay and career advancement; the right to attend military academies, as well as to serve; and the right to accessible, affordable, and representational health care.

The second wave helped launch women's studies programs and departments across the nation, creating a venue for women's contributions. Women's studies classes are often the first, and sometimes the only, place we learn women's side of history and perspective on current issues. Beyond women's studies, the second wave began the massive effort to put women into mainstream studies, so that our history textbooks, and sociology, psychology, anthropology, science, and books on every area of study, do not exclude women's perspectives or contributions. For the first time, women were able to widely publish and to be recognized as contributors to their fields. Chronicling and critiquing our past, as well as evaluating our present and visioning our future, women's studies professors and writers introduced a discourse that is woman-centered. This legacy continues today, as younger generations are now afforded the opportunity to earn degrees and build careers, specifically in women's/feminist studies.

Women's studies further gave rise to much of the activism of the feminist movement. While certainly women have raised awareness and called for change in multiple arenas of society, including factories, offices, and community centers and within religious institutions, colleges and universities have been a central training ground for activism. Typically places that encourage the questioning of the status quo and foster new ideas, college campuses are a prime locale for feminist organizing. This is a tradition that continues to live on as classic second-wave organizations such as NOW, the Feminist Majority, and Gloria Steinem's URGE: United for Reproductive and Gender Equality (formerly Choice

USA) have student chapters and campus task forces established throughout the nation.

The women's health movement also saw its rise during the second
wave. Reclaiming our bodies, demanding research and knowledge, and
calling for affordable and accessible health care are cornerstone issues for
the feminist women's health movement. Key organizations began in the
second wave and continue to work today to provide comprehensive health
care information and services for all. Among these organizations are the
Feminist Women's Health Centers, which put women back into the center
of our health care and empower women in the choices they make; the
Boston Women's Health Collective, which made woman-centered health
information widely available through classic publications like *Our Bodies, Ourselves*; the National Women's Health Network, which lobbies for
women's health priorities and is often the only voice women have on Capitol Hill; and the National Black Women's Health Project (now the Black
Women's Health Imperative), which is leading the way on education, advocacy, research, and leadership training for African American women's
health initiatives. These organizations, and many others, have changed the
face of health care for women. And, while the fight to protect women's
health is still being fought, the second wave put into motion the idea that
women, and only women, must control their bodies.

Perhaps the most classic battle of the second wave was the fight for
an Equal Rights Amendment (ERA). Drafted in 1923 by the first-waver
Alice Paul, the ERA battle was picked up by the second wave in the
1970s—a great example of intergenerational work. The Equal Rights
Amendment simply reads:

> Section 1. Equality of rights under the law shall not be denied or
> abridged by the United States or by any state on account of sex.
> Section 2. The Congress shall have the power to enforce, by appropriate
> legislation, the provisions of this article.
> Section 3. This amendment shall take effect two years after the date of
> ratification.

The quest for constitutional equality has been a long, controversial battle, with the most notable opposition coming from Phyllis Schlafly, of the Eagle Forum. She effectively argued against the ERA, claiming that feminists hated "men, marriage, and children."[2] Despite tireless efforts among members of the feminist movement, congressional approval, and ratification in thirty states, the ERA never achieved approval in the necessary three-quarters of the states to be adopted as an amendment to the Constitution. Perhaps activists today will continue the intergenerational efforts of the ERA by picking up this fight for constitutional equality— not just for women this time, but for all those who are marginalized and oppressed.

While much of the second-wave agenda has yet to be realized, there is no debate that the second wave established an expectation of equality. The second wave took the once-extreme notion of economic, political, and social equity for women and brought it into mainstream consciousness. The second wave taught my generation that we could do, and be, anything. But, despite their best efforts, they have not achieved every goal. The fight continues. While the vision, knowledge, and activism of the second wavers remain central to the movement, a new generation has joined them—bringing with them all that they have learned from the second wave while also introducing their own vision, knowledge, and activism to the movement.

THE THIRD WAVE

In the early 1990s, the next wave, the third wave, of feminism began to emerge. Frequently referred to as "third wavers," third-wave feminists dispel the myths of feminism, claim feminism for a new generation, and embrace and incorporate our diversity as people in a movement to bring gender equity throughout the globe. Third wavers confront the sentiment "I'm not a feminist, but . . . ," the attitude that young women want the benefits of feminism—fair pay, contraceptive equity, access to higher education, protection from sexual harassment—without recognizing the fight that was necessary to win these rights. Third wavers benefit from the gains of the previous waves but also recognize the importance of continuing the work and the legacy of a feminist movement. Third-wave feminism is a movement that is working alongside the activists of the second wave, and supporting the voices of those coming up in the movement.

As I mentioned earlier, I consider myself a third waver. I grew up in the feminist movement. This means that I grew up in a time of possibility and was frequently told that I could do anything. I was taught that my voice is powerful, that women's voices are powerful. But, as I grew up, I began to realize that not all little girls are told these messages and that even when they are, the world doesn't necessarily support them. One definition of "third-wave feminists" is that they are the children of the second wave of feminism—literally and/or figuratively. Either you were, as Rebecca Walker claims, a "movement baby" who was carted around to meetings, marches, and rallies or you simply grew up in a time that benefited from the efforts of second-wave feminism. Third-wave feminists, for example, were born, or came of age, after the passage of Title IX, the Supreme Court win of *Roe v. Wade*, and the general fight for equality for all women. Walker introduced the notion of a third wave through a 1992 article for *Ms.* magazine and later edited an anthology, *To Be Real*, which highlighted the perspectives of young women. She, along with others, built an organization dedicated to funding and sponsoring young women's projects. The Third Wave Direct Action Corporation was founded in 1992, then became the Third Wave Foundation a few years later, and is now the Third Wave Fund. Walker set the tone for recognizing the energy and activism of a new wave of feminists. For while the 1990s saw more freedoms than ever before, this was still a time when our political, economic, and social representation was marginalized. Still today, we live in a global community where our lives are in danger, we do not have adequate access to health care, our home labor is rarely recognized, and our paid labor jobs bring us inequitable salaries. While many of the issues are the same as those that faced earlier generations, third-wave feminists added their perspectives to the discussion and worked to address the criticisms of the first and second waves to build a stronger movement.

One way in which the third wave contributed to a stronger movement was by diversifying its approach to activism and social change. Organizations like the Riot Grrrls and the Third Wave Foundation brought youth culture into a political context. One approach was through zines— independent, low-budget publications that have few or no rules. Zines are an "anything goes" approach to creating a venue for young voices. Often seen as radical, zines and their publishers focus on personal experiences while connecting political thought about issues ranging from abortion to rape to poverty to war. Not unlike the first and second waves, as young women come into the feminist movement, they try not only to find their voices but to also understand the political nature of their experiences. Coming of age with the Internet has also affected the approach to activism taken by third wavers. Not only has the Internet been instrumental in the production and dissemination of zines, but the Internet has been a key source of outreach, education, consciousness raising, advocacy, and organizing in today's feminist activism.

I think my family background played a huge part in forming my feminist identity as I was raised by a very old-fashioned Mexican mother. Judith, 20, Mexican American, bisexual, Massachusetts

In conjunction with the politics of inclusiveness, another critical contribution of the third wave is the appreciation of and the emphasis on the intersection of race, class, sex, gender, gender identity, sexual orientation, disability, and age. Through anthologies like *To Be Real, Colonize This!, Listen Up!,* and *The Fire This Time* and with writers like Rebecca Walker, Jennifer Baumgardner, Amy Richards, Michele Serros, Daisy Hernández, and Joan Morgan, we hear the diverse voices of young women critiquing the movement and addressing how we view feminism. Among these writers, as well as among young feminist groups throughout the country, a debate came alive about the effectiveness of identifying the waves of the feminist movement, the importance of claiming feminism or the idea of creating new terminology, and the errors of the past and proposals for the future. Forums address white privilege in the movement and the lack of connectedness to feminism among women of color. As Daisy Hernández and Pandora Leong write, in an April 2004 article titled, "Feminism's Future Young Feminists of Color Take the Mic,"

> Many women of color, like their Anglo counterparts, eschew the term "feminism" while agreeing with its goals (the right to an abortion, equality in job hiring, girls' soccer teams). But women of color also dismiss the label because the feminist movement has largely focused on the concerns of middle-class women. . . . Attempts to address the racism of the feminist movement have largely been token efforts without lasting effects. Many young women of color still feel alienated from a mainstream feminism that doesn't explicitly address race. . . . Feminism in the United States has stagnated in part because it has largely neglected a class and race analysis.[3]

It is precisely this analysis that the third wave embraces in its feminist discourse and activism. Learning from the movement's collective past, third wavers include a racial consciousness in every aspect of gender discrimination.

Similarly, the third wave includes an internalization of a broader definition of gender, actively avoiding a limited male-versus-female dichotomy. A growing understanding of and focus on transgender issues is increasingly central to the work of third-wave writers, activists, researchers, and CR groups. Writers like Amy Bloom, author of *Normal*; Kate Bornstein, author of *Gender Outlaw* and *My Gender Workbook*; Jennifer Finney Boylan, author of *She's Not There*; and Jack Halberstam, author of *In A Queer Time and Place*, influenced third-wave activists, and those coming to the movement today, to delve into

The main issue of feminism that I fear is under-represented is the issue that race and class are seen as separate issues. There should be no separation.
Yun Jin, 21, Korean-American, bisexual, California

a wider understanding of gender and gender oppression. While a great deal of understanding is still to be gained and there is a tremendous amount of work to do before we legally and socially recognize multiple genders, more of the movement is incorporating challenges to gender within the fight for equality.

FOURTH, AND FUTURE, WAVES

Is there a "fourth wave," and if so, who are they? They may or may not call themselves feminists. Some are involved with feminist organizations; many are not. They join different causes. They see themselves in many different identities. Building upon the gains and learning from the mistakes of the first, second, and third waves, young activists today broaden our understanding of feminism and our definition of experiences. They bring with them their own perspectives and politics. As one key example, the conversation about gender has changed significantly and the consciousness of the fluidity of gender identities is far more embraced by young activists today than any prior "wave." As such, this generation stands to deeply impact gender politics in our society. Indeed, they already have.

As I mentioned earlier, organizing our conversation of the history of U.S. feminism into waves may have its place in just that, history. The language of waves seems less and less relevant as our movement ebbs and flows among generations. If we have a fourth wave today, where are the time markers? When did this wave begin, and when do we begin counting subsequent waves? As this movement grows, our generational experiences are merging, perhaps making the wave analogy less relevant today. This question, however, is best addressed by the youngest feminist generations. The right to define themselves and their place in the movement is something all generations can recognize. Certainly, it was a cornerstone for those among my generation. That said, how to mentor, learn, and share leadership among many generations and across many identities is an essential focus.

Whether over issues of race, gender, or economics; levels of activist experience; ideas for change; feminist discourse; and/or agenda, activists across generations are intersecting in a challenging, yet meaningful way. While we may not define every problem the same way or come to the same conclusion about what action to take, we must hear one another and commit to working together. For we cannot do this work alone; we need one another if we are to realize the goals of feminism.

MENTORING THE MOVEMENT

Today, the feminist movement is in an interesting position—one that allows for direct involvement of people of different generations. This presents opportunities and challenges. In the movement today, activists of many generations face one another in the same room and work collectively in the fight to end discrimination. We have the opportunity to share experiences with, and learn from, one another intergenerationally. We have the opportunity to change the misconceptions about feminism and to learn from criticism, bringing all women to the table. I have personally experienced both the challenges and the triumphs of intergenerational leadership. On the downside, I have experienced the marginalization that accompanied being a young feminist who was trying to legitimize her vision and leadership in a community of second-wave feminists who believed that I was too young to lead. But, on the positive side, I spent four years leading California NOW in an intergenerational partnership. My executive director, Helen Grieco, is twenty years older than I, and together we created a model of leadership that valued and honored our experiences as activists with respect to our age differences. Intergenerational leadership is a relatively new concept, for, as I mentioned, the waves of the movement are merging in way we have not previously experienced.

The challenge today is in learning how to share the movement—and to share leadership within the movement. Sadly, we face significant barriers to achieving this—both from outside and within the movement itself. From outside, there is a widely publicized perception that young people are apathetic or that they don't "get it." Often there is a lack of reporting or representation of young people working for social justice—or, when such activities are reported upon, the young activists are reported as representing an exception to the norm. From within the movement, we see a struggle between the older generation and the younger generation of women's rights activists. Young activists who join this movement often express feelings of being

> For my generation in urban California, I feel feminism tends to just be accepted as something our mothers did and we ignorantly reap the benefits of the struggle.
> Susannah, 32, white, straight, married

excluded and patronized and feel pigeonholed into specifically "young" issues, despite their expertise on a wide array of feminist issues. Veteran feminists—those who have been in the movement for a significant period of time—often feel threatened by the growing movement of young feminists and sense that they are being replaced and unvalued. Occasionally, I hear an expression of relief that young women are picking up the proverbial baton and that veteran feminists can finally "retire." To be fair, there are those veterans who have truly committed themselves to working with the next generation, but, unfortunately, this is too seldom the reality. Instead, I often hear stories of young women being told to sit on the side and learn from the older women as opposed to being integrated into the leadership of the movement. Subsequently, we see young women disregarding the women's movement because they don't find a place or see themselves reflected within it. Veteran feminists are frustrated because they cannot seem to recruit young activists. As a result, we confront a disconnect between generations of women and the women's movement. And we face the challenge of learning to share leadership intergenerationally in order to continue this movement and achieve the goals for which we strive.

SO HOW DO WE DO THIS?

Speaking to the next generation, the veteran feminist, author, and activist Phyllis Chesler writes in her book *Letters to a Young Feminist*, "You are entitled to know our war stories. We cannot, in good conscience, send you into battle without giving you a very clear idea of what may happen there."[4] Not only must young activists hear these "war stories," but veteran feminists must also hear those of younger activists, for we too have been in battle. Through these experiences, we have both something to share and knowledge to gain. To foster intergenerational leadership is to recognize the contributions that young activists have to bring to the table while honoring the work and perspectives of those who have built the modern movement. It is both of these sets of experiences and perspectives that collectively strengthen and further the women's movement. I believe that, as we move further into the twenty-first century and face the future of feminism, it is imperative that we hear the multitude of women's voices. In order for this movement to be relevant to the next generation, we need to engage, empower, educate, and train young people as activists committed to making a difference. We need to mirror their experiences, address their concerns, and validate their perspectives. Going beyond their general participation, we must respect their leadership and encourage their position within a movement that belongs not just to their mothers—or grandmothers—but also to themselves. Young women can be incorporated into the movement today and not just be seen as the future. We can also recognize and celebrate the gains of the women's movement—learning about both our history and the fight that achieved our rights today. We need to clarify and emphasize what is at stake for women and girls under conservative, anti-woman, and racist political administrations. Young voices must be raised; the feminist movement needs be passed onto the future, and its leadership must be shared intergenerationally. We need to continue to look at the criticisms of the past in order to build for the future. We can learn to mentor while supporting the efforts of the next generation. And we can honor the efforts of the second wavers without dismissing their relevance in current activism. Most important, we must never forget that we come from a continuum—that women who came before us fought for the rights that we enjoy today and that women today must fight for the rights of future generations. We need to recognize these contributions and the immense value of "veteran" feminists. And we need to learn how to mentor young activists while recognizing the importance of their roles in leadership of the feminist movement today. Most of all, we must recognize that we can join together in this movement—for its future and ours.

SISTERHOOD IS INDEED GLOBAL

We are experiencing an interesting contradiction today, one that is not all that new to the United States. On the one hand, we fight for boundary recognition, debate who can immigrate and under what circumstances, and wage war under the guise of protecting democracy and nationalism. On the other hand, the Internet has broken barriers down in ways our foremothers never imagined; as governments, we export and import products among nations and involve ourselves in the governing of others; in the name of business, we establish multinational corporations that employ host-country citizens, use (and abuse) host-country natural resources, and dictate local and global markets; we share medical knowledge and resources worldwide; we travel extensively; we forge personal relationships; and in many other ways we break the boundaries between nations. The contradiction lies in our quest to be independent and separate while also being an integral part of the global community. The reality is that what one does in one area of the world does affect another area—we are all interrelated on both the personal and the political levels. Nowhere is this truer than in relation to the issues of political and social justice.

As we become a more globalized community, our feminism has moved to a greater recognition of women around the world. There is much debate about the role of Western women in the lives and battles of women worldwide. Is the discussion about feminism too focused on the United States? What role should U.S. women take in the battles for freedom that are fought in Asia, Latin America, Eastern Europe, and Africa? Do U.S. women involve themselves ineffectively in global feminism— taking leadership in fights that belong to women elsewhere? Do U.S.

women focus on international issues to avoid the realities of struggle within their own country? These are all critical questions to address when exploring global feminisms and revisiting Robin Morgan's sentiment that sisterhood is global.

I believe that there are many issues to be addressed in our country—many fights still to be fought, much discrimination to be eradicated, and many people to lift up. But I also believe that sisterhood is global and that we must realize and appreciate that when women are oppressed anywhere in the world, their oppression contributes to an overall devaluing of women everywhere. Not only do these actions of oppression impact the global attitude about women, but they devastate the daily lives of women around the globe. From honor killings, dowry deaths, domestic violence, and female genital mutilation to rape and sexual servitude around the globe,[5] women are fighting battles for their lives. While I believe there is much to do and focus upon within the United States, when we hear the cries for help from women around the world, I believe that we have no other choice than to answer with action.

The action we take can be multifaceted. From influencing U.S. policies on foreign relations to joining global efforts, American activists can play an important role in eradicating global gender discrimination. We can explore the bias that we bring as American women into the debate about the status of women worldwide, listen to the voices of women from cultures different from our own, and honor the leadership from women in individual regions, joining their efforts as supporters and not in an effort to replace them as leaders. We can participate with women-led efforts such as the Beijing Conference and the fight to ratify the Convention on the Elimination of All Forms of Discrimination Against Women (CEDAW)—both here in the United States and worldwide.

In 1995, women from around the globe gathered in Beijing, China, for the United Nations World Conference on Women. The intent of the meeting was to reaffirm the conventions of the 1993 World Conference on Human Rights in Vienna and to "put women's human rights even more firmly on the world agenda."[6] Addressing the critical issues of health care, poverty, violence against women, armed conflict, economic inequalities, environmental degradation, and governance, the women in attendance argued not only for understanding and recognizing women's rights as human rights, but also for implementing such rights.[7]

One important measure to support the rights of women is the Convention on the Elimination of All Forms of Discrimination Against Women (CEDAW). Adopted by the U.N. General Assembly in December 1979, CEDAW is the first international human rights treaty to define discrimination against women. CEDAW "laid the foundation and universal standard for women's equal enjoyment without discrimination of civil, political, economic, social and cultural rights. . . . CEDAW seeks to advance women's human rights protection by applying a gender perspective to principles enunciated in the Universal Declaration of Human Rights. . . . CEDAW holds governments responsible for taking steps to modify practices based on stereotypes about women's roles as well as beliefs about women's inferiority."[8] As of 2018, 189 out of 194 countries have ratified CEDAW.[9] The United States has not.

> CEDAW: The Convention defines discrimination against women as "any distinction, exclusion or restriction made on the basis of sex which has the effect or purpose of impairing or nullifying the recognition, enjoyment or exercise by women, irrespective of their marital status, on a basis of equality of men and women, of human rights and fundamental freedoms in the political, economic, social, cultural, civil or any other field."

To support the activism of women around the world and to eradicate global gender discrimination, we must start at home. We can call on our government to stop profiting off the backs of women worldwide. We can call on our government to support the efforts of women's organizations, the United Nations, microcredit unions, nongovernmental organizations, women leaders, grassroots activism, and any efforts to accord women safety, respect, and equality. And we can call on our government to ratify CEDAW.

BUILDING THE MOVEMENT

The gains of the movement to date are the foundation for our future. We still have challenges—both within and outside the movement—to overcome before we are truly a diverse, inclusive, and widely successful movement. We each bring something unique and dynamic to the table, and with this we may realize a collective power that is immeasurable. But this power will be realized only if we set aside our fears, learn from our mistakes, and build upon our diverse strengths. We must be willing to get honest—not just about our struggles in society, but also about those struggles within the movement and among our greatest allies. We must all be vested in this quest, for the outcome—good or bad—deeply impacts each of us. The movement, and feminism, belongs to us all.

SPOTLIGHT ON ACTIVISM

In 2015, I was contacted by a local group of high school women. They were putting on their first feminist conference and asked if I would speak. On their own, they designed, organized, and delivered a day-long conference bringing together dozens of area teens who wanted to learn about feminism and challenge gender oppression. Co-founded by high school students Inga Manticas and Zelia Gonzales, the Sacramento Young Feminist Alliance is a collaboration of multiple identity students from area high schools who focus on the intersections of gender, gender identities, race, class, and sexualities. They have been featured in local papers, as well as on *Feministing* and MTV. "The feminism that we are practicing, in the alliance," stated Inga Manticas in a *Sacramento Bee* article, "is to look at the way women and people of genders experience social inequality."[10]

TAKE ACTION

Getting Started

Read *Ms.* magazine, *Bitch*, or any other great feminist magazine.

Read feminist blogs . . . Feministing, Girl w/ Pen, or RH Reality Check (just a few examples!).

Ask libraries and bookstores to make feminist magazines available. Learn our herstory.

Take women's or gender studies courses (either at your current college or university or at your local community college).

Search the web and research feminist organizations, nationally and in your local area.

The Next Step

Attend a meeting of a feminist organization; check out several and see which group best suits your philosophy.

Honor our foremothers, and register to vote. Make a commitment to vote in every election.

We need a two-thirds vote in the U.S. Senate to ratify CEDAW. Contact your U.S. senators and urge them to fight for CEDAW.

Many U.S. states are working on state-based CEDAW initiatives. Contact your state representative to find out what your state is doing to support CEDAW.

Getting Out There

Donate time or money to an organization that works to support feminist work.

Volunteer with a feminist organization.

Host a discussion group to discuss what is at stake today for women and girls.

Create a plan of action on how you can make a difference.

Participate in a march or rally. Organize one around an issue that you are passionate about.

Investigate international exchange programs, or consider spending a summer working for an international aid group.

FABULOUS FEMINIST WEB RESOURCES

Amnesty International

www.amnesty.org

An international campaign working for human rights and peace. The website includes a wealth of information, including information on campaigns to end violence against women, protect refugee rights, end torture, and control arms.

Bitch Media

www.bitchmedia.org

Both a print magazine and online blog community to present a feminist critique of popular culture.

#BlackLivesMatter

www.blacklivesmatter.com

Created in 2012 after the murder of Trayvon Martin, #BlackLivesMatter is a movement to challenge racism as it permeates the institutions of our society, not the least of which includes law enforcement and the prison system. #BLM is about broadening the black liberation movement and "affirms the lives of Black queer and trans folks, disabled folks, black-undocumented folks, folks with records, women and all Black lives along the gender spectrum" (blacklivesmatter.com).

Black Women in Sisterhood for Action

www.feminist.com/bisas1.htm

Founded in 1980, Black Women in Sisterhood for Action is a nonprofit organization providing education and career development; scholarship assistance; social assistance; and information and resources geared toward black women.

Black Women Organize for Political Action

www.bwopa.org

BWOPA is a great organization. It is committed to training black women in the political process, and works to increase the presence and voice of black women in the political system.

CEDAW

www.ohchr.org

The United Nations Human Rights Office of the High Commissioner website tracks the status of CEDAW internationally. It also addresses critical issues regarding CEDAW. Great source of information.

Feminist.com Activism Links

www.feminist.com/activism

A great site for links to a variety of feminist activism nationwide.

Feminist Majority

www.feminist.org

National and international information, resources, and activism. The Feminist Majority website is a great source of information on how to get involved and make a difference in the lives of women worldwide.

Feministing
www.feministing.org
An online blog community created by, run by, and centered around young feminists.

Guerrilla Girls
www.guerrillagirls.com
Their website gives information about Guerrilla Girls's history and current activism. The site also includes publications, stickers, and posters.

Human Rights Watch
www.hrw.org
Campaigns to ensure that human rights apply to all. The organization engages in fact-finding research to determine the treatment of peoples around the globe. Their website includes information about the status of human rights abuses throughout the world, organized by region and by issue.

Kiva
www.kiva.org
Kiva is an international non-profit that was founded to link individuals around the globe to support one another through micro loans.

MANA (a national Latina organization)
www.hermana.org
Emphasizes the empowerment of Latinas through leadership development, community service, and advocacy.

National Organization for Women
www.now.org
Nationwide organization working on a wide range of women's rights issues. Their website includes resources, links to other organization, activist campaigns, and a store of feminist goods.

National Women's History Project

www.nwhp.org

Great resources for educators! A wealth of information and resources about women's history.

PFLAG

www.pflag.org

A community of LGBTIQ+ folks, their families, friends, and allies. They have local chapters throughout the United States.

Third Wave Fund

www.thirdwavefund.org

Great source for grants and scholarships for third-wave work. The website also includes resources and public-education programs.

United Nations Women Watch

www.un.org/womenwatch/

A great source for resources and statistics on the status of women globally.

3

A MOVEMENT FOR EVERYONE

Extraordinary work is being done by women—internationally, nationally, and locally—that has changed policy, politics, programs, and perspectives. Women have changed not only their lives and the lives of girls today, but also the lives of future generations. Women have broken barriers, set records, and established their worth, their ability, and their strength. Tremendous dedication, time, commitment, and sacrifice have gone into raising consciousness and ending discrimination. But, in the history of the feminist movement, there seems to be a divide among women ourselves—a disconnect that keeps us from unifying our efforts and achieving our collective goals. This disconnect, I believe, is based upon the very issues against which we are fighting—racism, classism, ageism, homophobia, transphobia, ableism, and the like. Our disconnection is the result of a long history of oppression and segregation, of being socialized to gravitate toward those who are most like us.

I am saddened by the historical roots that have served to keep us from truly unifying, and I wonder whether we can ever resolve them. Even after multiple waves of the feminist movement, we are still divided as women in this country and worldwide. Can we ever come together? I have been a feminist all my life. I have been active in the feminist movement for over twenty-five years. And, while I am incredibly grateful for the gains that have been made and the work that has been done, there is still much to be done to make this a movement for everyone.

Rac·ism *n.* 1. a belief or doctrine that inherent differences among the various human races determine cultural or individual achievement, usu. involving the idea that one's own race is superior. 2. a policy, system of government, etc., based on such a doctrine. 3. hatred or intolerance of another race or races.

RACISM

Of the criticisms of feminism and the women's movement, the most poignant is that of racism. It is a myth that women of color are not involved in the women's movement. They are and always have been. Unfortunately, a division formed that served to separate women of color from white women. There are many questions to ask about this division—did white women honor the perspectives of women of color? Were women of color incorporated into, and respected in, the leadership of the movement? Whose issues were of primary focus? How did racism infiltrate itself into a movement determined to fight for equality? I feel as if I have inherited much of this strain and daily confront the past when mobilizing for change today. But, as a white girl, it is a challenge to talk about race. What do I know about being "of color" in this culture? How can I speak to the issue of racism, not having lived it myself? I used to want to be colorblind, not to see race, but then I realized that this was essentially ignoring the role of race in a society that is far from colorblind. I realized that to try not to see color in this culture is to ignore the challenges of race and ethnicity, to undervalue the struggle that has been waged to end racial discrimination, and to distance myself from the ongoing fight to end racism. To do so also ignores the importance of celebrating our differences as a means of expanding our individual and collective knowledge.

I recognize the power of growing up white in a racist society. And, in that, I recognize that I say and do prejudicial things without fully knowing the impact of my actions or words. While I work every day to unlearn racism, to listen without prejudice, to hear the realities of my sisters, I also recognize that in a global culture with such tense race relations, I am seen first as a white woman. The assumption by some, I believe, is that I have no greater commitment to inclusivity than that assumed by my foremothers. So, how do we break through this? How do we create a venue to get real with each other? To have a dialogue that understands that, while we may not say the right words, while we may not fully understand the realities of living with racism, we come into the conversation with honest intentions? How do we have a dialogue about the multitude of oppressions we face without valuing one over the other? How do we get to a respect- ful understanding that, while a person of color knows racism in a way that a white woman can only imagine, the op- pression of sexism is also real? I believe that we have come to a place of under- standing that no longer asks people to define narrowly who they are primarily—a person of color *or* a woman *or* a lesbian *or* a gay man *or* a person with a disability—but that recognizes our diversity and the importance of eradicating all discrimination and oppression. I own the fact that because I grew up white in a racist society, on some level I will have prejudice, and, though without the intent to offend, I sometimes say or do things that are offensive. In my quest for better understanding, communication, better partnership, I unknowingly tokenize—not because I believe that one person can speak for her group, but because I want the conversation to occur.

> *I think Indian people still have a hard time incorporating feminism into the conventional idea of what Indian women are supposed to be like. We worship our goddesses and confine our women to cultural straight* [sic] *jackets.* Sheethal, 23, Asian Indian, heterosexual, Ohio

I want there to be a place where we can all sit down and really talk it all out, where we come to the conversation with honest intentions. I want us to give one another the benefit of the doubt, understanding that fear of offending has kept us from meaningful interaction. I am not talking about truly, overtly racist people who hate on the basis of skin color and think they are right in doing so—they are a whole other, more obvious problem. I am talking about the people who care about equity, who are conscious of racism but who largely are ignorant of the implications of their own words and actions and their impact, or the people who spend so much energy searching for the right words that they say nothing. I realize that just sitting down together is not the solution, but it is an important step.

One of the greatest moments in my activist life occurred at the 1996 San Francisco "Fight the Right" March. As Californians, we were fighting two horrible propositions—Prop. 209, the "civil rights initiative" that proposed the elimination of affirmative action in the state, and Prop. 187, which proposed cutting health and social services (including public education) for immigrant populations in California. For the first time, at this march, I saw all the "groups" come together to fight discrimination. The women's movement, the civil rights movement, the labor movement, the immigration movement, the LGBT movement—six hundred different organizations were represented, and approximately fifty thousand participants were at the march. In that moment, we were powerful—instead of focusing on our differences and debating who had more at stake, we recognized that we were all oppressed by the power structure. Because we are female or gay or a person of color or an immigrant, we are denied access to full participation in society—we are denied housing, jobs, promotions, and free movement. We are disenfranchised, ignored, targeted, or denied basic rights because of characteristics inherent to who we are. We are divided and pitted against one another, fighting over a small piece of the social pie, while all the while the power structure takes the bulk of the pie. I believe that there is a conscious effort to divide our groups. But, if we can begin to recognize our commonalities rather than believe in the lines that divide us, we can share the struggle, unite forces, and emerge stronger. The power structure fears this most—fears an organizing of the oppressed who can rise up collectively and change the distribution of the proverbial pie. Unfortunately, in the end, both propositions were approved. The movements are still fractured and we continue with the struggle to see the importance of our diversity and to share leadership across the board. But we have our moments and I have to believe that every time we come together we build a stronger foundation for future efforts.

> As a woman, feminism obviously represents me. But as a Black American, I have goals that are much different than the goals of the feminist movement.
> Carita, 33, straight, California

The 2017 Women's March, following the inauguration of Donald J. Trump, was one of these moments. In communities all across the United

States, and indeed across the globe, people came together to protest the electoral college election of Trump. And in doing so, to collectively stand against all that he embodies: misogyny and sexual assault, racism and white supremacy, anti-immigration, anti-Islamism, and his attack against the poor. Millions marched, far exceeding the paltry numbers who showed for his inauguration. Trump's administration, his nominees, and his proposed agenda were so blatantly against the goals of social justice that people from across movements, and even those who have never joined a cause, stood together. The Women's March far from solved the challenges of racism, classism, ableism, and like within the feminist movement, and there are valid criticisms of the march, but it was a moment in time where many embraced the connection of oppression that brought us all together against a common enemy. We still have much work to do—within and outside the movement.

I have seen racism within the women's movement. I have heard the frustrations of women of color who come to the table only to be shut out by white reality. I have seen white women negate the importance of religion and faith to women of color who often hold these as central to who they are. I have seen many well-intentioned white women make racist remarks. But I have also seen women from all ethnic backgrounds sit together in a room and discuss the challenges to women today and collectively work toward a solution. I have seen the bridging of our lives, the raising of consciousness, and the commitment to band together. And it is a powerful sight.

The second wave's approach of consciousness raising is regaining momentum as young feminists are reviving the tradition and practice. And it is not just young people who need this consciousness raising; I see everyday examples of racial tensions among people of all ages and across all ethnicities. The reality is that we live in a multicultural, multiracial society. But, despite this diversity, when it comes to the debate about race, we tend to see and talk only in black and white. Certainly, historical and current tensions are significant between African Americans and whites, but these are not the only racial tensions that exist. Racism occurs between white people and people of every ethnicity, and it also exists among other ethnic groups. The idea of valuing one's skin color over another is not unique to white people. As JeeYeun Lee writes in her article "Beyond Bean Counting," "Issues of exclusion are not the sole province of white feminists."[1] We categorize and discriminate in all areas of race, creating a hierarchy of value within and among varying ethnicities. At the core are issues of power—getting it, having it, and keeping it. And, indeed, historically, white people have systematically held the most power. This is, of course, still true today. However, not all white people have power. Class, age, gender, physical and mental ability, and sexual orientation all come into play when determining power. But skin color alone does afford benefits for whites. Whiteness itself provides an unearned privilege for those who carry the pigmentation. In her book *Feminism is for Everyone*, bell hooks writes:

> *I am a white person, so in large part I believe that feminism does represent me, but it is not as inclusive as it needs to be to really represent all women. Jennifer, 31, Caucasian white girl of Italian heritage, California*

> No intervention changed the face of American feminism more than the demand that feminist thinkers acknowledge the reality of race and racism. All white women in this nation know that their status is different from that of black/women of color. They know this from the time they are little girls watching television and seeing only their images, and looking at magazines and seeing only their images. They know that the only reason nonwhites are absent/invisible is because they are not white. All white women in this nation know that whiteness is a privileged category. The fact that white females may choose to repress or deny this knowledge does not mean they are ignorant: it means that they are in denial.[2]

I believe that white women must confront this denial and deconstruct our role in racism. In her writings on white privilege, Peggy McIntosh encourages looking beyond individual acts of racism to invisible systems of privilege and dominance of whites. She writes, "As a white person, I realized I had been taught about racism as something that puts others at a disadvantage, but had been taught not to see one of its corollary aspects, white privilege, which puts me at an advantage."[3] White people must begin (and continue) to deconstruct and understand this privilege if we are to be true allies in ending racism and the discrimination that accompanies it. If you are white, consider these statements when evaluating your benefits as a white person:[4]

I live in a school district where more money is spent on schools that white children go to than on those that children of color attend.

I went to a school where the textbooks reflected my race as heroes and builders of the United States, and there was little mention of contributions of people of color.

I work in a job, career, or profession where there are few people of color.

I can always vote for candidates that reflect my race.

My race needn't be a factor in where I choose to live or where I send my children to school.

I don't need to think about racism every day.

For a white person, examining these statements is the start to unlearning racism and beginning to look critically at the tensions we keep at arm's length—because we are certain (and often loudly proclaim) that we are not racist. In meeting after meeting of "progressive-minded" activists, I hear white women argue against concerns brought forward by women of color. Perhaps this happens because progressive white women have a lot invested in being politically correct. Perhaps it happens because there is a lot of guilt about being white among those whites who fight for equality. But fear of being accused of being racist gets in the way of *hearing* the points and views of women of color. And, instead of building a bridge, we deepen the divide.

White people need to get beyond their feelings of guilt and understand that guilt for being white (or male or straight) is self-indulgent and paralyzing. This isn't about you. It is about the structure of society and your actions within it. Feel guilty if you are not contributing to the solution, but not over something over which you have no control. Energy is much better spent working to be allies of people of color in ending racial discrimination. In his book *Uprooting Racism: How White People Can Work for Racial Justice*, Paul Kivel sets forth some important guidelines for being a white ally to people of color:

1. Assume racism is everywhere, every day.
2. Notice who is the center of attention and who is the center of power.
3. Notice how racism is denied, minimized, and justified.
4. Understand and learn from the history of whiteness and racism.
5. Understand the connections between racism, economic issues, sexism, and other forms of injustice.
6. Take a stand against injustice.
7. Be strategic. Decide what is important to challenge and what's not.
8. Don't confuse a battle with the war.
9. Don't call names or be personally abusive.
10. Support the leadership of people of color.
11. Learn something about the history of white people who have worked for racial justice.
12. Don't do it alone.
13. Talk with your children and other young people about racism.[5]

As a white woman, let me add another guideline: Don't look to people of color to educate you on racism. It is not the job of people of color to take care of white folks. It is the job of white folks to raise their consciousness, to reach out and partner with people of color, to consult, include, and take the lead from people of color on the issues of racism . . . and on other issues of social justice, as well. As McIntosh asks, "having described [white privilege], what will I do to lessen or end it?"[6] White people need to share positions of power and support and encourage the leadership of people of color in organizations and in the larger society.

RACISM AND THE FEMINIST MOVEMENT

What about the feminist movement? Does it truly represent all women? Like many of us, I have learned the history of exclusion and the politics between white women and women of color. I have heard the arguments that white women focused on issues about their lives—for example, fighting for the rights to abortion—while women of color were fighting for their rights to have children; white women have neglected to embrace and support the issues of women of color. I have seen conflict arise when white women focus solely on their gender as their oppression, putting gender above all else. All the while, women of color fight to be recognized as such and resist being forced to choose their ethnicity over their gender or vice versa. I have seen the fighting between women, and, more tragically, I have seen women give up and move further away from one another. The conflict for feminists today is in knowing this past and respecting the feelings and opinions that came from that time, while living our commitment to a more inclusive movement, doing this work every day and confronting and changing this heritage. Many young activists today are acutely aware of the reality of racism and the history of exclusion of women of color by so-called mainstream organizations—it has been taught to us through women's studies and is present in our day-to-day interactions, our writings, our dialogues, and our activism. The discussion of race is integral to all that young feminists do, as are gender politics, class, sexuality, and disability. Many today are coming into feminism at the same time they are aligning with #BlackLivesMatter, #MeToo, homelessness, and trans-inclusive movements. And, while we certainly don't have everything figured out, we have had the benefit of learning from the women who came before us, and, as a result, we recognize and appreciate the inadequacy of valuing gender as the only oppression.

> *I have mixed feelings about whether the movement represents me or not. I feel that it does represent me individually, but not some of my black sisters. There is more happening to include women (and men) of every race, but it's not there yet.*
> Nicole, 25, heterosexual, Connecticut

White women need to recognize and respect that women of color have always been involved in social justice movements—for suffrage, women's rights, civil rights, LGBTIQ+ rights, disability rights, and so on. There is a misconception that women of color are not interested in the feminist movement; quite the contrary, they are leaders and visionaries working for change every day. This, of course, is not news to women of color, but it just might be news to those who know of the feminist movement only what they see on TV or read in history books. In fact, this movement is multifaceted—from nationally based mainstream organizations to local, grassroots efforts, we all contribute to this fight for equality. We need to come together to define feminism, to define our work, and to commit to working together. Collectively, we can reclaim and redefine the image of feminism and women's rights—so that all women, all experiences, and all perspectives are represented. We are in this together, not in spite of but because of our differences and because of our commitment to justice. We must ensure that this is the foundation upon which we build and that the images of the movement reflect all women.

Feminism is very inclusive as far as addressing the rights of women no matter their race, gender, ethnicity, income level, marital status, sexual orientation, etc. etc. etc. Christina, 22, straight, Greek, California

One of the greatest contributions of the Third Wave was to begin to close the gap across ethnicities, to build upon the failures and successes of this movement, and to live a politic that is about, and represents, all women. To continue these efforts, and expand upon them, we need to be willing to join together, to be honest with one another, to build and share a dream together. And we need to tell the true story of feminism, one that is not controlled by the media, does not put forth one leader but rather reflects the contributions, the perspectives, and the lives of us all. I see today's feminists attempting to do this work everyday, choosing not to inherit this divide but to learn from our foremothers and change the course of this movement. We need to be able to call one another on our misconceptions and inaccuracies, to hold each other accountable, to listen and hear one another—each of us, across all ethnic and racial lines. It is difficult, it is confusing, it is sensitive, it is raw, but it is also vital.

WHAT CAN YOU DO?

Listen. Read. Support. Advocate. Join multicultural efforts to address issues as defined by those affected. Hold your own organizations, friends, school, and family accountable for racism, exclusion, and ignorance. Get honest with yourself and about your actions. It is not enough to believe that you are not racist; you must deconstruct racism within our culture, your role, and how you benefit from it. We need to question the structure of society and the hierarchy of race. We must raise our racial consciousness. We need to get honest about this, about who

> I identify as a feminist to a certain extent. I believe the term womanist was coined by Alice Walker to more accurately reflect the unique struggle of Black women who suffer discrimination both for being female and non-White; that term might more accurately reflect my identity. Cheria, 31, Black/African American, heterosexual, Ohio

benefits and who does not—even when this system is not what we wish for or consciously support. We *all* need to do this. I do hold the feminist movement to a higher standard, as I do all social justice movements, but I believe that we must also recognize that racism is a challenge throughout our culture, that there is not an answer out there that the feminist movement is choosing to ignore. Which means that we—the multiracial, multicultural, multigendered, progressive masses—need to lead the way in finding the solutions.

TIMELINE OF RACIAL AND ETHNIC JUSTICE IN THE U.S.

The following is nowhere near a complete timeline, but I hope that it piques your interest and encourages you to continue to research and learn. Malcolm X said, "Armed with the knowledge of our past, we can with confidence charter a course for our future. Culture is an indispensable weapon in the freedom struggle. We must take hold of it and forge the future with the past."[7] It is important to know that which came before us; the fights that ensued;

the losses and the victories. The story of those who seek to deny civil liberties is long and powerful, but those who have individually and collectively stood for justice is stronger. While I have included a few key court cases and events that limit freedom, I have tried to focus primarily on those events that worked toward, or achieved, justice and equity.

1790—Benjamin Franklin's petition to abolish slavery is ridiculed. Instead, the Naturalization Act is passed, limiting citizenship to whites only.

1851—Freed slave and abolitionist Sojourner Truth delivers her powerful speech "Ain't I a Woman" at the Ohio Women's Rights Convention.

1865—The Thirteenth Amendment abolishes slavery, though Southern states continue in practice, establishing "Black Codes" until the first Civil Rights Act the following year, invalidating those codes. June 19th, known as Juneteenth or Freedom Day, commemorates the end of slavery in Texas, and emancipation throughout the former Confederacy of the Southern states. In 1980, Texas was the first state to officially recognize this day as a state holiday. Congress recognized the holiday through joint resolution in 1997. In 2018, Apple added the day to the official holidays in its iOS calendar.

1868—The Fourteenth Amendment grants due process and equal protection under the law to African Americans.

1870—The Fifteenth Amendment grants the legal right to vote to black men, including former slaves. Access to voting proves to be an ongoing struggle.

1886—The U.S. Supreme Court rules in *Yick Wo v. Hopkins* that a San Francisco laundry ordinance enforced solely against Chinese is unconstitutional.

1896—The U.S. Supreme Court rules in *Plessy v. Fergusson*, upholding racial segregation in public facilities and effectively solidifying "separate but equal" and validating Jim Crow practices in the South.

1898—The U.S. Supreme Court rules in *Wong Kim Ark v. United States*, that children born in the U.S. to parents of Chinese descent cannot be denied citizenship.

1909—The National Association for the Advancement of Colored People (NAACP) is formed.

1924—Congress passes the Indian Citizenship Act, granting citizenship to all American Indians. Tribal membership and land rights are maintained, though many tribes remain wards of the U.S. government and the right to vote is still barred for many Native Americans at this time.

1944—Four hundred Japanese Americans protest their draft order because they are simultaneously being denied constitutional rights. The U.S. Supreme Court rules the Japanese internment camps constitutional in *Korematsu v. United States*. The *Korematsu* case becomes the test case for forced internment in the U.S. The National Congress of American Indians is formed.

1945—The last Japanese internment camp officially closes, in Tule Lake, Utah.

1948—Executive Order 9981 ends racial segregation in the Armed Forces.

1950—The Chinese Hand Laundry Alliance strikes in New York City, seeking wage increases and benefits.

1952—In *Sei Fujii v. California*, the U.S. Supreme Court rules the Alien Land Law of 1913 racially discriminatory and unconstitutional. The McCarran-Walter Act allows Asian residents to become naturalized citizens.

1954—In *Brown v. Board of Education*, the U.S. Supreme Court ends legal racial segregation in schools.

1955—Rosa Parks's refusal to give up her seat on a bus kicks off the year-long Montgomery Bus Boycotts.

1957—The "Little Rock Nine" are blocked while trying to integrate Central High School. President Eisenhower eventually sends federal troops in to escort the students. The Civil Rights Act of 1957 is signed into law.

1960—Four black college students refuse to leave the "whites only" Woolworth lunch counter in Greensboro, North Carolina. The

Student Nonviolent Coordinating Committee (SNCC) is formed by students at Shaw University in North Carolina. Six-year-old Ruby Bridges is escorted by four armed federal marshals to desegregate William Frantz Elementary School in New Orleans.

1961—The Freedom Rides kick off to test the 1960 U.S. Supreme Court ruling in *Boynton v. Virginia*, banning segregated interstate bus travel. The National Indian Youth Council is formed.

1962—The United Farm Workers (UFW) labor union is formed by Cesar Chavez, Dolores Huerta, and Gilbert Padilla.

1963—President Kennedy sends the National Guard to the University of Alabama when Governor George C. Wallace refuses entry of two black students into the university. Nearly 250,000 people attend the March on Washington for Jobs and Freedom in Washington, DC, where Martin Luther King Jr. delivers his now-famous "I Have a Dream" speech.

1964—President Johnson signs the Civil Rights Act of 1964. The U.S. Equal Employment and Opportunity Commission (EEOC) is formed. Activist Aileen Hernandez is the only woman appointed to the EEOC when formed.

1965—The Selma to Montgomery march in protest of black voter suppression is brutally interrupted and impacted by police. Weeks later, after a court win, civil rights leaders are able to reach Montgomery, Alabama. President Johnson signs the Voting Rights Act of 1965. The five-year-long Delano Grape Boycott kicks off, joining the efforts of the UFW and the Agricultural Workers Organizing Committee. Patsy Takemoto Mink becomes the first Asian American to serve in Congress (and the first woman to represent Hawai'i).

1966—Huey Newton and Bobby Seale form the Black Panther Party. To raise awareness of the farm worker movement, Cesar Chavez and others embark on a 340-mile *peregrinación*, or pilgrimage, from Delano to Sacramento, the California state capitol.

1967—The U.S. Supreme Court rules in *Loving v. Virginia* that barring marriages among interracial couples is unconstitutional.

1968—The Fair Housing Act, or the Civil Rights Act of 1968, is signed into law. Cesar Chavez fasts for twenty-five days to help recommit the movement to the tenets of non-violent protest inspired by Gandhi and MLK Jr. Shirley Chisholm becomes the first black woman elected to the U.S. Congress. The American Indian Movement is started by Dennis Banks, NeeGawNwayWeeDun, Clyde H. Bellecourt, and George Mitchell. The controversial Indian Civil Rights Act is passed, guaranteeing the rights of individual Native Americans living under tribal governments.

1968–69—Student protests at UC Berkeley and San Francisco State University lead to the first Ethnic Studies programs at college.

1969–71—The "Indians of All Tribes" occupation of Alcatraz occurs.

1970—The American Indian Movement occupies Plymouth Rock and kicks off the first annual National Day of Mourning.

1972—The "Trail of Broken Treaties" cross-country protest is organized by Native American tribes and organizations. Groups siege the Bureau of Indian Affairs building in protest. The Indian Education Act is passed that, among other things, requires culturally relevant education and establishes the Office of Indian Education.

1973—Over 200 Sioux Indians occupy Wounded Knee for a seventy-one-day protest.

1974—The Asian American Legal Defense and Education Fund is started, working to protect the civil liberties of Asian Americans.

1975—The UFW wins passage of the Agricultural Labor Relations Act, which establishes collective bargaining for farm workers in California. Chavez, with thousands of others, marches for 1000 miles over fifty-nine days to educate farm workers on their rights.

1978—Asian Pacific American Heritage week is officially recognized by Congress. The American Indian Movement organizes the "Longest Walk" from California to Washington, DC, calling attention to housing, health care, employment, and legislative issues impacting native communities. The American Indian Religious Freedom Act is passed, recognizing the rights of American Indians to practice the religion of their choice.

1980—The Refugee Act is passed in Congress, giving specific status to refugees.

1981—The Fort McDowell Yavapai Nation of Arizona wins a long battle preventing the building of the Orme Dam, which would have flooded more than half of their reservation.

1982—The U.S. Supreme Court rules in *Plyler v. Doe* to uphold the rights of the children of undocumented immigrants to attend public school.

1985—Wilma Mankiller becomes the first woman principal chief of the Cherokee.

1986—The UFW kicks off the Wrath of Grapes campaign to call attention to pesticide poisoning of grape workers and their children.

1988—Congress overrides a veto by President Reagan, passing the Civil Rights Restoration Act, which expands non-discrimination policies in private institutions that receive federal funds. Cesar Chavez does his longest, and last, fast for thirty-six days to protest pesticide poisoning. The Civil Liberties Act is passed, ruling that Executive Order 9066 was wrong and officially apologizing for the internment of thousands of Japanese Americans during WWII.

1989—Ileana Ros-Lehtinen becomes the first Latina elected to Congress (also the first Cuban American elected to Congress and first woman Republican elected to the House from Florida).

1992—People in Los Angeles, CA, take to the streets in protest following the acquittal of four white police officers in the beating of Rodney King. The National Coalition of Racism in Sports and Media is formed in response to a growing movement challenging the use of Native American imagery as team mascots.

2011—The Keystone XL Pipeline protests kick off. This becomes a massive joint movement among native groups and environmentalists protesting a new phase in the pipeline project. In 2015, President

Obama rejected the pipeline proposal by vetoing the related Congressional bill. However, in 2017, Donald Trump took action to support the continuation of the Keystone XL Pipeline (and the Dakota Access Pipeline).

2013—Alicia Garza, Patrisse Cullors, and Opal Tometi form Black Lives Matter in response to the acquittal of George Zimmerman, who killed Trayvon Martin. Integrating women, queer, and transgender people, #BlackLivesMatter quickly grew to a national movement protesting police brutality and anti-black racism in the U.S. The Havasupai Tribe leads efforts to prevent uranium mining near the Grand Canyon National Park.

2015—The African American Policy Forum kicks off #SayHerName to bring attention to the fact that black women are also the targets of racialized police brutality.

2016—After UFW activist efforts, the first law in the country providing farm workers with overtime pay is passed in California. Standing Rock Sioux kick off a protest that soon gains national and international attention regarding the Dakota Access Pipeline. Over 200 other tribes and allies join the protest.

2018—Deb Haaland and Sharice Davids become the first Native American women to be elected to Congress. Rashida Tlaib and Ilhan Omar become the first Muslim women elected to Congress.

INTERGENERATIONAL PARTNERSHIP

One of my first memories of being a leader was in first grade. Normally, story time involved a gathering on the floor around our teacher's feet. Instead, I convinced a table of fellow six-year-olds that we were "close enough" to hear the story and had no need to leave our table for the cold hardness of the floor. I convinced the kids at my table to stay put, even in the face of losing recess. We sat together in quiet resolve. And, of course, after story time we spent our recess practicing how to get up from our table and sit on the floor, how to get up from the floor and sit back at our table. The point wasn't that we lost our recess; the point was that they did what I said. I was thrilled; I intuited that I had a "gift." I was a leader—or, perhaps, a little dictator!

After a few years of principal-parent conferences (don't all good activists end up in the principal's office?), I began to learn that making people follow me was not as interesting as inspiring change. Controlling people's actions wasn't as interesting as creating a dialogue about a situation and encouraging a collective solution. I realized that I still had a lot to learn from other leaders before becoming one. I could not have become who I am today without the presence of very important mentors in my life to guide me. My most successful mentor relationships were ones that not only guided me but, more importantly, allowed me to lead. Mentoring is an exchange, an egalitarian relationship based upon support and collaboration. As the waves of the feminist movement intersect, mentoring is crucial for the movement's growth. One of the greatest challenges any new generation of activists is charged with is to continue to expand upon the movement of our foremothers, as well as to learn from their mistakes and to actively counter the misconceptions about feminism more generally. We come to this movement energetic and idealistic—we've heard the stories of our mothers, learned our history in women's studies, and grown up expecting equality with men. We come from all races, all countries; we speak a variety of languages, practice a number of different religions and faiths; we have different economic and educational backgrounds; we have different opinions. We are active in our communities, in politics, and in organizations because we want to make a difference. Some of us identify as feminists; some of us do not. We debate the word—its connotations, its meaning, its history. Wherever we enter this movement, we share the commonality of being the children of feminism, of civil rights, of lesbian and gay rights, trans rights, disability rights, the fight for economic justice . . . and all the movements that occurred before us to bring true social, economic, and political equity to us all. We benefit from these movements and inherit a unique perspective on politics today. And, while we are afforded a different life from that of our mothers—through better laws, court decisions, legislation, social consciousness shifts, and the like—we are also in the unique position of being able to critique the movement without having lived through our mothers' experiences firsthand. This perspective both hinders us and provides us the objectivity with which to examine the movement constructively.

However, new activists risk offending veteran activists if opinions or views differ. As younger women are trying to make names for themselves, to make a difference, they may fear offending the leaders of the movement and thus being rejected or shut out by the very people they respect and with whom they dream of shared leadership. If they don't follow the party line, will they still be allowed at the table? If they question the status quo or offer a new way, what do they risk?

We wouldn't have the freedom that we had today if it wasn't for the women who fought for our rights. I believe this movement represents all women and men of all ages. Gabriella, 19, Hispanic, heterosexual, California

Many young activists have turned away from mainstream organizations largely because they do not see themselves reflected within them—they don't represent the issues in the manner that they see them. They don't feel that leadership or respect is attainable in mainstream organizations that carry with them years of set history and entrenched authority. Still others do join these organizations, and within them find both mentors and resistance. With mentors they find a place of encouragement and support—a place at the table.

Young women encounter a wide variety of resistance. Some of this resistance is intentional, and some of it is not. There is a gap in understanding between generations; in many ways, we don't speak the same language. New views on old ideas are presented; a new perspective is shared and a new reality is addressed in relation to the issues that veteran feminists have long been fighting. There is a great deal that younger activists can learn from veteran feminists. Agreed. But there is also a great deal that younger feminists can teach veterans. The dilemma is that the movement finds itself in new territory, merging voices as we continue to confront our common battles of discrimination. Whenever a new voice emerges, tension arises, sometimes out of fear and threat and other times out of ignorance. Young activists often report feeling isolated, undervalued, and unwelcome.

Sometimes 2nd wavers seem to think they know it all, and I think they need to step back and let some of us take leadership roles. Juli, 34, white, bisexual, Massachusetts

While veteran or older feminists have a responsibility to the movement in mentoring, supporting, and embracing young activism, young women also have an obligation to learn about and respect the work and contributions of veteran feminists. We all need to appreciate that this work is ongoing. We need to recognize that this work enables us to be who we are and to have what we have today but also that the gains of the movement are not just for us. We need to recognize that we are part of a continuum and that we have an obligation, a responsibility to join with and continue the work of feminism, contributing our perspective, our voice, and our vision. As generations merge, we struggle to find tangible ways to share leadership intergenerationally. Collectively now, we are charged with addressing these challenges and learning how to not just co-exist in this movement, but to learn from and support one another. Young activists don't want to replace older women; they want to sit at the table with them. They don't want to be expected merely to show up for events, but rather want to be included in the design and creation of the event. They don't want to be considered the future of the movement; they want to be a part of the movement today and help build for the future.

Earlier in the book, I spoke a bit about building bridges between generations and fostering true intergenerational leadership. At the core, it really comes down to respect—respecting that we have different experiences with similar issues, that we bring with us unique perspectives based upon our individual histories, cultures, and religions, and respecting the reality that, while we may come at a situation differently, we all want to end oppression, hate, ignorance, and dis-

I was raised not to need to be a "feminist" to believe that I am equal, to be able to KNOW without having to identify as such. Karen, 26, Aleut, heterosexual, Alaska

crimination. I've put together a Do's and Don'ts list to help facilitate the growth of intergenerational partnership, noting, of course, that this list is in no way exhaustive. These are my suggestions; they are based on my own experiences and on the numerous experiences shared with me— from both younger and older activists. Feel free to add to, change, alter, adapt—whatever is needed to further the conversation.

DO'S AND DON'TS FOR VETERAN FEMINISTS

Do give the benefit of the doubt, and ask questions before you make assumptions.

Do empower young activists to run with their ideas.

Do recognize that age doesn't equal experience—young feminists join this movement with a wide array of experiences and expertise. They reach their feminist consciousness at different points of their lives. In other words, just because they're young doesn't mean they don't know things.

Do ask what young activists need from you.

Do share your histories, experiences, failures, and successes, while sharing your expertise, ideas, and knowledge today.

Do recognize and respect the diversity of younger feminists—in terms of demographics, identities, ideas, and approaches to activism.

Don't accuse young feminists of "not getting it"—if they're at the meeting, march, action, they do "get it."

Don't pigeonhole young feminists into specifically "young feminist" issues— they have many areas of knowledge and interests.

Don't dismiss ideas just because they "have been tried before."

Don't overlook leadership ability in young people.

Don't assume that young activists are here to take over, or that they don't value your work, past and present, or that they don't want to work with you today.

DO'S AND DON'TS FOR YOUNG FEMINISTS

Do give the benefit of the doubt, and ask questions before you make assumptions.

Do respect the energy and work—past and present—of veteran feminists.

Do recognize that you are a part of a continuum—the movement that happened before you but also the responsibility that you have to those who are coming up behind you.

Do speak your mind, bring your ideas to the table, and take leadership.

Do your share of the work, but don't be a "gopher" to do all the trivial tasks.

Do celebrate and honor the diversity of the movement today—in terms of both identities and ideas.

Don't apologize for your age.

Don't exclude older feminists from your discussions or action plans; we have a lot to learn from one another. And we have a lot to gain from working collectively.

Don't ignore the political context of our lives. This movement is not just about reclaiming knitting or wearing pink, and it is not just about our pursuits or our careers; it is about a system of oppression and the need for collective action.

Don't dismiss the ideas of veteran feminists with the assumption that "they're out of it."

DISABILITY RIGHTS

Despite the passage, in 1990, of the Americans with Disabilities Act (ADA), which prohibits discrimination in employment against those with a disability, disabled people in the United States continue to experience discrimination and abuse—with women facing the greatest challenges. Women with disabilities face multiple discriminations—their disability and their gender, and for some the added discrimination

---

Americans with Disabilities Act (ADA)—July 26, 1990
101st Congress of the United States
An Act: To establish a clear and comprehensive prohibition of discrimination on the basis of disability.

of race, ethnicity, sexuality, gender identity, and more. They are stereotyped and stigmatized, resulting in inequitable treatment, including barriers to equal employment and educational opportunities. According to a Center for Women Policy Studies *Briefing on Girls and Young Women with Disabilities*, young women are underrepresented in special education programs, are less likely to find images of themselves or role models in education, are less likely to receive sex education, have lower employment rates, receive lower pay, and face a greater likelihood of being employed in low-status jobs than do disabled males.[8] According to December 2017 statistics from the U.S. Bureau of Labor Statistics, women with disabilities have an unemployment rate nearly two and a half times that of their non-disabled female peers.[9] According to the U.S. National Institute on Disability and Rehabilitation Research's *Chart Book on Women and Disability*, of children who participate in special-education programs, about two-thirds are male.[10] Additionally, women with disabilities working year-round earn seventy-six cents to every dollar earned by men with disabilities working year-round.[11]

Clearly, the challenges faced by disabled women are central to the issues championed by the women's movement. Unfortunately, the women's movement has not always centralized these concerns, and women with disabilities often still feel invisible in the movement. Able-bodied feminists are often guilty of perpetuating stereotypes and using ableist language. From inaccessible meetings and events to phrases like "fall on deaf ears," "blind to privilege," or "such and such is crazy," disabled women have been marginalized both in society and within the movement. Feminist disability studies, activists' blogs, and organizational conferences such as the Disabled People's International World Summit, which focuses on women and disabilities, have challenged the dehumanization of disabled peoples and pushed for the recognition and understanding of disability as identity. The intersection of disability and feminism must be fully integrated into social justice work, with disabled peoples framing the conversation and leading the way.

LESBIAN, GAY, BISEXUAL, TRANSGENDER, INTERSEX, QUEER+

I remember sitting on old couches in the women's center at the heart of campus and engaging in long, detailed conversations in which we debated where we all fell on the Kinsey scale of sexuality, the spectrum of sexual orientation developed by Dr. Alfred Kinsey in the 1940s and 1950s. We spent hours debating whether or not there was truth to the idea that everyone is bisexual. We shared a collective outrage at the religious right, which argued that being gay is immoral and against God. We discussed the fluidity of gender and the influence and power of socialization. We argued the power of the media and the paucity of images of gay and lesbian characters. We discussed the misconception that all feminists are lesbians and fought against the notion that being a "dyke" is negative. We discussed the impact of these misconceptions on the public perception of feminism and their impact on the future of the movement.

TIMELINE OF LGBTIQ+ RIGHTS

1924—The Society for Human Rights, the first openly gay American organization, is formed in Chicago.

1955—Del Martin and Phyllis Lyon form Daughters of Bilitis, the first lesbian organization in the United States, in San Francisco.

1958—The nation's first gay periodical, *One*, is allowed by Supreme Court decision to be distributed through the mail.

1961—José Sarria, the country's first openly gay political candidate, runs for office in San Francisco.

1961—Illinois becomes the first state to abolish laws against consensual gay sex.

1964—The New York League for Sexual Freedom protests the military's antigay policies by picketing the Whiteball Induction Center.

1967—*The Advocate* is founded.

1969—The Stonewall Riots kick off the "gay and lesbian liberation movement" in the United States.

1970—New York City hosts the first Gay and Lesbian Pride March. Sylvia Rivera and Marsha P. Johnson start the Street Transvestite Action Revolutionaries (STAR), later to be called the Street Trans Action Revolutionaries, serving homeless queer youth.

1973—The American Psychiatric Association removes homosexuality from classification as a mental disorder. The Lambda Legal Defense Fund is founded.

1974—Kathy Kozachenko becomes the first openly lesbian elected official when she is elected to the Ann Arbor, Michigan, City Council.

1975—Santa Cruz County becomes the first county in the United States to ban discrimination against gays and lesbians.

1976—The first Michigan Womyn's Music Festival is held.

1977—Harvey Milk is elected San Francisco City Supervisor, the first openly gay elected official in any large U.S. city.

1981—PFLAG (Parents, Families and Friends of Lesbians and Gays) is founded.

1981—Barney Frank is elected to the U.S. House of Representatives; he continues to be one of the most prominent openly gay politicians holding elected office.

1987—ACT-UP is formed.

1991—The first Black Lesbian and Gay Pride event takes place in Washington, DC.

1992—The Lesbian Avengers are founded in New York.

1994—During the 1994 Gay Games in New York, Olympic gold medalist Greg Louganis publicly comes out. This follows the much-watched 1988 Olympic Games in Seoul, South Korea, where Louganis won the gold medal for diving after hitting his head on the diving board. In 1995, he announced that he was HIV+ and addressed concerns he had during that 1988 Olympic accident.

1996—GLSEN's first annual Day of Silence is held to raise awareness about bullying and harassment of LGBTIQ+ youth. Intersex Awareness Day begins (October 26).

1997—An eager public watches as character Ellen Morgan "comes out" on the TV show *The Ellen DeGeneres Show*, mirroring Ellen DeGeneres's real-life "coming out."

1998—Tammy Baldwin becomes the first nonincumbent openly LGBTIQ+ person to win election to Congress. National Coming Out Day begins. Mathew Sheppard is brutally killed; his story ignites national outrage at hate crimes.

1999—First Transgender Day of Remembrance. Dot Nelson-Turnier founds the National Organization Of Lesbians Of Size Everywhere (in 2011, the organization changed its gender policy to include all genders).

2000—Vermont becomes the first U.S. state to offer civil unions for same-sex couples.

2003—The U.S. Supreme Court case *Lawrence v. Texas* overturns a Texas law banning gay sex.

2004—San Francisco issues marriage licenses to same-sex couples. Massachusetts becomes the first U.S. state to legalize same-sex marriage.

2005—Civil unions become legal in Connecticut. Illinois adds sexual orientation and gender identity to the Illinois Human Rights Act.

2006—Washington state passes a bill to prohibit discrimination based on sexual orientation and gender identity.

2008—New York Court of Appeals decision requires that NY employers recognize same-sex marriages from other states. California voters pass Proposition 8, banning same-sex marriage after a California Supreme Court decision allowed same-sex marriage, sending California into intense conflict. Florida and Arizona voters pass initiatives to ban same-sex marriage. Connecticut becomes the second state to legalize same-sex marriage. Stu Rasmussen becomes the first openly transgender person elected as a city mayor in the U.S. Blogger TigTog (Viv Smythe) first coins the controversial acronym "TERF" for "trans-exclusionary radical feminist."

2009—Iowa becomes the third state to recognize legal same-sex marriage. Vermont becomes the first state to recognize same-sex marriage through legislative act (not court decision). President Obama signs a referendum allowing benefits to same-sex partners of federal employees. Harvey Milk is posthumously awarded the Presidential Medal of Freedom. The first annual International Transgender Day of Visibility is recognized (March 31).

2010—The Clinton-era "Don't Ask, Don't Tell" military policy is repealed.

2011—New York legalizes same-sex marriage.

2012—California's Proposition 8 is ruled unconstitutional by the Ninth Circuit Court of Appeals. Tammy Baldwin (D-Wi) becomes the first openly gay politician elected to the U.S. Senate.

2013—California's Proposition 8 and the 1996 Defense of Marriage Act (DOMA) go to the U.S. Supreme Court. In June, DOMA is ruled unconstitutional. This ruling also impacts states' rights to define marriage. Minnesota, Rhode Island, New Jersey, Illinois, and Hawai'i all legalize same-sex marriage. Queen Elizabeth II and the British Parliament both confirm the right of same-sex couples to legally marry. California passes the School Success and Opportunity Act, the first legislation nationwide protecting transgender students. In a landmark case, the Colorado Civil Rights Division rules in favor of six-year-old transgender student Coy Mathis.

2014—The U.S. Supreme Court intervenes in Utah, South Carolina, and Kansas. Additional courts intervene in Pennsylvania, Oregon, and Montana. Laverne Cox is the first openly transgender person to be nominated for an Emmy in an acting category. Cities across the U.S., such as Austin, San Francisco, Portland, and Washington, DC, approve laws requiring gender-inclusive signage on single-user bathrooms.

2015—In a 5–4 ruling, in *Obergefell v. Hodges*, the U.S. Supreme Court rules that same-sex couples have a fundamental right to marry. Justice Anthony Kennedy writes the majority opinion, stating, "Under the Constitution, same-sex couples seek in marriage the same legal treatment as opposite-sex couples, and it would disparage their choices and diminish their personhood to deny them this right." President Obama opens the first gender-neutral bathroom in the White House. Democrat Kate Brown, in Oregon, becomes the first openly bisexual governor of a U.S. state (she won re-election in 2018).

2016—Oregon becomes the first state to allow an individual to register as gender non-binary. Misty Snow becomes the first openly transgender individual to win a major party primary for U.S. Senate. The U.S. Department of Justice issues a joint statement with the U.S. Department of Education arguing that Title IX protections apply to transgender students (later repealed by the Trump administration in 2017). President Obama names the Stonewall Inn a national monument.

2017—Residents in the District of Columbia become the first in the United States to be able to designate a gender-neutral option on their driver's license/identification cards. Danica Roem becomes the first openly transgender candidate elected to a state legislature.

2018—In Colorado, Jared Polis becomes the first openly gay man to be elected governor to a U.S. state.

As previously mentioned, the equating of feminists with lesbians or dykes has long been used as a way to discourage women from fighting for equality and claiming feminism. I've discussed how this impacts straight women and their involvement with the movement, but, additionally, how do these messages impact lesbian women and their place in the feminist movement? Certainly, lesbians and straight women, by the very nature of being women, share a mutual interest in the fight for equality. While issues may vary in their focus, intent, and priority, people of all sexualities have a vested interest in working together to combat the use of our sexuality against us. Like with all oppression, whether one is straight or gay, homophobia works to devalue us all. As Urvashi Vaid argues, "there is an intimate connection between homophobia and sexism: Homophobia maintains gender inequality. Labels like 'fag' or 'dyke' are deployed to police the boundaries of sexual and gender expression."[12] Unfortunately, however, like other groups within the feminist movement, lesbians have been marginalized. This marginalization can result from a heterosexist norm both within and outside the movement.

[A key challenge that I face is] the transition from Female-to-Male and wanting all women to know that it's not that I want to have the so-called privilege of being male. It's something I need to do to bring my mind and my body closer spiritually, physically, and mentally. I'm not giving up any of my roots in the women's movement. Shaun, 27, Native American and Caucasian, pansexual, Rhode Island

Considering heterosexualism as the norm creates an "othering," much like the othering of women to men, making lesbian women second to heterosexual women. Instead, we need to recognize that, as Kristin Severson writes in "Identity Politics and Progress: Don't Fence Me In (or Out),"

> ... as the feminist movement is learning the hard way, women's issues include homophobia, racism, classism, xenophobia, etc., because a feminist movement MUST include ALL women. It is when identity politics sells out "Others" by not being inclusive that we realize our political movements are more like that which we are fighting against than we wish to realize. But to be truly progressive, it seems we must go one step further than including all the diversity within our own identity movement, we must create a belief system that everyone can adopt as their own whatever their identity.[13]

In adopting this system, we need to also embrace all the issues faced within our community as they are our own issues: gender identity, transphobia, homophobia, sexual oppression, gender-based violence, discrimination in the workplace, and political rights such as marriage equality, access to adoption, gender inclusive bathrooms, and protection from police brutality.

From the denial of lesbian and gay leadership within most traditional faiths to the extremist antigay organizations like GodHatesFags. org, religion is inevitably at the core of the debate surrounding the morality and legitimacy of lesbians and gays. These arguments are present among school boards, in day-care centers, within city councils and state legislatures, and in Congress. It is argued over and over that gays are a threat to American family values, to the health of our children, to our educational system, and to our political structure—it's amazing the power that lesbians and gays hold! Most recently, these arguments of immorality extend to the transgender community, specifically into our bathrooms. But let's be clear, immorality is not the driving force behind these arguments; rather, it is the unfounded fear behind the accusation. This fear is deeply rooted in lack of knowledge or understanding. As we continue to tell our stories, fight for changes in our courts and legislatively, and take a stand for the rights of all, our country's narrative begins to change.

After years of fighting locally and on the state level, the movement for marriage equality achieved a huge victory. In 2015, the U.S. Supreme Court ruled in *Obergefell v. Hodges*, affording gay couples the same rights and privileges as those in heterosexual relationships. More than one thousand specific rights are now granted to same-sex married couples, including the right to make medical decisions for the partner, the right to hospital visitation, the right to insurance benefits, social security, and inheritance among partners—hardly radical notions.

With the rise of gender studies and with issues of gay marriage taking political center stage, the fight for gay rights has gained a recognition like that accorded the civil rights and women's rights movements of the 1960s and 1970s. Importantly, marriage has long been debated within feminist circles, as some have argued that the institution itself is inherently patriarchal and inequitable for women and so have questioned whether the gay community should in fact fight for marriage at all. Others argue, however, that gay marriage both signifies and affords social and political equality with heterosexuals. Whatever your perspective on marriage itself, it is clear that the fight for marriage equality has been a pivotal effort to integrate same-sex relationships into the public fabric of our society. We see evidence of this in our popular culture television shows, like *Modern Family*, in commercials for mainstream organizations like Kaiser, and among our CEOs and elected officials.

The publication of books like *Princess Boy* and *I am Jazz* have introduced truths about gender non-binary and gender non-conforming children, effectively creating a broader awareness, understanding, and acceptance for gender diversity and the trans community. And while we are far from full integration, recognition, and rights, advocates are moving the nation toward greater equity for all genders. In 2014, the U.S. Justice Department asserted that Title VII of the Civil Rights Act of 1964 applied to discrimination based on gender identity. In 2016, the Justice and Education departments issued an advisory extending the protections of Title IX to transgender students. The fight for gender-inclusive bathrooms has made it into many communities. Schools and college campuses have committed to converting single-user bathrooms for all genders. In March 2017, a California law went into effect mandating all single-user bathrooms be converted into gender-inclusive bathrooms. These are important gains, but the fight for true gender equity is far from achieved. States like Texas, North Carolina, and South Dakota have considered and/or passed legislation requiring transgender individuals to use bathrooms that match their biological sex. More recently, the Trump administration reversed Obama-era nondiscrimination positions, particularly those that impact transgender students. Advocates have shifted energy to the U.S. Supreme

> *[The Massachusetts] ruling gave me a sense of equality to heterosexual couples that I never knew I wanted or needed. It truly made me feel like more of a whole person . . . now that I have tasted that sense of equality there is no going back. Nothing less than marriage rights will ever create that equality and any attempt to amend the state or federal constitution to keep marriage from us will be seen as blatant discrimination and unacceptable.* Nina, 30, Italian, lesbian, Massachusetts

Court. Additionally, it is time to revisit a comprehensive Constitutional amendment that would guarantee rights for all genders.

> Transgender is a broad term that can be used to describe people whose gender identity is different from the gender they were thought to be when they were born. "Trans" is often used as shorthand for transgender . . . Gender identity is your internal knowledge of your gender—for example, your knowledge that you're a man, a woman, or another gender. Gender expression is how a person presents their gender on the outside, often through behavior, clothing, hairstyle, voice, or body characteristics . . . Some transgender people identify as neither a man nor a woman, or as a combination of male and female, and may use terms like non-binary or genderqueer to describe their gender identity. Those who are non-binary often prefer to be referred to as "they" and "them." (Definitions come from The National Center for Transgender Equality.)

I believe that the feminist movement must embrace and actively participate in the fight for the rights of all people—all genders, gender expression, and gender identity. We should:

- Demand that our political representatives actively oppose any federal legislation that limits or denies the rights of gender non-binary and gender non-conforming peoples;
- Demand that federal hate-crimes legislation include hate crimes motivated by gender, gender expression, gender identity, and sexual orientation and that conviction for such crimes carries serious punishment for offenders;
- Protect and defend the right of gay, lesbian, intersex, and transgender people to parent, whether through pregnancy, adoption, assisted reproductive technology, or surrogacy;
- Support sexuality education in schools that is comprehensive, including education about sexual orientation;
- Incorporate intersex in our understanding of gender and sex categories;
- Support, respect, and defend the right of people to express their gender and sexual orientation in any manner that does not harm others, as we do heterosexual folks;

- Require all colleges, universities, schools, and workplaces to adopt non-discrimination policies that include gender, gender expression, and sexual orientation;
- Treat gender and sexual orientation as civil rights issues, defending them against discrimination; and
- Fight for a Constitutional equity amendment that incorporates people of all sexes, genders, sexualities, and gender expressions and identities.

We must also encourage and create a safe place for personal exploration of gender. It is the norm in a society like ours to accept, force, and/or assume the gender labels we were given at birth. But, as Kate Bornstein writes in their book *My Gender Workbook*, "it's when we begin to poke around in the piles of accumulated emotions, mannerisms, attitudes, and values, when we really let ourselves look at what we've gotten ourselves into; that's when we can begin to get some clarity on gender. That's when we can construct a gender identity for ourselves that best lets us express our needs and wants in this world."[14] In order to fight for political and social recognition, we must first understand our own gender identity and the sociopolitical constraints that inevitably follow its definition.

A WORD REGARDING MEN IN THE MOVEMENT

Men are not the enemy. They, too, are at a disadvantage in a patriarchal society. Men in the feminist movement can take a stand against gender-based oppression and speak out about the cult of masculinity that boxes them into a very narrow accepted norm. The feminist movement needs to do a better job in welcoming and incorporating men. We need to do a better job in changing the cultural interpretation of feminism that hinders male involvement. That burden is on us. But, I also believe that men need to do a better job of addressing their role in, and their experience with, gender oppression. The feminist movement should stop celebrating men's presence, but at the same time it should welcome men's involvement. It is possible to incorporate men into feminism without falling over ourselves to thank them. I find that we're either *so* happy that men have become involved that we become obnoxious or we are suspicious and/or irritated by their presence. Both of these reactions have to stop. Let's be partners—equal partners—and let's model within the feminist movement what we would like to see outside the movement.

Similarly, men need to stop expecting that women will work it all out for them. I am asked frequently what I am going to do for men. There seems to be a rising accusation that the feminist movement left the men behind. I have three nephews whom I adore beyond words. I want them to grow up in a culture that allows them to define themselves and does not require them to be macho, über-masculine men. I embrace my role in their learning. But I am tired of being expected, as a feminist, to raise the consciousness of all men. I am sick of people demanding that I create a progressive men's movement. Women have not achieved true equality; my own movement is not yet over. Even if it were, I would still be hesitant to take responsibility for a men's movement. I am not a man, did not grow up a man, do not know what it is like to be a man. Why should I create or lead a men's movement? I shouldn't, any more than I would expect people of color to teach me how to unlearn racism. However, I would support a pro-feminist men's movement to detoxify masculinity. I'd come to your rallies, distribute your materials, vote for your initiatives and your candidates, support your legislation; I'd work as a partner, just as I hope that you will work with me.

Besides, the reality is that there are men who are doing great work to address masculinity and feminism. Men are feminists—both within and outside the feminist movement. And feminist men, like Jackson Katz, Kevin Powell, Michael Kimmel, Tony Porter, Greg Tate, and Scott Coltrane, to name a few, are writing, speaking, and acting to de-

> *I grapple with the notion that men can be feminists. While they can definitely identify with the movement's ideal and goals, men will never truly know what it feels like to be a woman.* Milton, 23, African American, Louisiana

construct the notions of masculinity and the intersection of race, sex, class, pop culture, and feminism. Unfortunately, however, there seems to be a notion that men, by nature of being male, cannot be feminists. Or that men who are feminist are not "real" men; they are gay or "girlie men." This is related to the culture of sexism and homophobia in which we live. And it is linked to the rampant myths about feminism. Fortunately, more and more men are breaking the stereotypes and standing up for equality. The reality is that until men recognize the importance of sharing partnership with women, honoring our differences rather than highlighting them as justification for discrimination, and begin to fight a patriarchy that hurts not just women but also men, we—of all genders—will not achieve true equality and the endless benefits that go along with it.

Organizations such as the National Organization for Men Against Sexism (NOMAS) are working to address the challenges to masculinity and the role men have in ending sexism and discrimination. NOMAS is an activist-based organization committed to pro-feminist, gay-affirmative, antiracist ideology that is dedicated to enhancing men's lives.[15] NOMAS works to challenge the traditional stereotypes of masculinity that plague men and boys in our society. They believe in working alongside women to oppose gender discrimination, eradicate gender-based violence, and challenge social injustice, such as racism, sexism, and homophobia. Whether in organizations or individually, men are actively working to counter sexism, end discrimination, and create a new generation without gender bias.

> I identify as a feminist but I feel that the word feminism pushes a lot of men away because of the labels attached to it. David, 21, black, heterosexual, New Jersey

Organizations like NOMAS, and the individual efforts of men working to end discrimination, serve as a vital resource for men who want to effectively work to end discrimination against women. And they serve as an important alternative to oppressive organizations of men that work to enforce male-dominated traditional roles, such

As a black person who suffers from mental illnesses, and is a progressive Christian who is lower class, I suffer in this society. But as a cis-gender, heterosexual, progressive Christian, high-income nation resident, I gorge on immense privileges. So, with all these realities I understand some privileges are rewarded rather than others, so therefore I find the deep understanding of intersectionality. This quote sums up my point perfectly, "I am not free while any woman is unfree, even when her shackles are very different from my own." Audre Lorde Terrance, 24, California resident in the USA, high-income nation resident, Black, cis-gender male, heterosexual, living with mental illness, working class.

as the Promise Keepers. Founded by the conservative Bill McCartney, the Promise Keepers are backed by Jerry Falwell (of Jerry Falwell Ministries), Bill Bright (of the Campus Crusade for Christ), and James Dobson (of Focus on the Family). The Promise Keepers, unlike pro-feminist organizations, advocates that men take back their "rightful" role as head of household by any means necessary and require that women unquestioningly follow men. Such organizations and attitudes deepen the divide between men and women, protect and advance the theory and practice of patriarchy, continue to place women in positions of subordination to men and deny the fluidity of gender and legitimacy of trans people.

Fortunately, these groups represent only a minority of men. The fact is that men have always worked alongside women for justice. They continue to have the opportunity to do so.

MOVING FORWARD

As we continue to address the challenges both within and outside our movement, it is important to remember that together we are strong. Our fight is a collective one—for any to be free from oppression, we must *all* be free from oppression. Everyone deserves a seat at the table. We simply need more chairs.

MEN SPEAK OUT TO WOMEN

Sometimes, I am treated far too well simply because I am a man. Men should be feminist, and realize their male privilege, and use that to enhance sexual equality. Fareed, 18, Hispanic/West Indian, gay, Colorado

We have to lead other men by example. We have to have the presence of mind to learn from women leaders and to apply that learning to our male peers and ourselves. Zafar, 23, South Asian American, heterosexual, Texas

As a man who identifies as feminist, I feel that I have a responsibility to not only self-identify as a feminist, but to publicly identify—even to proclaim myself—as a feminist, to help other men (and women) realize that men can be feminists too, and give support to feminist women. Jesse, 21, white, straight, Arizona

I am a gay man and realized that sexism was intertwined with heterosexism, I realized that the taunts I received had to do with my not being perceived as a "real" man and that I was being seen as a sort of woman which was seen as bad, so obviously women were hated too. Chris, 33, Latino/Anglo, HIV+, Michigan

When you can see inequities it does not matter which side of the scale you are on, it is your duty as a decent human being to point out those inequities and fight for change. James, 25, white, straight, Illinois

WOMEN SPEAK OUT TO MEN

Men should actively discourage sexism in their social circles and peers . . . they should teach their children men's role in standing up for women. Emma, 21, white, heterosexual, Michigan

It is crucial to realize that women are fighting against patriarchy, not men. Lina, 21, South Korean (studying in U.S. since eighth grade), heterosexual, Massachusetts

In patriarchy, men are just as trapped as women. Amy, 22, mixed ethnicity, heterosexual, Mexico and California

I wish that men would stop being threatened and just be supportive. They should get out of the way and realize that they would be taking the same action if they were the ones being marginalized. Sara, 19, Caucasian, bisexual, California

I think that men are critical allies in the feminist movement . . . I do not think that we will ever achieve widespread change in sexism without partnership with men. Nicole, 32, white, heterosexual, Illinois

I think it's most important that men know that they can play a role in the feminist movement. In my experience, many men are unaware that they can be feminists. Because so many of the major decision-makers in this country are men, their involvement in the

feminist movement is crucial. Erin, 23, Japanese American/Chinese American, heterosexual, California

Men should play a supportive role in the feminist movement. The leadership and the major voices should be female, because the movement is about empowering women. The movement is not about keeping men in charge and just asking a male-run society to treat its women better. Laura, 20, white, straight, New York

Men should play as much of a role as possible. They should show their support and voice their beliefs. Charrise, 19, Black, heterosexual, Maryland

I think men need to acknowledge their privilege and recognize women's specific struggles. They need to constantly challenge themselves to be anti-sexist in an environment that does not require this of them and in fact encourages sexism. They need to never stop listening to women as we articulate feminism. At the same time, they should point out ways in which gender politics and norms harm men. They need to maintain their feminist ideals even when inconvenient (as do we), and this means challenging other men's sexism. Rosalie, 22, white, straight, Maine.

SPOTLIGHT ON ACTIVISM

Based in Atlanta, Georgia, SisterSong is an organization dedicated to lifting "the voices of women of color to have an impact on reproductive justice issues that affect women of color." SisterSong is a collective of seventy-six local, regional, and national grassroots organizations representing five primary ethnic populations and indigenous nations in the United States, including Native and Indigenous Americans, Asian/Pacific Islanders, Middle Eastern/Arab Americans, Latinas, and Black/African Americans.

Formed in 1997, SisterSong works on public policy and advocacy, educational programs, and community organizing and has collaborated on national political efforts. It publishes a national newspaper, *Collective Voices,* which is created by and for women of color. For more information about, and to support the efforts of, SisterSong, visit www.sistersong.net or phone the group at 404.344.9629.

TAKE ACTION

Getting Started
Listen.
Read.
Reach out.

The Next Step

Question racist, sexist, ageist, homophobic, or transphobic jokes. Redefine what is funny.

Question racist, sexist, ageist, homophobic, or transphobic language. Changing language can change assumptions.

Explore your own privilege—examine your status in society, what you have been able or not able to do because of your gender, race, ethnicity, ability, religion, age, sexual identity, and so forth.

Actively unlearn racism (and ageism, homophobia, transphobia, etc.) by getting informed, challenging your own assumptions, and examining your position in society.

Go beyond tolerance. Be a model of acceptance and respectful behavior.

Celebrate and take action on the International Day of Action Against Racism, August 31. Celebrate International Women's Day, March 8.

Getting Out There

Ask your local school board and/or schools if their curricula and textbooks are equitable and inclusive.

Examine the membership of the groups, schools, businesses, and organizations that you are a part of—does everyone look like you? Is the group committed to inclusivity? Raise the issue if it has not been raised.

The next time you are in a public place that isn't accessible, ask the management why not.

Celebrate Freedom to Marry Day, February 12, each year. Plan special events, write editorials to your newspaper. Honor the work that achieved marriage equality and address the ongoing barriers to access. And work every day to ensure that lesbian and gay couples are afforded the same recognition, rights, and respect as straight people.

Recognize one of the important days acknowledging the LGBTIQ+ community. Host an event in your community or on your campus. Share information, lend support.

- March 31—International Transgender Day of Visibility
- April—Day of Silence
- May 17—International Day Against Homophobia
- May 22—Harvey Milk Day
- June—Pride Month
- Sept 23—Celebrate Bisexuality Day
- October 11—National Coming Out Day
- October 20–26—Asexuality Awareness Week
- October 26—Intersex Awareness Day
- November 8—Intersex Day of Remembrance
- November 20—Transgender Day of Remembrance

Host an intergenerational dialogue in your community or organization or on your campus. Pick an issue to focus on, and share perspectives from a variety of generations.

FABULOUS FEMINIST WEB RESOURCES

Asian Americans Advancing Justice
www.advancingjustice-aajc.org
Formerly the National Asian Pacific American Legal Consortium, AAAJ is a nonprofit organization focused on civil rights for the Asian American community through education, public policy, and litigation.

ASTRAEA Lesbian Foundation for Justice
www.astraeafoundation.org
Based in New York, Astraea works globally to advance LGBTIQ human rights.

Black Lives Matter
www.blacklivesmatter.com
Created in 2012 after the murder of Trayvon Martin, Black Lives Matter is a movement to challenge racism as it permeates the institutions of our society, not the least of which includes law enforcement and the prison system. #BLM is about broadening the black liberation movement and "affirms the lives of Black queer and trans folks, disabled folks, black-undocumented folks, folks with records, women and all Black lives along the gender spectrum" (blacklivesmatter.com).

Black Women Organized for Political Action
www.bwopa.org
BWOPA supports, educates, and promotes black women in the political process.

Bitch magazine
www.bitchmedia.com
Bitch Media, a Feminist Response to Pop Culture, includes a magazine and online presence.

Equality Now
www.equalitynow.org
Founded in 1992, Equality Now is a global organization promoting the human rights of women around the globe.

FRIDA: Young Feminist Fund
www.youngfeministfund.org
Located throughout the world, FRIDA stands for Flexibility, Resources, Inclusivity, Diversity, Action. FRIDA focuses on supporting young feminist activism around the globe.

Girls Incorporated
www.girlsinc.org
National nonprofit youth organization focused on girls, including mentor and leadership programs.

Grrrl Zines
www.grrrlzines.net
No longer maintained, this site archives resources, zines, information about the feminist, trans, queer, women in publishing, and similar topics.

Hadassah
www.hadassah.org
Hadassah, the Women's Zionist Organization of America, focuses on the empowerment of Jewish women.

Lesbian Herstory Archives
www.lesbianherstoryarchives.org
Website housing collections, exhibits, resources, and materials chronicling lesbian herstory.

Mexican American Legal Defense and Education Fund
www.maldef.org
The U.S.'s leading Latino civil rights organization, founded in 1968.

Ms. magazine
www.msmagazine.com
The classic feminist magazine. First published in 1972, Ms. magazine has been a staple in feminist households and women's studies departments.

National Association for the Advancement of Colored People
www.naacp.org
A rich history of fighting for political, educational, social, and economic equality for all, with a specific focus on eliminating race-based discrimination.

National Congress of American Indians
www.ncai.org
The NCAI's mission includes protecting and enhancing treaty and sovereign rights, securing traditional laws and culture, and improving the quality of life for native communities.

National Congress of Black Women
www.nationalcongressbw.org
Non-partisan organization focused on the political empowerment of Black women.

National Council of Jewish Women
www.ncjw.org
A progressive, grassroots Jewish women's organization working for social justice.

National Center for Transgender Equality
www.transequality.org
A national social justice organization fighting to end discrimination and violence against the transgender community.

Native American Rights Fund
www.narf.org
Nonprofit legal assistance to Indian tribes.

New Moon magazine
www.newmoon.org
An advertisement-free magazine for girls ages 8–14.

OlderWomen's League
www.owlca.org
Now primarily located in California, OWL focuses on the rights of women as they age.

Palestinian American Women's Association

www.pawasca.org

Based in Southern California, PAWA is a non-profit, community-based organization focused on the empowerment of Arab women and children.

Southern Poverty Law Center

www.splcenter.org

Champions of civil rights, the Southern Poverty Law Center takes on pro bono cases fighting for justice. It was instrumental in implementing the Civil Rights Act of 1964. Website provides resources and information.

Third Wave Fund

www.thirdwavefund.org

Youth activism for gender justice. Great source for grants and scholarships for third-wave work. Website also includes resources and public-education programs.

Tolerance.org

www.tolerance.org

Educational resources focus on a variety of topics including race and ethnicity, activism, ability, immigration, bullying, gender, and sexual orientation.

UnidosUS

www.unidosus.org

Formerly the National Council of La Raza, UnidosUS is a non-partisan Latino organization focused on research, public policy, and advocacy.

Women as Allies

www.women-as-allies.org

Woman As Allies brings women from multiple backgrounds together to dialogue and work for social justice.

4

AT THE TABLE

WOMEN AND SOCIETY

To achieve true social, political, and economic equality for all women, we must have equal representation in the institutions that shape the face of our society. We need to have a place at the table of decision-making. Women's ideas, perspectives, and vision need to be considered in all social and political realms of society, and we need to have an equal role in government, education, the media, labor, religion, and the military. We must be at the tables of corporate and union workplaces, on the floor of Congress and in the Oval Office of the White House, in our churches, temples, synagogues, and mosques, in our academies and at every level of military leadership, in our colleges and universities, in our classrooms, in administration, and on our school boards. Women's voices must be not only heard, but equally counted when deciding the future of this nation—and in nations around the world.

In 1776, when this country was writing its Declaration of Independence, Abigail Adams wrote to her husband:

> By the way, in the new code of laws which I suppose it will be necessary for you to make, I desire you would remember the ladies and be more generous and favorable to them than your ancestors! Do not put such unlimited power in the hands of husbands. Remember, all men would be tyrants if they could. If particular care and attention is not paid to the ladies, we are determined to foment a rebellion, and will not hold ourselves bound by any laws in which we have no voice or representation.[1]

No longer must women wait for husbands, or men, to "remember the ladies." We are now in positions of leadership and have more political and economic power than ever before in modern history. But we are still bound by laws in which we have little voice or representation, and there is still work to be done to change the consciousness about gender roles and to achieve proportional representation and true equality in all facets of society. Our history is rich with revolutionary events. We have made gains because people fought for them, and that fight continues.

> Politics can help us change what is going on within our lives, if we don't agree . . . CHANGE IT. Vickie, 22, Korean, California

While there is not room in this book to fully explore every key institution that shapes our society, my goal is to present an introductory look at how women are represented in society. Like all rights afforded women, the right to have a voice—politically, economically, academically, spiritually—is the result of the efforts of women who stood against individuals and a society that said no.

THE RIGHT TO VOTE AND OTHER POLITICAL ACTION

Politics and political activism are critical for our future. From the price of milk or soda pop to the rise in tuition this semester, from the pharmacist who won't fill your prescription for emergency contraceptives to the health center that can't keep its doors open, from the cuts in welfare or financial aid to tax cuts for the wealthiest few in the nation, from campaign ads to who runs for president, it is all politics. We may be frustrated with what we see as corruption and lack of representation, but if we do nothing we only contribute to the problems about which we complain. If this system of ours is supposed to be "of the people, by the people" then let's claim the system for ourselves.

I never feel alone at the polls. In fact, my booth always feels so crowded, packed with the ghosts of the suffragists who fought for me to stand there, and heavy with the thought of future generations that my vote will impact.

Following her election as the Democratic whip in 2001, Nancy Pelosi, the highest-ranking woman ever in Congress, met at the White House with the president and top congressional leaders. Noting that everyone at the table but her was male, she recounts that this meeting was unique both for her and for the White House. Of the experience, she says:

> It sounds strange, but as I sat down, I felt that I was not alone. For an instant, I felt as though Susan B. Anthony, Lucretia Mott, Elizabeth Cady Stanton—everyone who'd fought for women's right to vote and for the empowerment of women in politics, in their professions, and in their lives—were there with me in the room. Those women were the ones who had done the heavy lifting, and it was as if they were saying, *At last we have a seat at the table*.[2]

Indeed, women's right to vote was fought for—not assumed, not granted or handed out. Women died fighting so that we would have the right to participate in our political system today. And, despite the conflicts within the movement, the lack of inclusion, the racial and generational politics among the suffragists, they achieved lasting change. These women were the first to ever picket the White House; they suffered violent attacks, imprisonment, even force-feeding during hunger strikes, all because they believed that women must have a voice in a political system that sets out to make decisions on their behalf. To waste that right today is an affront to their memory, a disregard of all they lost to give us this right. Wasting this right is disrespectful to ourselves and to the women around the globe who are still fighting this battle. I realize that time is tight, child care is hard to come by, candidates, issues, and initiatives are confusing, poverty and lack of education stand in our way in accessing the polls, but we collectively need to ensure that everyone's voice is heard on election day. We can share resources, pool child care, demand that polling places be fair and accessible, carpool, register for absentee ballots, and initiate discussion groups on the issues. We need to support one another because we owe it to ourselves to vote.

OK, soap box aside, I hope I have convinced you to register and to vote in every election. Now let's talk about whom to vote for and our representation in our political system. In 2019, women held 27.6 percent of statewide elective executive offices in the United States, with women of color accounting for 4.5 percent of those statewide officeholders.[3] Additionally, women make up about 23.7 percent of the members of Congress, with women of color constituting only 8.8 percent of the members of Congress.[4] Only nine states have women governors, and only two woman of color have ever served as a governor for her state.[5] Despite making up nearly 51 percent of the U.S. population,[6] women have never come close to achieving proportional representation in politics. Our representation is crucial, since we cannot leave it to others to make policy that directly impacts our lives.

I find it hard to be a feminist and not have some sort of interest in politics . . . it is far too important. Michelle, 22, female-ish, queer, Florida

Fortunately, we do have noteworthy women who paved the way for women in politics; we need only to follow their lead. In 1916, Jeanette Rankin, of Montana, was the first woman elected to the U.S. Congress. Since then, many women have made important contributions as members of Congress, including Bella Abzug, Barbara Boxer, Shirley Chisholm, Diane Feinstein, Geraldine Ferraro, Barbara Jordan, Barbara Lee, Carolyn Maloney, Patsy Mink, Eleanor Holmes Norton, Nancy Pelosi, Hillary Rodham Clinton, Linda and Loretta Sanchez, Patricia Schroeder, Kamala Harris, Elizabeth Warren, Maxine Waters, and Diane Watson. In addition, women have served as governors and in local and state office. Most recently, the nation witnessed Hillary Rodham Clinton, after being First Lady, a U.S. Senator, and Secretary of State, become the first woman to earn a major party's presidential nomination. Though she won the popular vote, Clinton was denied the presidency by elec-

I never saw politics relevant in my life until I started to see that the rights that I have taken for granted for my entire life can be taken away just as quickly as a vote can be taken in Congress. I am registered to vote and use my right willingly. Rachel, 24, Caucasian, heterosexual, California

toral vote. Despite all that has been proven by these women, we still have yet to have a woman president. In other countries—Finland, Iceland, Israel, Panama, India, Latvia, Canada, and New Zealand— women have served as presidents and prime ministers and as leaders at all levels of government. These women are to be honored as leaders and as pioneers. But while these are amazing women who have significantly contributed to their nations, overall, women currently fill only 22.8 percent of the world's parliamentary seats.[7] The National Organization for Women, Emily's List, the Feminist Majority, the National Women's Political Caucus, and Black Women Organized for Political Action are just a few of the organizations that are working to further women's roles in government. We need to train women in politics, put them in the political pipeline, and help those who run for office to raise money and win their campaigns. Further, when women are in office, their voices must matter and be respected. In 2017, Senate Majority Leader Mitch McConnell silenced Massachusetts Senator Elizabeth Warren during her testimony regarding the nomination of then-Attorney General nominee, Jeff Sessions. Senator McConnell stated, "She was warned. She was given an explanation. Nevertheless, she persisted," and Senator Warren was no longer allowed into the hearings on Session. Thanks to feminist colleagues in the Senate, like California Senator Kamala Harris, and to activists throughout the country, Warren's silencing was not ignored. Among other impacts, the phrase "Nevertheless, she persisted" has become a unifying quote for women who won't give up.

Our equal representation is critical. With that said, it is also important to note that not all women leaders support gender equity or have progressive politics. While it is important that we celebrate the gains of any woman elected to office, it is also important to recognize that the feminist agenda is a progressive one. We need to elect leaders, of any gender, who support and fight for equity for all. This must be our commitment, as it is the only way to achieve truly equal representation in our political system.

WOMEN LEADERS

In 1916, Jeannette Rankin (R-MT) became the first woman elected to the U.S. House of Representatives.

In 1960, Siramavo Bandaranaike became the first woman prime minister in modern times when she became prime minister of Ceylon (now Sri Lanka).

In 1964, Patsy Takemoto Mink (D-HI) became the first woman of color elected to the U.S. House of Representatives.

In 1966, Indira Gandhi became the first female prime minister of India.

In 1969, Golda Meir became Israel's first female prime minister.

In 1974, Maria Estela (Isabela) Martínez de Perón became the first woman president of Argentina.

In 1975, Elisabeth Domitien became the first woman to serve as prime minister for the Central African Republic.

In 1979, Maria de Lourdes Pintasilgo became the first woman prime minister of Portugal.

In 1979, Lidia Gueiler became the first woman elected president of Bolivia.

In 1979, Margaret Thatcher became the first woman elected leader in Europe when she became prime minister of the United Kingdom.

In 1980, Jeanne Sauvé was the first woman appointed speaker of the House of Commons in Canada.

In 1980, Eugenia Charles of Dominica became the Caribbean's first female prime minister. She was also Dominica's first female lawyer.

In 1980, Vigdís Finnbogadóttir became the first woman president of Iceland and the world's first democratically directly elected female president.

In 1981, Gro Harlem Brundtland became the first woman to become prime minister of Norway.

In 1982, Milka Planinc became the first woman prime minister of the Socialist Federal Republic of Yugoslavia.

In 1982, Agatha Barbara became the first woman president of Malta.

In 1984, Maria Liberia-Peters became the first woman prime minister of Netherlands Antilles. Wilma Mankiller became the first woman elected to serve as chief of the Cherokee Nation.

In 1986, Corazon Aquino became the first woman president of the Philippines.

In 1988, Benazir Bhutto became the first woman prime minister of Pakistan.

In 1990, Kazimira Prunskienė became the first prime minister of Lithuania after their declaration of independence.

In 1990, Violeta Barrios de Chamorro became Nicaragua's first female president and the first woman president in Central America.

Elected in 1990, Mary Robison was the first woman president of Ireland, and Ertha Pascal-Trouillot was the first woman president of Haiti.

In 1991, Edith Cresson of France and Khaleda Zia Rahman of Bangladesh became the first woman prime ministers for their countries.

In 1992, Betty Boothroyd became Great Britain's first woman speaker of the House of Commons.

In 1992, Hanna Suchocka became Poland's first woman prime minister. Carol Moseley Braun (D-IL) became the first woman of color elected to the U.S. Senate.

In 1993, Toujan Faisal became the first woman elected to Jordan's Parliament.

In 1993, Tansu Ciller of Turkey, Sylvia Kinigi of Burundi, and Agathe Uwilingiyimana of Rwanda each became their country's first prime minister.

In 1994, Reneta Indzhova served as Bulgaria's first female prime minister.

In 1994, Chandrika Kumaratunga, daughter of Sri Lanka's first female prime minister, became the country's first female president.

In 1995, Claudette Werleigh became the first woman prime minister of Haiti.

In 1997, Jenny Shipley became the first woman to serve as prime minister in New Zealand.

In 1997, following her husband's death, Janet Rosenberg Jagan was elected president of Guyana. She became the first American-born woman to be president of any country.

In 1998, Tammy Baldwin (D-WI) became the first openly gay person to serve in the U.S. Senate.

In 1999, Vaira Vike-Freiberga not only became president of Latvia, but also became the first woman president of a former Soviet state.

In 1999, Mireya Elisa Moscoso de Arias became the first woman president of Panama.

In 1999, Ruth Dreifuss became the first woman president of Switzerland.

In 2000, Tarja Kaarina Halonen became Finland's first female president.

In 2001, Senegal appointed Mame Madior Boye as their first female prime minister and Megawati Sukarnoputri became Indonesia's first woman president.

In 2002, Maria das Neves became the first woman head of government in Sao Tome and Nataša Mićić became the acting president of Serbia.

In 2003, Anneli Tuulikki Jäätteenmäki became Finland's first female prime minister and Beatriz Merino became the first female prime minister of Peru.

In 2005, Massouma al-Mubarak became the first female cabinet member in Kuwait and Yulia Tymoshenko became the first woman appointed prime minister to Ukraine.

In 2005, Angela Merkel became Germany's first female chancellor.

In 2006, Chile elected Michelle Bachelet as its first female president (and only the third woman to serve as president of a Latin American country). Ellen Johnson Sirleaf was elected president of Liberia, becoming the first woman to be elected a head of state in Africa. Han Myung-Sook became the first prime minister of South Korea. Portia Simpson Miller became Jamaica's first female prime minister.

In 2006, Dalia Itzik became the first speaker of the Knesset in Israel. In 2007, she served as interim president of Israel, making her the first female president of the country.

In 2007, Prabitha Patil became India's first female president.

In 2008, Zinaida Greceanii became Moldova's first female prime minister.

In 2009, Jóhanna Sigurðardóttir became Iceland's first female prime minister and the world's first openly gay head of state. Jadranka Kosor became Crotia's first female prime minister. Dalia Grybauskaite became Lithuania's first female president.

In 2010, Laura Chinchilla became Costa Rica's first female president. Kamla Persad-Bissessar became the first female prime minister of Trinidad and Tobago. She was also the country's first female attorney general. Julia Gillard became Australia's first female prime minister. Iveta Radičová became

Slovakia's first female prime minister. Dilma Rousseff became Brazil's first woman president (and the world's first democratically elected female president to be impeached and removed from office).

In 2011, Atifete Jahjaga became Kosovo's first woman president. Yingluck Shinawatra became Thailand's first female prime minister. Helle Thorning-Schmidt became Denmark's first female prime minister.

In 2012, Joyce Banda became Malawi's first female president.

In 2013, Park Geun-hye became South Korea's first female president. Alenka Bratušek became Slovenia's first female prime minister. Sibel Siber became the first woman prime minister of Northern Cyrus.

In 2014, Laimdota Straujuma became first woman prime minister of Latvia.

In 2015, Kolinda Grabar-Kitarovic became the first woman president of Croatia. Namibia appointed Saara Kuugongelwa-Amadhila, the country's first female prime minister.

In 2016, Hillary Rodham Clinton became the first woman to win a major party's presidential nomination.

In 2018, Danica Roem became the first openly transgender woman to be elected to, and to serve in, a U.S. state legislature. New Zealand's prime minister, Jacinda Ardern, becomes the first world leader to take maternity leave while in office, after the birth of her daughter in 2018.

To increase our political representation, we must secure a voice for women in politics. Passing a constitutional amendment for gender equity is an important step to ensure that women, men, and LGBTIQ+ in the United States are afforded full equality under the law. We need to insist that the United States support CEDAW to help free the world's women from discrimination. We need to engage politically on local, state, federal, and international levels. We need to make politics integral to our daily lives. There are, and have been, great women leaders. We have proven ourselves and our capabilities beyond any question. As young women, we have role models to look up to, but we also have a responsibility to participate in our democracy. Get political if you aren't already. Get louder if you are!

WOMEN IN THE WORKPLACE: INTEGRATING WORK, FAMILY, AND CIVIC LIFE

Women have always worked.[8] Our work has not always been publicly recognized, valued, or paid. But our work has always contributed to the economic health of our families and our nations. Women's labor, both paid and unpaid, must be recognized and respected. The feminist movement has advocated for this recognition of women's labor, including the right to work outside the home, and for safe and fair working conditions for those in the paid labor force. Additionally, feminists fought for the overall economic rights and health of all women, including the right of women to own property, to keep the money they earned, to have credit in their own names (a right not afforded women until 1971!), the right to join and participate in unions, and the right to be free from sexual harassment. The efforts of the feminist movement changed the consciousness of society and in turn created a work environment that is increasingly fair.

> Glass ceil·ing *n.* an upper limit to professional advancement, esp. as imposed on women, that is not readily perceived or openly acknowledged.

There is still a ways to go to achieve full equality for working women—in both the paid and the unpaid labor forces. Most agree that there is still a glass ceiling—a barrier between women and senior levels of employment. The glass ceiling is invisible, and it is not until one tries to pass through it that its impermeable nature is discovered. For those at the top, there is a responsibility to identify who is coming up the path. We then must mentor, hire, and advocate for other women so that the glass ceiling is broken permanently.

In addition to creating networks within business, we need to address the societal factors that work to keep the glass ceiling intact. Gender socialization continues to be powerful and is often used to categorize people and determine their abilities. When we first learn of the birth of a child, often the first question is, Is it a boy or a girl? Immediately, and almost involuntarily, we begin to associate behaviors and qualities with that child. In fact, a famous study, known as the "pinks and blues,"[9] showed how society sees girls and boys differently. Using the same baby, the study evaluated how people respond to gender-specific cues. Researchers wrapped the child in a blue blanket and then asked a group of people to apply adjectives to the baby; they found that the group described the baby as strong, big, and alert. However, the same baby wrapped in a pink blanket elicited descriptive terms such as sweet, quiet, little, and weak. From birth, we are assigned gender-specific attributes that in many ways determine how we are viewed throughout our lives. Women, for example, are assigned certain qualities that can prescribe nonthreatening and disempowering roles for them in society.

> I don't necessarily feel represented by the feminist movement since I am one of the women who is viewed as rather spoiled to be able to stay at home with my children and "dabble" in my career. Aimee, 34, Washington

These stereotypes follow us into adulthood. Women constitute the majority of those in lower-paying careers and jobs. For example, 95.6 percent of childcare workers are women, and disproportionately workers of color,[10] and 88 percent of maids and housekeeping workers are women.[11] According to the Bureau of Labor Statistics, maids and housekeeping cleaners make an average of $10.49 an hour, whereas janitors (a separate category and one dominated by men) make an average of $11.63 an hour.[12] Compare the salary and status of the person who cares for children with those of someone who cares for cars—a mechanic makes an average hourly wage of $18.50 an hour, whereas a child day-care provider makes an average hourly wage of $10.18.[13] Women with master's degrees still make less than men with bachelor's degrees. According to the Center for American Progress, while women make up the majority of the nation's population and about 52 percent of the professional-level jobs, they lag significantly in representation in leadership positions. Women make up only 25 percent of executive and senior level positions, 20 percent of the board seats, and merely 6 percent of CEO positions.[14]

Women of color fair even more poorly in terms of representation, making up only 3.9 percent of executive and senior level management and 0.4 percent of CEO positions.[15]

While these statistics are daunting, the good news is that women and people of color continue to make gains and to change the demographics of the workplace. Citing studies by Morrison, White, and Van Velsor, Catalyst, and McKinsey and Company (a European study), Merida Johns argues that "the business case for women in senior leadership is compelling. Studies conclude that inclusion of women in the top ranks of company leadership has a direct and positive impact on a company's bottom line and risk management."[16] These studies show that companies with strong representation of women perform better financially, including such measures as profitability, competitiveness, and total return to shareholders (TRS). Yet, the structure of the workplace has not kept pace with the value of integrating women into the workplace. We need to have flexible work hours, comprehensive paid family leave, child care available or compensated, strict sexual harassment policies and prevention, institutionalized mentor programs, and benefits for all family members, including domestic partners. If such changes can be put into place, not only can women begin to realize their full potential in the workplace, but the workplace can become more representative and accessible to today's worker.

Feminists need to concern themselves with putting feminists in positions of political, economic, and media power. By placing feminists in control of these vehicles, a diversity of perspectives may be introduced to our insular society. This has the potential for revolutionary change. Bronwyn, 26, Caucasian, heterosexual

In addition to structural changes, we also need to change cultural attitudes and informal networks. For example, as Debra Meyerson and Joyce Fletcher write in their report, "A Modest Manifesto for Shattering the Glass Ceiling":

. . . mentoring programs may help women meet key people in a company's hierarchy, but they don't change the fact that informal networks, to which few women are privy, determine who really gets resources, information, and opportunities. Launching family-friendly programs doesn't challenge the belief that balancing home and work is fundamentally a woman's problem. And adding time to a tenure clock or providing alternative career tracks does little to change the expectation that truly committed employees put work first—they need no accommodation.[17]

In order to truly support a diverse work environment, corporations, unions, employers, employees, family members, and society as a whole must participate in this shift of consciousness. While revolutionary in their goals, Meyerson and Fletcher do not advocate revolution. Rather, they encourage small, incremental changes in deeply imbedded discrimination, arguing that "gender inequity is rooted in our cultural patterns and therefore in our organizational systems."[18] Further, they argue that "existing systems can be reinvented by altering the raw materials of organizing—concrete, everyday practices in which biases are expressed."[19] Small victories are the steps to cultural change. Passing legislation and corporate policy are important steps, but we need to also include a daily practice that supports integrating work, family, and civic life.

I don't know anything about political stuff, but I do see that politics is relevant to my life. And I do plan to [vote]. Kelly, 24, Asian

MEDIA: THE POWER OF TELLING OUR STORIES

The media impact the way we view the world around us and, more importantly, who we are in that world. We grow up in a media-rich society, with radio, magazines, movies, billboards, and TV readily present at every turn. Indeed, the media have a powerful influence on our idea of reality. Far too often, however, women are not in the positions of leadership that would permit them to determine and direct our stories and images in the media. In 2016, women compromised merely 17 percent of the directors, producers, executive producers, and cinematographers in the top 250 domestic grossing films of that year.[20] Unless women are in positions of leadership and decision-making, our stories are not told and our lives are often misunderstood and misrepresented. If we turned to the media to learn about women, we would believe that men outnumber us two to one.[21] We would learn that 68 percent of us are white, 16 percent of women are African American, 7 percent are Asian-American, 7 percent Latinas, and 2 percent are classified as "other."[22] We would discover that 71 percent of women are under the age of forty.[23] Very few of us are lesbians, or lesbians with a sex life (with very few exceptions), and virtually none of us have disabilities. This is hardly a true and accurate representation of women in this country.

Women's involvement in the media is critical. Not only must we hold positions of leadership, but we must also familiarize ourselves with the media well enough to become media activists—not only to get our stories in the news, but to democratize the media. The third-wave writers Jennifer Baumgardner and Amy Richards have a great section about the relationship between feminism and the media in their book *Manifesta: Young Women, Feminism and the Future*. In their chapter "Feminists Want to Know: Is the Media Dead?" they write, "The media doesn't know how to deal with feminism, and feminists haven't mastered the media."[24] Pointing to the fact that we have never owned a significant portion of the media, Baumgardner and Richards use this chapter to flush out media myths about feminism. Indeed, many of the myths of feminism are rooted in the media's portrayal of feminism. The media not only have a history of ignoring and misrepresenting us, but they also have an incessant need to *soften* our image—focusing on trivial issues of make-up and clothing, rather than on the political and economic issues for which we work. For example, when I was first elected as president of NOW in California, I did a newspaper interview in which the writer spent a significant part of the article detailing what I looked like and what I was wearing, including describing me as wearing the ever-feminine color pink (which I was not), rather than using the space to discuss the agenda that California NOW was putting forth. Despite the many challenges posed by inaccurate and biased media coverage, feminists need to learn how to effectively use the media to their advantage. Women need to be media savvy—we need to know how to get our message across and our stories told. The media are a powerful vehicle in our society, and indeed in the global community.

Perhaps activists today are finding social media and blogging the most effective vehicles of media. These forms of media give content control to the writer and are in many ways far more accessible to today's activist. While it can be argued that online activism cannot replace in-person activism, together they are a powerful mechanism for creating change. For many, online activism is a good entry point to social movements, giving the activist an opportunity to engage in debate, surveys, and petitions, as they develop their comfort and knowledge base.

In general I still believe that people are wary about feminism. We have been so saturated with stereotypes about feminists that it prevents us from understanding the movement. Rebecca, 22, white, Virginia

Finally, in addition to putting women in positions of media leadership and practicing media activism, we must be knowledgeable about our pop culture. Music, television, and movies set a tone for behavior, style, sexuality, and gender. Whether we personally follow the trends or not, it is important that we be able to critique their impact on the public perception of women and our lives as women. From the lasting impact of *Leave It to Beaver* to the shows that redefine family for the twenty-first century, from the movies that reinforce a narrow stereotype of femininity to the indie films that show another image, the media create a definition of woman to which we often turn to find our own definition. We idolize our celebrities as American royalty, we are obsessed with their every move—what they eat, what they wear, how they live—they set our trends and impact how we define ourselves. Far too often, these images are unrealistic and misleading. But every once in a while we hear a song that declares our independence, a movie that shows that "real women do have curves," television that inspires our political nature and shows our intelligence, and we are proud to be women. We need to celebrate these occasions and demand that they become the norm.

GREAT MEDIA FOR WOMEN

Bitch magazine—a great third-wave, feminist magazine.
Fairness and Accuracy in Reporting: Women's Desk—a national media watch organization.
Media Education Foundation—a great source of films that examine social issues.
Ms. magazine—the classic feminist magazine.
Wolfe Video—video distributors with a focus on lesbian films and filmmakers.
Women in Film—a nonprofit networking organization for women in the film industry.
Women Make Movies—a nonprofit organization that promotes media projects by and about women.

RELIGION: TO EACH HER OWN

Another key institution that shapes the face of our society and impacts the lives and status of women is religion. Indeed, women come to feminism with a great diversity of backgrounds, including religious beliefs. Many people seem to think that feminism and religion do not go together. But if feminism is to protect and support women in their pursuits, then feminism needs to do a better job of embracing women of faith. It is true that there is much to question when it comes to religion and the roles and treatment of women within it—from the reinforcement of traditional gender roles within the home to the debate about whether women should be allowed to be religious leaders—but it is a mistake of the feminist movement to assume that women within religions are not questioning these very things and working to change the structure from the inside out. Many women, particularly white women, came to feminism in the 1960s and 1970s as refugees from rigid religious doctrines. Many have wounds from these experiences. And feminism is a great place to address the gender bias in upbringing and in the houses of religion. However, we need to recognize that feminism is multifaceted, as are the people within the movement. And, for many women, faith is central to their identities and ways of life. One's religious choices are deeply personal, and one's beliefs and practice should be left to the individual. That said, religion itself can be used in ways that can discriminate against individuals, even serve as a justification for killing.

While the Civil Rights Act of 1964 prohibits discrimination in employment on the basis of race and gender, section 702 of the Act exempts "religious corporations, associations or societies with respect to the employment of individuals of a particular religion to perform work connected with the carrying on by such corporations, associations, or societies of their religious activities." In 1972, this act was expanded to allow religious groups to discriminate in all employee activities, as opposed to just those within religiously oriented venues. It is on this basis that religious institutions are allowed to refuse the ordination of women as leaders within religious organizations. Despite this, women have begun to join the clergy, which is certainly a gain, but in 2012, women comprised only 11 percent of the leaders in American congregations, and many faiths continue to prohibit women's leadership altogether.[25]

> I identify as a feminist because I think that everyone should be equal. . . . However, as a Christian I sometimes feel like feminists marginalize those that believe in the Bible because they have written it off as an oppressive text. Sarah, 23, straight, Wyoming

Throughout the world, in many cultures, there is an expectation that women are to be the keepers of the faith in their families and that they carry the responsibility to pass on these traditions to their children. It is an important role, yet women are still not permitted to join the upper-level leadership within the church itself. Indeed, around the world, religion—from Catholicism to Islam—is used as justification to treat women as second-class citizens. The Roman Catholic Church is one of the strongest opponents of women's leadership within the church and has issued strong policy statements against the ordination of women priests. However, many Catholics throughout the world disagree with the pope's position. "We Are Church" is an international organization working for equal rights for women within the Catholic Church. It believes in the admission of women to all Church ministries and argues for a positive attitude toward sexuality. It believes in making change within the Church, while working toward a "Council of all Christian churches, which will regard each other as equals in their search for peace and friendship among themselves."[26] Like the Vatican, Eastern Orthodox, Greek Orthodox, some of the Anglican Communion, the Church of Jesus Christ of Latter-day Saints, and many fundamentalist and evangelical Protestant denominations also oppose women's leadership and the ordination of women. However, many religious sects and organizations support, and are working toward, an increase in women's participation in religious leadership. Reform Judaism and the Baptist, Lutheran, Presbyterian, Methodist, and Episcopal churches, as well as the Church of Pakistan and some Anglican churches, have all allowed women to become priests, bishops, rabbis, or deacons. The Unitarian Universalist faith is founded upon tenets of equality and is the first church to have a clergy made up of a majority of women. Some women of faith have chosen traditional religions in which they maintain traditional gender roles, while others have gravitated toward reform religions, reclaiming the role and importance of women within that faith; still others have turned to a revival of Goddess, Wiccan, or Neopagan faiths, creating their own spiritual practice or rejecting religion and/or spirituality altogether. In any case, many are working to support the leadership of women in religious orders.

I realize that as a country we have never had true separation between church and state. Religion has always been influential, even foundational, to our political system. But, short of protecting one's right to voluntarily practice and participate in a religion, while not controlling or limiting the action of others, I believe that the government should stay out of religion and religion out of government. I do not look to my elected officials to represent, design, or enforce my morality, and I do not believe that they should be allowed to. Since when do those who call themselves the "moral majority," or Christian conservatives, have the market on values and morality? Who are they to decide? I believe that morality is up to the individual, and as long as someone is not harming or restricting another's right to be, believe, or act, then to each her own. But do not be mistaken; there is a strong morality among feminists and the progressive left. Great activism and social service come from religious institutions full of folks working for justice. We must stop allowing the conservative right to define faith in only evangelical Christian terms. We must stop allowing conservatives to narrowly define our nation's morality. We must remember that conservatism and religion do not always, or even usually, go hand in hand.

JUST DO WHAT? EDUCATIONAL AND ATHLETIC EQUITY

I'd like to end this chapter on women's roles and representation in society by focusing on Title IX. After forty-plus years of Title IX, as of this writing, how are women and girls faring in athletics? Is there educational equity? Who is most likely to be called upon in the classroom—boys or girls? How do teachers respond to girls' ideas in school? How are girls faring in math and science? How gender-specific are examples used in classes or textbooks? What sports do girls have access to? How do sports impact a girl's self-esteem and self-concept? How equitably distributed are college scholarships? These are just some of the questions that activists and academics focus on when talking about Title IX. Arguably, if there has been a significant change in women's participation in society, it can be seen in those thousands of little

Title IX, Educational Amendments of 1972: No person in the United States shall, on the basis of sex, be excluded from participation in, be denied the benefits of, or be subjected to discrimination under any educational program or activity receiving federal financial assistance.

girls now running around on soccer fields throughout the nation—a sight that was just not seen forty years ago.

Although mostly associated with athletic equality, Title IX of the 1972 Education Amendments is a federal statute that prohibits sex discrimination in education. Title IX includes all educational programs and activities in federally funded schools. Title IX prohibits discrimination based on gender, marital, or parental status. According to the American Association of University Women (AAUW), "Title IX applies to all areas of education, including:

- recruitment, admissions, and housing;
- career and technical education;
- pregnant, parenting, or married students;
- science, technology, engineering, and math (STEM);
- sexual harassment and assault;
- comparable facilities and access to course offerings;
- financial assistance;
- student health services and insurance benefits;
- harassment based on gender identity; and
- athletics."[27]

Title IX also prohibits sexual harassment by employees or agents of a school. In 1981, the U.S. Department of Education's Office for Civil Rights required that schools bound by Title IX have a policy and procedure in place to address complaints of sexual harassment.[28] In 1999, in *Davis v. Monroe County Board of Education*, the U.S. Supreme Court ruled that school districts can be liable for student-to-student sexual harassment if the school district had knowledge of the harassment and did not effectively address the problem.[29]

Within coeducational schools, Title IX prohibits single-sex classes or programs unless these programs are "designed to overcome the effects of past discrimination."[30] The intent is to allow schools to address the problems of inequitable access to programs, activities, and classes that have historically disadvantaged one sex. I wrote in the first edition of *Fight Like a Girl* that perhaps one day we would also work to remedy the exclusion of those who do not identify as male or female, and under the Obama administration we did just that. Title IX, under the Obama administration, was determined to extend to the rights and protections of transgender students. This is now challenged under the Trump administration. It is ever more clear that politics do matter. Exceptions to this single-sex rule include contact sports, sex education in elementary and secondary schools, and choral groups; these areas may remain segregated.

Numerous studies, including those done by the California Women's Law Center and the Women's Sports Foundation, show that many women and girls who participate in sports have increased self-esteem, improved academic performance, better scores on standardized tests, higher rates of high school and college graduation, and higher rates of college attendance than their nonathletic female counterparts; they have lower rates of teen pregnancy and are less likely to stay in abusive relationships.[31] Additionally, we know that girls who are involved in sports have a more positive body image and better overall health. Given these results, it is concerning that we don't do a better job at encouraging and supporting girls' athletics. Are we frightened by the prospect of girls defining themselves, feeling strong in their bodies, bench pressing 250, or running a minute mile?

In recent years we have seen a rise in women's professional sports—from the Women's National Basketball Association (WNBA) to the Women's Professional Football League (WPFL)—further providing young women with healthy images and models to emulate. But, despite the move into professional sports and the known positive effect that sports have in the lives of women and girls, we are still fighting for equal access, recognition,

It bothered me, especially in high school and college, that my peers took boys and men more seriously than girls and women. Catherine, 23, white, lesbian, California

and funding. In addition to educational equity, Title IX seeks to create athletic equity. In fact, athletics is the most immediately visible part of Title IX requirements. Under Title IX, educational institutions must provide equitable athletic opportunities to all students, regardless of sex, in three specific areas: participation, treatment of athletes, and athletic scholarships. In order to evaluate a school's compliance with Title IX in athletics, the Office of Civil Rights established a three-pronged test, and schools must meet one of the three criteria in order to be compliant. The three prongs are these:

1. Proportionality: assessing whether male and female students are participating in athletics proportional in numbers to their enrollment at the school;
2. History: a school must show a history of expanding opportunities in athletics for the underrepresented sex;
3. Meeting interest and abilities: a school must fully meet the interest and abilities of the underrepresented sex.

For a long time, many schools chose proportionality to test their compliance. Unfortunately, instead of truly ensuring access to athletics, this criterion means that women and girls are often blamed for cuts to men's sports. In response to demands for Title IX compliance, schools often cut men's teams to "make room" for women's teams—thus pitting men against women. The media tell the tragic stories of the men's lacrosse team being axed because those greedy women want a softball team. But what we rarely hear are stories of hotel rooms for football players who are playing at-home games, or the practice of purchasing new uniforms and multiple practice uniforms every season; or examples such as these, found by the Women's Sports Foundation:

- One university spent $300,000 putting lights on a football practice field that has never been used for football practice. It wanted to be able to impress potential recruits.

- One college housed the whole football team in a hotel for the entire preseason football camp because dorms were not available for the last two days and the coach didn't want the interruption. The snack bill alone was $86,000.
- A university dropped its men's swimming and diving program, citing economics. That same university found the means to (1) renovate the outdoor track, (2) renovate the indoor track, including the installation of hydraulic banked turns, (3) build a multifield baseball complex with heating elements under the soil to keep the grass growing year round, (4) add a new row of sky-boxes to the football stadium, and (5) install new state of the art turf in the football stadium.[32]

We also rarely hear of the challenges faced by women athletes—challenges like those faced by the women's swim team that has to share parkas between races; or the women's diving team that has to practice in the dark with flashlights after the men's water polo team has finished practicing even though they are off season; or the teams that are told that women's uniforms must to be self-funded or that the costs of travel to games are the individual responsibility of team members. We also don't hear about who is awarded the majority of athletic scholarships—despite comprising 52 percent of the student body, women received only 43 percent of college athletic scholarships and only 31 percent of the dollars spent to recruit athletes.[33] Scholarship awards are often a deciding factor in college attendance. The truth of the matter is that for colleges and universities the issue is about prioritizing—and it is clear that even after more than forty-five years of Title IX, women are still not a priority. Despite the assertion that women's sports have caused the demise of men's sports, both women's and men's participation in athletics has increased under Title IX—women's participation in intercollegiate sports increased from 90,000 in the 1981–82 school year to 163,000 in 1998–99, and men's participation went from 220,000 to 232,000 in those same years.[34] These numbers continue to grow. In the 2015–16 academic year, the number of women participating in collegiate sports grew beyond

214,000, nearly 7 times that of pre-Title IX participation.[35] The numbers of male collegiate athletes also continued to grow, exceeding 256,000 in 2015–16.[36] These numbers show us that it is possible to increase the number of women's teams without cutting any men's teams; indeed, men's participation in sports has also grown with Title IX. If we are to believe that girls and women have as much a right to play competitive sports as boys and men, and that the word "athlete" is not exclusively for men, then we must continue to support Title IX.

I realized about halfway through my undergraduate degree program that there was no representation of women in the subjects I was studying, and that the teaching methodologies were biased and patriarchal. . . . I knew something was very wrong. Sarah, 22, white, California

CHALLENGES TO TITLE IX AND WOMEN'S SPORTS

While gains have been made in women's participation in sports, we still have a way to go before we see true proportionality and representation for women athletes. And, while we have made gains in many areas, we are losing ground in coaching and leadership positions for women. Women coaches are paid less than men and face significant barriers to advancement in their fields. In college athletic programs, women account for only 13 percent of sports information directors, 31 percent of all head athletic trainers, and continue to face significant wage disparities compared to their male counterparts.[37] Further, women comprise a mere 3 percent of the coaches for men's teams.[38] In contrast, men now hold the majority of coaching positions for women's teams. In the 1970s, with the passage of Title IX, 90 percent of women's team were coached by women.[39] As of 2014, only 43 percent of coaches of women's teams are women.[40]

On the professional level, we are finally seeing the emergence of women sports stars. Venus and Serena Williams, Annika Sorenstam, Laila Ali, Michelle Kwan, Mia Hamm, Sue Bird, Sheryl Swoops, Lindsey Vonn, Hope Solo, Maya Moore, Lisa Leslie, Carli Lloyd, Megan Rapinoe, Diana Taurasi, Natalie Coughlin, and the many WBNᴬ, NCAA, and

WPFL players all give us heroes to watch in sports. But, as in the other arenas in which women serve as heroes, they are neither recognized nor awarded the same status as their male counterparts. The minimum NBA salary in 2015–16 was $525,093, compared the 2015 minimum WNBA salary at $38,913; the 2014 PGA total prize money amounted to $340 million, which was five times that of the WPGA in 2015.[41]

Pay inequity in sports is real. When a man argues for a higher salary, we give him props, sing his praises, and never doubt his worth. When a woman does, we tell her that she is lucky to be playing a sport she loves. When a male sport star is accused of rape, domestic violence, or even murder, we usually allow him to continue playing—and often rearrange his court dates (if there are any) to avoid disrupting the season. But when a woman star poses for *Playboy*, we are outraged at her indecency. You'd think if we were going to hold women to such a higher standard, we'd pay them better!

When I was 7 years old I wanted to play ice hockey, my hometown only had a boys' team and I was therefore not allowed to play. That day it really meant something to me, how it is different to be a girl. Just because I was a girl I couldn't play even though I was a better skater than most of the boys. Anna, 22, bisexual, Nebraska and Sweden

These issues are not going unnoticed, however. Tennis was widely recognized as paying out grossly inequitable in winnings. Despite television ratings being higher for women's tennis matches, female tennis players made significantly less than their male counterparts in major international tennis matches. After years of fighting this, women won parity. In 2007, Wimbledon, the last holdout, finally agreed to equal winnings. Now all four Grand Slam events (Wimbledon, the French Open, the Australian Open, and the U.S. Open) offer equal prize money.[42] The U.S. women's soccer team is fighting a similar battle. Citing sex discrimination and the fact that the women's soccer team is paid 40 percent less than that of their male counterparts, five members of the U.S. women's soccer team filed suit with the Equal Employment Opportunity Commission (EEOC) in 2016. The suit is publicly supported by the entire team. The U.S. women's soccer team is fighting for equal bonus structure, and while the EEOC complaint was not yet resolved as of this writing, the women were able to win a significant gain in 2017 through collective bargaining. Though not yet at equal pay, the women's soccer team is taking an important stand for fairness.

THE STATUS OF TITLE IX

In theory, Title IX means great gains for women and girls in education. Unfortunately, theory is not the same as practice. Four decades after the passage of Title IX, women and girls still don't enjoy equal, or even adequate, access to participation in sports; they are still being barred from activities in school because of their gender; and a reported 56 percent of girls experience sexual harassment at school.[43] While the rate of girls taking classes in STEM/STEAM classes is increasing and we are starting to see parity among women and men graduates in some of these fields, we continue to see a significant lack of representation in post-college jobs. Women make up merely 12 percent of engineering professionals; even less when accounting for race and ethnicity. Black women and Latinas make up 1 percent, respectively, while American Indian and Alaska Native women make up a fraction of 1 percent.[44] Women continue to be underrepresented in computer science, earning only 17.9 percent of the bachelor's degrees in this field.[45] And in terms of who is doing the teaching, women make up less than a third (32.4 percent) of the nation's professors, and are more likely to be non-tenured compared to their male colleagues.[46] Black women make up 2.3 percent, Asian women 3 percent, and Latinas 2.4 percent of the tenured faculty members in academia.[47] The disparity in education in the representation of women and men, particularly when

I was sitting one day in my high school English class listening to my teacher lecture on Great Expectations *and the archetypes of women. . . . It suddenly dawned on me that in the entire four years . . . not one book we had read had been by a female author. My teacher's explanation was that there were just not as many female authors to choose from. That summer I read Sylvia Plath, Virginia Woolf, Joyce Carol Oates, Jane Austen. I've been a feminist ever since.* Lindsay, 21, Euro-mutt, California

you account for race and ethnicity, is shameful, and yet we excel. Women's excellence in education should not be used as an argument that they don't face discrimination, and it should not be used to argue that women don't need equality of opportunity to get by. Rather, we should imagine what could be, if we truly supported and funded women and girls in all arenas of education.

ACHIEVING EQUALITY

Equality is our right. There can be no compromise. Our very lives depend upon it. Within the United States and throughout the globe, we must fight until all women, all people, have true social, political, and economic equality. Many came before us, and I suspect that many may need to follow us on this journey. Women have been imprisoned, harassed, threatened, brutalized, ignored, celebrated, honored, and victorious in this fight for equal rights. The question is, what will your contribution be to the lives of women you know? And to the lives of women whom you do not know but with whom you share a common plight? What will you do for justice?

SPOTLIGHT ON ACTIVISM

Thousands of workers across hundreds of cities in the United States have joined the Fight for Fifteen. In their book, *$2.00 a Day: Living on Almost Nothing in America*, authors Edin and Shaefer write, "In no state today does a full-time job paying minimum wage allow a family to afford a one- or two-bedroom apartment at fair market rent. But a family with a full-time earner making $15 an hour can afford a two-bedroom apartment at the fair market rent in twenty-two states and can come very close in another four."[48] Indeed, it has long been recognized that minimum wage is inadequate and nowhere near a living wage in America.

In 1994, Baltimore became the first city to pass a living wage. And while this law ultimately impacted few employees, it did trigger an important conversation on working poverty. In 2011, the growing disparity among economic classes in the United States became a national conversation with the 1 percent versus the 99 percent consciousness raised by Occupy Wall Street. Then, in 2012, fast food workers, big box chain workers, janitors, and other low-wage workers began to mobilize for better pay and working conditions. Seattle became the first city to win a citywide $15-an-hour ordinance. This prompted cities across the nation to take up the fight. Vocal socialist and key activist in Seattle's campaign Kshama Sawant argued, "People don't need some kind of detailed graduate-level economics lesson; they understand that the market is not working for them. The market is making them homeless. The market is making them cityless. And they're fed up, and they're angry."[49] Sawant was elected to the Seattle City Council.

To date, the Fight for 15 has been taken up in 300 cities across the United States. Seattle, California, and New York have made it law. Pennsylvania has done so for nursing home and hospital workers. And initiatives are pending in many other city councils and state governments.

TAKE ACTION

Getting Started

Register to vote. Register others to vote. Remember, if you have moved or changed your name, you must re-register.

Realize that all women's work is valuable, whether paid or unpaid.

If you attend a religious institution, inquire about its policies and practices in support of women's leadership.

The Next Step

Vote. Vote in every election. Sign up for an absentee ballot if transportation, child care, time, or whatever has made it difficult for you to vote in the past. Coordinate group child care with your friends—watch each other's children and take turns voting. Or, better yet, take your child(ren) with you to impress on them the value of practicing democracy.

Write your U.S. senators and urge them to support the ratification of CEDAW.

Call or write the White House to encourage the administration to support CEDAW.

Support paid-family-leave benefits in your state and on the federal level; write your elected officials and ask for their support.

Getting Out There

Volunteer to work on a campaign—phone bank, precinct walk, stuffing envelopes.

Get involved with living wage campaigns in your city and state.

Get involved with media activism—write an editorial, call into a radio talk show, or write letters to television studios about their programming. See Fabulous Feminist Web Resources for more resources.

FABULOUS FEMINIST WEB RESOURCES

AlterNet
www.alternet.org
A great source of independent news.

American Association of University Women
www.aauw.org
With a mission of "equity for all women and girls, lifelong education, and positive societal change," the AAUW website provides information on grants, educational programs, and research on educational equity.

American Civil Liberties Union
www.aclu.org
Protecting constitutional rights, the ACLU takes on legal battles to protect due process, First Amendment rights, rights of privacy, and the many other freedoms that we hold essential to our society. The ACLU website includes information about legislation, the Supreme Court, and legal activism in the United States.

Bitch magazine
www.bitchmedia.com
Subtitled "Feminist Response to Pop Culture."

Black Women Organized for Political Action
www.bwopa.org
Focus on training, supporting, and promoting black women's leadership.

Center for American Progress

www.americanprogress.org

Great progressive site for current information on domestic politics, the economy, and national security. Includes "Campaign for Women's Lives," about medical privacy and reproductive rights.

Center for Digital Democracy

www.democraticmedia.org

Activist-based, the Center for Digital Democracy focuses on Internet and broadband media. Their website has information about activist campaigns, media/market watch, media ownership, and other areas of digital media.

Code Pink

www.codepink.org

More radical in nature, Code Pink is an activist organization working for peace and social justice. It promotes creative and visually innovative protests against war and injustice.

Common Cause

www.commoncause.org

A nonprofit, nonpartisan organization working to encourage "citizen participation in democracy."

Disability Rights Education and Defense Fund

www.dredf.org

Working to extend civil rights to people with disabilities, DREDF provides information on advocacy, legislation, and legal cases.

Dyke Action Machine

www.dykeactionmachine.com

Primarily focused in New York City, Dyke Action Machine "is a public art collaboration which critiques mainstream culture by inserting lesbian images into a recognizably commercial context."

Emily's List

www.emilyslist.org

A grassroots political network, providing resources to pro-choice, Democratic women running for elected office.

Equality Now
www.equalitynow.org
Promoting human rights for women around the world, their website includes information about international campaigns to advance the status of women worldwide.

Fairness and Accuracy in Reporting
www.fair.org
A national media-watch organization. Their website includes a Women's Watch and Racism Watch Desk.

Feminist Majority
www.feminist.org
Great site for current campaigns—local and global. Also has information about the group's campus activism program.

Fight for Fifteen
www.fightfor15.org
Collaborative effort to fight for living wage and unionizing workers across the United States.

Gay and Lesbian Alliance Against Defamation
www.glaad.org
"Dedicated to promoting and ensuring fair, accurate and inclusive representation of people and events in the media as a means of eliminating homophobia and discrimination based on gender identity and sexual orientation," GLAAD is a leader in gay and lesbian rights. Their website has a great deal of information, including information on a variety of campaigns hosted by GLAAD.

Global Exchange
www.globalexchange.org
"Global Exchange is an international human rights organization dedicated to promoting political, social and environmental justice globally."

Their website includes information on international campaigns, eco-nomic and human rights, speakers bureau, and volunteer and job opportunities.

Global Fund for Women
www.globalfundforwomen.org
Grant-based organization, working to provide resources for women's groups fighting for human rights around the world.

International Association of Women in Radio and Television
www.iawrt.org
International organization dedicated to ensuring women's representation in media. Holds consultative status with the United Nations Economic and Social Council.

International Women's Media Foundation
www.iwmf.org
"The IWMF's mission is to strengthen the role of women in the news media around the world, based on the belief that no press is truly free unless women share an equal voice." IWMF's website includes a variety of pro-gram initiatives, training, and news and research resources.

Lambda Legal Defense Fund
www.lambdalegal.org
Lambda Legal works for civil rights for LGBT and HIV+ communities, through litigation, education, and public policy work.

League of Women Voters
www.lwv.org
Nonpartisan organization working to bring women's voice into the politi-cal system through voter information, campaign finance reform, and election reform.

Media Education Foundation
www.mediaed.org
Great source for films—including Tough Guise 2, Killing Us Softly 4, Reviving Ophelia, *and* The Purity Myth.

MoveOn.org
www.moveon.org
Voter information and campaign organization. Hosts "meet-ups" in communities around the United States for GOTV (Get Out The Vote) activities. Great source for electoral politics.

Ms. magazine
www.msmagazine.com
The classic! Many of us cut our teeth on our mother's copies. As always, a great source of feminist news.

National Committee on Pay Equity
www.pay-equity.org
Great source for information on pay equity, including statistics, research, Equal Pay Day campaign, and tips for activism.

National Gay and Lesbian Task Force Policy
www.ngltf.org
Founded in 1973 as the first LGBTQ task force for civil rights and advocacy. Their website includes information on campaigns, research, issues, and community action.

National Low Income Housing Coalition
www.nlihc.org
Dedicated to ending the affordable-housing crisis in the United States. Their website includes research, public policy, and up-to-date information on housing access.

National Organization for Women
www.now.org
Check out its "Merchants of Shame" and "Women-Friendly Workplace Campaign" for information and activism on Walmart. Also a good source of information on a wide array of issues pertaining to women's equality.

National Partnership for Women and Families
www.nationalpartnership.org

Nonpartisan, nonprofit organization focused on meeting the dual demands of work and family.

National Public Radio
www.npr.org
Publicly controlled radio. Check its website for local listings.

National Women's Law Center
www.nwlc.org
Public education and advocacy promoting fairness in the workplace and family-friendly policies in the workplace.

National Women's Political Caucus
www.nwpc.org
Multicultural, intergenerational, multi-issue organization working to get women involved in politics. NWPC puts women in the political pipeline through recruitment and training.

9 to 5: National Association of Working Women
www.9to5.org
Working for women's economic justice, 9 to 5 is an advocacy organization that addresses workplace issues, including sexual harassment, pay equity, and work/home challenges.

Pacifica Radio
www.pacifica.org
Progressive, alternative radio. Stations in Berkeley, Los Angeles, Houston, New York, and Washington, DC.

Parents, Family and Friends of Lesbians and Gays
www.pflag.org
Nonprofit, grassroots organization providing support and advocacy.

Religious Tolerance.org
www.religioustolerance.org
Website for tolerance and acceptance of multiple religious ideologies. Includes articles about women, faith, and religious leadership.

United Nations—Women Watch

www.un.org/womenwatch

A section of the United Nations website with a focus on women. Good site for information about the status of women globally, particularly with regard to CEDAW.

Webgrrls International

www.webgrrls.com

Webgrrls provides a network of resources for women in media—includes job and internship opportunities, business networking, and skills building.

Women in Film

www.wif.org

Networking for women in the film industry, dedicated to mentoring and promoting women.

Women's International League for Peace and Freedom

www.wilpf.org

Founded in 1915 with Jane Addams as its first president, WILPF is still going strong. Calling for "peaceful means world disarmament, full rights for women, racial and economic justice, an end to all forms of violence, and to establish those political, social, and psychological conditions which can assure peace, freedom, and justice for all." WILPF's website provides issue and campaign information.

Women's Sports Foundation

www.womensportsfoundation.org

Founded by Billie Jean King in 1974, the Women's Sports Foundation is a nonprofit charitable organization providing resources, advocacy, and education for women in sports.

5

GOOD ENOUGH

I remember reading once that "getting my head out of the toilet bowl was the most political act I ever committed"[1] and thinking—this is my life. For years I struggled with an eating disorder, bulimia, that consists of a cycle of binging and purging. I was bulimic for much of my activist life—during the grape boycott, at the same time I sat in on Bettina Aptheker's classes, and even as the president of my college NOW chapter. At my worst, I was throwing up a dozen times a day. I could throw up with no noise. I could throw up on command. I could even throw up out the car door while driving down the road. I'm not claiming braggin' rights. I was becoming more involved in the women's movement, working toward the empowerment of women and girls, and falling deeper and deeper into a pit of self-hatred.

> Eat·ing disor·der *n.* any of various disorders, as anorexia nervosa or bulimia, characterized by severe disturbances in eating habits.
> An·or·ex·ia ner·vo·sa *n.* an eating disorder characterized by a fear of becoming fat, a distorted body image, and excessive dieting leading to emaciation.
> Bu·lim·ia *n.* 1. also called bu·lim·ia ner·vo·sa, a habitual disturbance in eating behavior characterized by bouts of excessive eating followed by self-induced vomiting, purging with laxatives, strenuous exercise, or fasting.

I was plagued by this question: How is it possible that someone with a growing feminist consciousness can be binging and purging while remaining a staunch feminist? I was regularly talking with young women about eating disorders and media images and their harmful effects on our self-esteem, urging them to increase their empowerment and work on their sense of self—all the while feeling like a hypocrite. The more

I encouraged others, the more I felt like a failure. Imposter phenomenon[2] is what it is called. It's the notion of hiding your true self from others while fearful that people will find out that you are not what you seem, that you've had them all fooled. Who was I to talk about empowerment? To criticize media images or advocate change? I threw up so much my voice was raspy. I lived on throat lozenges. And the barfing was only part of it— body obsession, working out, dieting, dieting, dieting. The saddest part was that I was more worried that someone would find me out, uncover the sham that I thought I was, than concerned for my health, my self-esteem, my self-definition, or even my life.

I do not think a woman's body needs to be super thin or adorned with makeup and "sexy" clothes, yet I still have lingering issues with my body and body image in general. Heather, 22, European American, Illinois

When I first became bulimic, I don't remember knowing if there was a label or an understanding for what I was doing to myself. I thought that I had discovered the perfect solution to my fat ass—I could eat in social settings, I could binge on my "forbidden foods," and then I could *just take care of it*. It seemed like the perfect solution; no one would have to know. But I also felt isolated by this secret. When I reluctantly went to a group session—because a friend needed me to go to support *her*—I was shocked that others did the things that I did. There was even a word for it. Bulimia. I began to understand but remained ashamed. I felt that I had a different standard to live up to. *I* was a feminist. I knew better. I was supposed to embrace my fat ass—hell, celebrate it!

Later, in hushed conversations with feminist friends, I began to note that I was not alone. They too confessed feelings of body hatred, acts of yo-yo dieting, binging and purging or self-starvation. I believe that there is a special type of pressure for self-proclaimed feminist women. We understand that non-feminist-identified women struggle with self-image—look at our culture! Diet fads, personal trainers, and cosmetic surgery. Between 4 and 32 percent of college-age women are estimated to have an eating disorder,[3] and approximately 80 percent of fourth graders are dieting—they're nine years old![4] But feminists don't recognize themselves in those statistics—we're the ones who *know* the statistics; we're not supposed to be part of those statistics. And so we continue to harbor the secrecies of our betrayal. We fear betraying a movement that has spent so many years working to give us a better life, a better identity, a movement that has worked for decades to create an acknowledgement of, and resources for, those with eating disorders, a movement that was the first and loudest voice to critique the social pressures for women to fit the thin, white ideal and that countered the messages of advertising, film, television, and beauty pageants—in short, a movement that proudly said that women, in all their shapes, sizes, and colors, are beautiful.

The life event that turned me from just another Sassy *reader into a committed, self-identified, and active activist was my own personal struggle with bulimia nervosa. I credit feminism for a large part of my successful recovery.* Sarah, 28, Irish/English, straight but open, Oregon, originally from Tennessee

I worried about writing this in a book about feminism. I worried about being this exposed. I worried that the antifeminists would use this story as an argument to prove that feminism failed. Then I realized that these fears are the same fears that kept me silent for so long. Eating disorders and body hatred are not the fault of the feminist movement; quite the contrary. The feminist movement has struggled to provide women and girls with resources and support to fight the hidden tortures within our psyches. The fact that feminist women have eating disorders is evidence of the strength of a culture that continues to send the message to women that as we are is not good enough. The culture is what needs to change, not women and not feminism.

THE FLAPPER, ROSIE THE RIVETER, MARILYN MONROE . . . AND ME

After reading books like Mary Pipher's *Reviving Ophelia* and Laura Fraser's *Losing It* and seeing the work of documentary filmmakers like Jean Kilbourne, I realized that there is a correlation between the social and political power we hold as women and the projection of an ideal body size fed to us through popular culture. This emphasis is so intense that it can, and does, detract from our quest for political, economic, and social representation. For example, American women won the right to vote in 1920. This was a seventy-two-year battle, one that was indeed hard fought. As a result, women had more political representation and thus more social power than ever before in our modern history. But around the 1920s, who was the major fashion idol? First the "Gibson Girl," with her tall, slender frame, and then the widely popular "flapper," who was even thinner, more boyish, and without curves. And, while the flapper fashion was a response to the corset and the desire for freedom from gowns and petticoats, it also came with a requirement of whiteness, a small body size, and an emphasis on weight control. As the fashion feminist Valerie Steele writes in her book, *The Corset: A Cultural History*, "Although the traditional boned corset gradually disappeared during the 1920s, most women still wore some kind of corset, corselette, or girdle."[5] She notes that fashion magazines and advice books continued to stress exercise and diets and reinforced the fear of fat internalized by women throughout American society. Steele further writes, "The corset did not so much disappear as become internalized through diet, exercise, and [more recently] plastic surgery."[6]

Additionally, as Susan Bordo, author of *Unbearable Weight: Feminism, Western Culture and the Body*, reminds us, "the flapper's freedom, as Mary McCarthy's and Dorothy Parker's short stories brilliantly reveal, was largely an illusion—as any obsessively cultivated sexual style must inevitably be."[7] Despite freedom from the corset and a growing quest for sexual equality, women began to experience a backlash. Once again, their physical beauty and worth, rather than their independence and intelligence, became paramount. After all, let's not forget that 1921 was the year of the first Miss America pageant, the start of the practice of formally rewarding women for their physical appearance, as opposed to establishing a scholarship program (a common defense of beauty pageants) based upon intellect and scholarly merit.

Moving forward in history, during World War II, the strong, muscular image of Rosie the Riveter took hold. This can-do image was appropriated by the government to convince women to enter the paid labor force to support the U.S. economy, industry, and war efforts while the men were away fighting. Women were told that they could do a "man's job." I should note that this effort, like Rosie herself, was largely aimed at white women, as most women of color in the United States were already working. In her study *Creating Rosie the Riveter: Class, Gender and Propaganda During World War II*, Maureen Honey writes that "the woman in a nontraditional job was portrayed as valiantly leading the nation to victory. Women were provided with positive role models for entering male occupations, and the public was given a standard-bearer of home-front solidarity and protection."[8] Like Rosie, most of this imagery portrayed white, middle-class women and virtually ignored the contributions of women of color. Honey writes that "racial prejudice precluded using blacks in [heroic roles] because they were perceived by a racist culture as inferior to whites and therefore inappropriate figures of inspiration or national pride."[9] Women of color were inaccurately and unjustly left out of images of women supporting the war effort, and white women were sold the notion of nationalism and valor through their war work, along with the expectation that they would maintain their home, their family, and their femininity. After World War II, when women were essentially kicked out of the factories to make room for the returning soldiers, they returned home, and the baby boom exploded. The icon of the 1950s, Marilyn Monroe, a voluptuous size 14 or 16 by today's standards, suggested a return to femininity and the acceptance of a larger body size. Of course, Marilyn was also seen as a "dumb blonde" who didn't ask too much, didn't demand too much, and didn't know too much. Marilyn's image provided for a less threatening image of white women, one that posed a smaller economic and political threat within American society.

As we moved into the 1960s, with the women's movement taking off again and women demanding equal pay, equal representation, and equal rights, the fashion icon was Twiggie—rail thin, white, boyish, with no curves. Chris Strodder, author of *Swingin' Chicks of the '60s*, writes that "with 31-22-32 measurements and barely 90 pounds on her 5'6" frame, Twiggy in a lime-green mini and green tights represented a bold departure from the softer, rounder shapes on the 50's and early 60's."[10] Still referenced today, Twiggie and her waiflike appearance set a norm for ultrathinness.[11] Women fighting for equal rights and representation were quickly confronted with an ideal that emphasized slenderness—an ideal for which we were, and most of us still are, expected to strive. However, within the Latina and African American communities, a fuller figure is more often the norm. As Christy Haubegger put it in her essay "I'm Not Fat, I'm Latina," "Latinas in this country live in two worlds. People who don't know us may think we're fat. At home we're called *bien cuidadas* (well cared for) . . . there is a greater 'cultural acceptance' of being overweight within Hispanic communities."[12]

Fast-forward to the twenty-first century: women have won more elected offices and thus more recognition politically than ever before, and have begun to move up the corporate and union ladders, represent a greater proportion of enrolled students in colleges and universities, and so on—and yet we see "heroin chic" on the pages of our magazines and the much-talked about "Lolliwood" and the shrinking actresses of Hollywood. "Lolliwood" refers to the image of the celebrity woman who has lost so much body mass that her head looks out of proportion to her body, making her look like a "lollipop." You see, your body can lose a great deal of mass, but your head, your cranium, will not shrink in size. One contrast to these images of heroin chic and Lolliwood are women in professional sports. With an emphasis on strength and ability, women athletes give girls a powerful alternative to look up to. With the increasing success of Title IX, we are beginning to see stronger, more positive images for young women through sports. Venus and Serena Williams, Simone Biles, Abby Wambach, Laila Ali, Danica Patrick, Annika Sorenstam, and Michelle Wei are just a few women in sports who present images of confident, powerful women who are comfortable in their bodies. Still, while it is true that the U.S. women's soccer team's multiple Women's World Cup wins and the growing popularity of the WNBA have greatly impacted girls in the United States, the bigger message to women, particularly young women in the midst of adolescence, is that "thin is in." And at any cost.

Throughout history, when women have not possessed much political, economic, or social power—when we

I was seen as the odd ball. I was the only girl in my class who did not wear tight clothes, starve myself, and wear make-up. Madelon, 18, bisexual, Massachusetts

did not run for political office, when we did not demand equal pay for equal work, when we did not control our own reproductive lives, when we did not vote—then we did not determine our lives. If we are not involved, then we present little or no threat to the patriarchal power structure that supports and protects male dominance. But, as women and girls become more empowered, we confront a contradictory message about our value. We must begin to counter the notion that to be worthy is to look like the "ideal woman" delivered to us through television shows, movies, music videos, newscasts, magazine covers, and video games. And, in doing so, we begin to experience a shift in power; instead of being valued solely because of a physical image, we promote one that recognizes our other contributions. Here's the deal—when women are required—even informally—to meet an unattainable body size ideal, our energy is sucked away. Like the Barbie doll, usually even heavily promoted "role models," be they actresses or fashion models, do not naturally meet the image they project—airbrushing, computer altera-tion, piece modeling, lighting, make-up,

I get in seventh grade and my mother buys me makeup. I was like what do you want me to do with this then she wanted me to start wearing high heels to church. NOT. I feel bad for my mom she tried so hard to turn me into this little prim and proper lady. I am so not that. Serena, 26, Hispanic, straight, single mom, California

surgery, and semi-starvation are all part of the process of creating an image that can sell the average woman an unattainable ideal that often looks quite natural. When we are obsessed with this ideal, we have little time, or confidence, for anything else—including fighting for equality.

More and more of our celebrities—most notably Oprah Winfrey, Jamie Lee Curtis, Margaret Cho, Kate Winslet, Gabourey Sibide, Mindy Kaling, and Jennifer Lawrence—have begun to speak out about this ideal, some going so far as to chronicle their transformation from their normal selves to the image we see on the cover of magazines. But the more likely story to grace our magazine racks is of the weight gains and losses of our most beautiful. Played out in the public is the accusation that eating disorders are rampant among the women on popular sit-coms and in our favorite movies—and a denial that this is the case. The media industry pits one woman against the other—on the one hand publicly condemning extreme weight loss but on the other requiring extreme thinness among actresses who appear on television and on the big screen. This added pressure, in such a public position, creates an unfair demand on, and a bit of a contradiction for, famous women. Not only are they subject to this requirement, but they are in the position of projecting this unattainable ideal. Instead of endlessly targeting famous, thin women, we should recognize that they too are pressured by the media. Why condemn a woman who is also struggling with her self-concept and body size—as well as with her job? My point is not to encourage the furthering of celebrity exaltation—certainly they have enviable lives in many ways—but rather to assert that we need to change the politics of beauty, challenge the ideal, and create more room for our diversity. We must celebrate the images of larger women in the media, and we must do so unapologetically—in other words, we must end the ubiquitous notion that if she is fat, she cannot be beautiful or that if she is fat, she is unhappy.

IMAGE OBSESSED—OR "YOU CAN RUN BUT YOU CAN'T HIDE FROM MEDIA IMAGES"

So why do we buy it, this image of an ideal woman? Oh, so many reasons. Family. Friends. High school. The media. For many of us, we begin to learn these patterns of body hatred from family and friends. We hear our mothers, or our fathers, self-criticize. Our friends are dieting. We are ridiculed at school. Our histories with body hatred, dieting, and eating disorders are as unique and as diverse as our bodies themselves. But the common denominator for American women is the media. When looking at body image, I often focus on the media because, while our family and friends are significant, they too are affected by the constant barrage of media images. In the United States, about 97 percent[13] of households have a television, and it is on for an average of five hours every day;[14] 58 percent of households have some type of tablet; 50 percent have some sort of subscription service (like Netflix); and 50 percent of households have a DVR.[15] When you combine these sources of media with television, the average number of media consumed increases to nearly eleven hours a day.[16] We are all impacted by the "ideal beauty" images, so that those images get projected back to us through our own and others' comments, pressures, and expectations.

The media are driven by advertising. According to Jean Kilbourne, a media expert and the creator of *Killing Us Softly: Advertising's Image of Women*, Americans see an average of three thousand advertisements a day.[17] Advertising is powerful and works best when we are convinced that our lives would be better with whatever product is being sold. Whether it talks to us about the cleanliness of our homes, the safety of our cars, the health of our families, or the beauty of our bodies, advertising sells self-worth through good old-fashioned American consumerism. And, with this, we transition from what we truly need to what we want to what we believe we must have, all to survive in a culture that judges and ranks us on the basis of appearances.

Every year in the United States, $250 billion is spent on advertising.[18] And where there is that much money at stake, you can bet everything is intentional—even coordinated. From the placement of a hand to the shape of the product to the race or ethnicity of the model, images are created to catch the attention of the consumer. Today's use of logos as branding has taken advertising to a whole new level. Where logos were once discreet, they now take center stage on our clothing, accessories, television screens, and products.[19] As Naomi Klein, author of *No Logo*, writes, "The effect, if not always the original intent, of advanced branding is to nudge the hosting culture into the background and make the brand the star. It is not to sponsor culture but to *be* the culture."[20] It is interesting when you add to the prevalence of this branding the fact that we, as consumers, spend a tremendous amount of money paying for the privilege to advertise for these companies. In other words, we pay inflated prices for a basic t-shirt that sports a product logo and then walk around advertising that company to all with whom we come in contact. In doing so, we create a hierarchy among our peers in terms of who wears what brand—categorizing one another on first sight by the logo on our t-shirt, shoes, or handbags. The company benefits twice—once from our purchase and once from our "free advertising." But the cost for this is far greater than what we spend in the stores. This pressure to wear the right name and to mimic the image of models (although fashion models are thinner than 98 percent of American women[21]) carries with it the price of our self-esteem and our health. According to the Centers for Disease Control, about half of all women, and a quarter of all men, in the United States are dieting—and I suspect that this is a significant underestimate.

A DANGEROUS TREND

Obsessed with weight loss and a thin ideal despite the harmful effects of dieting, we continue to seek the ultimate weight loss miracle. We have spent decades dedicated to a variety of trend diets—the cabbage diet, the grapefruit diet, the Hollywood diet—not to mention the endless diet pills, programs, and promises ("lose thirty pounds in thirty days"). In fact, in 2017, Americans collectively spent an estimated $66.3 billion in the weight loss market.[22] But not only are we *not* attaining the unattainable; we are less and less satisfied with ourselves.

The prevalence and acceptance of prescriptive and over-the-counter diet pills and programs has gotten out of hand. Even in the face of fatalities and severe health complications, as occurred with Fen-Phen, women continue to swallow danger every day. Web-based pharmacies sell diet drugs and supplements at discount rates, chat rooms for the latest diet trend regularly pop up in web communities across the Internet, weekly weigh-ins at Weight Watchers, Jenny Craig, and L.A. Weight Loss centers nationwide have increasingly become women's social network, and the newest trend, the newest diet is surely just around the corner as Americans respond in desperation to the endless reports of America's obesity "epidemic." I say "epidemic" because this is how these issues are referred to, particularly in reference to the CDC's estimate that over one-third of American adults are categorized as obese.[23] Particular attention has also been given to the rise of obesity among children, with the increase in juvenile diabetes posing the most serious health risk. While I do not want to deny that there are real concerns here, most media stories seem to use the topic of obesity as just another way to shame us about our bodies. See, for example, the Children's Health Care of Atlanta 2012 campaign against childhood obesity that featured billboard ads with warning messages across children's bodies with copy like "it's hard to be a little girl, if you're not." The ad campaign triggered a strong feminist response, not the least of which was activist Marilyn Wann's I Stand campaign. The I Stand campaign modeled the Atlanta posters in image but countered fat shaming messages with messages like "I stand for healthy, happy children—no matter their size," "I stand for unconditional body love," and "I stand against social stigma and the right to be happy just as you are." Certainly, shaming people has proven ineffective.

> I didn't realize it at the time, but I now understand that in many ways my eating disorder was a way for me to gain control and a sense of self in an environment where my selfhood as a woman was denied and devalued. Gayle, 32, Euro-American, lesbian, California

The institutional and societal factors that contribute to obesity are often ignored; instead, we perpetuate a culture of sizeism by pointing fingers at those who are overweight and reinforcing the notion that the thinner, the better. In turn, not only do we overemphasize the issue of obesity, we overlook the epidemic of Americans, primarily women, who often turn to dangerous measures to "get thin." We know that these diets and drugs are not achieving our goal of thinness, and we know that yo-yo dieting, chronic dieting with repeated weight losses and gains, is much more harmful than fat itself. Yet, the pressure against women to meet the ideal outweighs any concern for health. I think that it is tragic that we consistently send the message to women that their health is secondary and that their appearance is where their worth lies. Why do we, as a culture, continue to endorse and perpetuate these "requirements"— especially when women's lives are literally in jeopardy?

Young women are particularly at risk. They are targeted heavily by advertisers at a time when they are still struggling through adolescence. While diverse images of older women, women of color, and, in rare cases, women of larger body sizes are beginning to be more common on television, this diversity of size and appearance does not seem to be the case for young women. Young women are bombarded with images of thin, young, and increasingly sexy female bodies on television, in movies, on the pages of magazines, and in music. In an Internet survey of four thousand teens, researcher Ann Kearney-Cooke found that "nearly half of the 14- to 18-year-olds said they were dissatisfied with their bodies, and a third of the teens said they were considering some type of plastic surgery."[24] Studies in recent years show a slight decrease in rates of plastic surgery among women eighteen years and younger, who now make up less than 2 percent of plastic surgery patients, but the desire to alter one's body is still very real. Disturbingly, young women now make up 5 percent of all labiaplasty, showing a significant increase in this

---

Body Dysmorphic Disorder: "A woman with this disorder sees herself as extremely ugly. . . . Seventy percent of the cases occur before the age of eighteen. . . . BDD sufferers are at elevated risk for despair and suicide. . . . In some cases they undergo multiple, unnecessary plastic surgeries." (Definition from the National Organization for Women's Love Your Body Campaign)

particular surgery over the last ten years.[25] Let's be clear, folks . . . that's surgery on your genitals. Additionally, according to a 2012 study, over 70 percent of teens between the ages of twelve and twenty report shaving and/or waxing their genital area.[26] As a result of her study, Kearney-Cooke said, "What's most disturbing to me is that this is a time when their bodies aren't fully formed, yet teens feel so much pressure to be instantly perfect."[27] Perfection is a dangerous game—unfortunately, a game that too many young women play.

UNDER THE KNIFE

One of the most physically dangerous outcomes of this epidemic of body hatred is the rising popularity of plastic surgery. Plastic surgery puts women under the knife in far greater numbers than men—and more often than not for "beauty" purposes—liposuction, breast augmentation, tummy tucks, nose jobs, and more. In fact, according to the American Society of Plastic Surgeons (ASPS), women accounted for 92 percent of the more than 15.8 million plastic surgery procedures in 2017.[28] The ASPS also found that there was a 127 percent increase in women patients between 2000 and 2017, with liposuction and breast augmentation the most common surgical procedures, and Botox injections, which saw an 876 percent increase in these same years, the most popular "minimally invasive" procedure.[29] But is surgery the problem? I am sure that many would say that being able to afford these surgeries and take charge of our appearance—and, in a sense, our destiny—is empowering. Women today have bought into the message that their power lies in their physical bodies and, more specifically, their physical beauty. I don't think that surgery is the problem per se; rather, the problems go back to my initial argument—the message that *as we are is not good enough*. We have set an extremely limited standard for female beauty, and, while we have begun to push back against this standard, allowing greater diversity among models and actors, the truth remains that American women are under tremendous pressure to look a certain way. Rather than emphasizing the unique beauty within us all, the media, society, and women themselves have sought to change women's bodies and appearance through increasingly extreme measures.

With the highly publicized case of the singer Carnie Wilson (who broadcast her procedure on the web), bariatric surgery is growing in its popularity for weight loss, with an estimated 196,000 procedures performed in 2015.[30] Bariatric surgery includes varied approaches, including laparoscopic gastric bypass, laparoscopic adjustable gastric band, and sleeve gastrectomy. With a cost of $11,500 to $26,000 per procedure, bariatric surgeries have become a new benchmark in the hierarchy of beauty. And, with an increasing number of stars taking this route, the message that you can never be too thin is clear. While newer bariatric surgeries have lower complication rates than previous procedures, bariatric surgery is hardly a complication-free procedure. Gastric bypass surgery, studies have found, leads to the greatest weight loss but still carries the higher risk. A study by the American Society of Metabolic and Bariatric Surgery found a thirty-day complication rate of 1.25 percent versus 0.96 percent for sleeve gasterectomies and 0.25 percent for gastric banding.[31] Bariatric surgery is one of the most extreme acts for weight loss—and, while it is targeted at those at least one hundred pounds overweight, it is becoming increasingly common. Media showcasing of gastric bypass surgery, combined with the creation of shows such as *Extreme Makeover, The Swan, Nip/Tuck*, and *Dr. 90210*, make surgery increasingly favored as the ultimate quick fix to an undesirable appearance. And women comprise 80 percent of those having gastric bypass surgery.[32] Rather than blaming ourselves and putting our bodies under the knife, I suggest we look at the larger institutional question of how American culture promotes and reinforces an unhealthy lifestyle. Americans are inundated with fast-food commercials, with added messages that fast food is the American way. Fast food is encouraged, accessible, and convenient. Rarely is there a healthy alternative to the quick and convenient roadside stop while driving down the freeway on your way to or from work or even on vacation. Culturally, Americans shop for convenience, buying meals in a box or ready for the microwave. Just add water and we have instant dinner. Boxed, shelf-stable foods, which are usually less nutritious, are an economic necessity for many; particularly those living paycheck-to-paycheck, living in motels, or in transitional living situations. Little emphasis is placed on nutrition in school, with many medical schools providing less than the recommended twenty-five hours of nutrition curriculum for medical degrees—and these are our health professionals![33] We live in a culture where exercise is generally not incorporated into our daily lives. Even the most basic of exercise, walking, often is replaced by driving cars; Americans drive more often than they walk. The U.S. Department of Transportation Bureau of Transportation Statistics reports that 87 percent of daily trips were made in personal vehicles and 91 percent of people commuting to work do so in a personal vehicle.[34] There is no federal law requiring minimum standards or directives for physical education programs in American schools,[35] and fast-food and soda companies often contract with schools to provide their products directly to students on elementary, middle school, and high school campuses. Additionally, in 2017, 11.8 percent of households in the U.S.[36] were living with food insecurity, meaning that they lived without regular access or resources for sufficient nutrition. In the United States, 2.3 million people live more than a mile from a supermarket and do not have access to a vehicle,[37] resulting in what is referred to as a food desert. Food insecurity and food deserts have a direct impact on access to healthy food and the sustainability of individuals and families. Further, communities of color and those with low socioeconomic status are disproportionately impacted by food insecurity and

> The CDC defines food deserts as "areas that lack access to affordable fruits, vegetables, whole grains, low-fat milk, and other foods that make up a full and healthy diet. Many Americans living in rural, minority, or low-income areas are subjected to food deserts and may be unable to access affordable, healthy foods, leaving their diets lacking essential nutrients."

are disproportionately likely to live in food deserts. Clearly, body size is compounded by multiple factors. This is a social issue. Sizism exists at the intersection of gender, race, and class. What we need are healthier alternatives and better resources, as well as changes in our own attitudes about our bodies.

EMBRACE YOUR SIZE—EVERY BODY IS BEAUTIFUL

In the sea of restrictive images and harmful practices, there is hope. More and more activists are rejecting the narrow definitions of beauty and advocating for embracing and celebrating bodies in all their diversities. Further, the writings of authors such as Charlotte Cooper, Marilyn Wann, Marianne Kirby, Kate Harding, Jes Baker, Sonya Renee, and Lindy West assert that size is linked to discrimination and that fat bodies are a target of hatred and oppression. A growing movement is challenging the social politic that allows for oppression against fat bodies. Organizations like the National Association to Advance Fat Acceptance and communities like Health At Every Size advocate for a more inclusive acceptance of the body.

The size acceptance movement argues that fat phobia is a deeply embedded social norm. We see evidence of this in our media, schools, families, and medical communities. Images of fat bodies are almost always presented as a problem to be solved and messages that one will only be happy when they lose the weight are plentiful. Larger bodies are negatively targeted at the doctor's office, on airplanes, and in stores. These experiences and the resulting discrimination create a hostile environment where fat bodies are ridiculed, pitied, and denied equal access to transportation, employment, medical care, and housing. Fat activists argue that policies and practices are often based on misinformation and stereotypes around fat bodies and that our medical definitions and understandings of obesity are exaggerated.

Discrimination against someone because of their size is real. Currently, only one state (Michigan) and six cities (Santa Cruz, CA; San

Francisco, CA; Madison, WI; Urbana, IL; Washington, DC; and Bing-hamton, NY) have laws protecting against weight discrimination.[38] Citing a number of studies, the National Association to Advance Acceptance argues that discrimination against one's size is prevalent in the workplace and schools. Citing a number of studies, NAAFA argues that fat people get fewer promotions, can be terminated or suspended regardless of job performance, and are more likely to be bullied in school.[39] In fact, in elementary school, fat children are 63 percent more likely to be bullied than their "non-overweight" peers.[40] Sixty-nine percent of fat patients report having been stigmatized by doctors, and more than half of nurses in a 2014 U.S. survey indicated that they carried negative attitudes when dealing with fat patients.[41] NAAFA asserts that workplace and school policies along with legislation are key to protecting "the rights of all citizens independent of the size of their bodies"[42] and education is key to promoting size diversity.

Indeed, the structural protections achieved through policy and legislation are critical to confronting size discrimination. Additionally, challenging our cultural attitudes about weight and size are key to the overall health of individuals. Author of *Body Respect* and *Health at Any Size*, Linda Bacon argues that *"Health at Every Size* does not claim that everyone is at a healthy weight. What it does do is ask for respect and help people shift their focus away from changing their size to enhancing their self-care behaviors—so they let weight fall where it may naturally."[43] Bias against, and stereotypes around, body size are key factors in whether or not people go to an exercise class, jog in public, participate in sports, or go to the doctor. And the often harmful practices that we engage in to force our body into an ideal end in futile efforts, or dangerous results. Many studies have shown that dieting doesn't work,[44] "yo-yo" dieting or what is referred to as weight cycling can lead to adverse effects,[45] and as previously mentioned, weight loss surgeries are very problematic. Rather than targeting our bodies, perhaps a more effective approach is to target sizism as the problem. What would life be like if all bodies—shapes, sizes, colors, abilities—were allowed to exist without bias? What if, instead of being bombarded with restrictive and narrow definitions of beauty, we learned at a very young age that beauty is broadly defined and all around us? What if, instead of being trained to look for love and acceptance through others, we were shown that self-love and self-acceptance was the most powerful act we could take? In her book, *The Body is Not an Apology*, Sonya Renee Taylor argues, unapologetically, "Liberation is the opportunity for every human, no matter their body, to have unobstructed access to their highest self; for every human to live in radical self love."[46]

WOMEN AND THE GLOBAL MARKET—THE COST OF GLOBALIZED FASHION

The fashion industry not only has a huge impact on body image and the diet industry, but also contributes significantly to globalization and the existence of sweatshops. To provide rich nations affordable fashions, women throughout the world, in poor and underdeveloped nations, work in substandard and abusive conditions for below-poverty-level wages. Women, mostly between the ages of fifteen and twenty-two, make up 90 percent of all sweatshop labor.[47] Women are often lured to sweatshops under false pretenses, having been promised jobs in wealthy countries for good wages and better opportunities.[48] Instead, they find themselves in forced servitude, controlled by coercion, threat, and violence.[49] Women working in garment and textile factories are commonly subjected to sexual harassment, rape, and sexual assault, as well as mandatory pregnancy testing and forced abortion.[50] Many women and girls are forced into the sex trade.[51] Factory labor wages can be as low as six cents an hour, far less then the average minimum wage for most countries, and nowhere near a living wage.[52] Of course, living needs and standards differ greatly in the United States and in the lower-wage countries. The cost of living varies tremendously between developed and developing nations. But there are some important questions to ask:

1. Should wealthy nations continue to profit from the economic situations of poorer nations, particularly if our acts of colonialism and imperialism have significantly contributed to their undeveloped or underdeveloped status?
2. Do wealthy countries' multinational corporations have an obligation to adhere to fair labor practices, safety provisions, and environmental protections?
3. Should multinational corporations serve as ambassadors from the countries in which they are headquartered—incorporating similar practices around the globe as are required at home? Or is this a violation of sovereignty and an infringement on the rights of host countries?
4. Should corporations provide a living wage to the workers they employ?

What is our obligation to our sister nations? How much profit is enough? Or too much? Even at one of the highest rates of pay cited—$1.75 an hour—laborers employed by our corporations cannot afford to purchase the products they create and cannot afford housing, clothing, or food for their families in their home countries—which often forces women and children into shanty-town dwellings and permanent states of hunger and further marginalizes them in the global economy. So, while the cost of living may be less in these countries, laborers are still not fairing well. One option women take is to go abroad looking for work, leaving children with older relatives and becoming a part of the low-wage immigrant labor pool whose members seldom see their own children, family, or homes while spending years caring for and cleaning for the homes and families of wealthy nations. In these situations, far too often, women end up with few or no rights; their passports and visas are "safeguarded" by their employers, strict house rules are enforced, prohibiting lives outside their employers' homes, and communication is monitored, keeping workers from engaging in true and honest dialogue with family or people who could help them improve their situations.

Of course, wealthy nations are not the only parties responsible. Many questions should be asked of the host country. For example, how is wealth distributed from the government to the people? Are leaders chosen by popular elections? Are elections safe and fair? What human rights (and let's remember that women's rights are also human rights) violations occur? What are the protections for the people when multinational corporations set up shop? What protections exist and are enforced for the environment? There is certainly a two-way street between governments and corporations. As consumers, we need to ask these questions to better understand where our money goes and what it supports. We must advocate for women's voices to be heard and so that women are a part of the decision-making process—which means improving women's status so that their daily lives are about not mere survival but also quality and equality.

Campaigns for livable wages have grown, taking root throughout the globe. Activists propose a wage that allows families to live adequately and safely. A livable wage may be one of the key answers to providing people, especially women, with access to participate in that decision-making process. iSeal Alliance, an international, nonprofit collaboration of six key organizations, is working globally on establishing a common definition of living wage. Comprised of Fairtrade International, Forest Stewardship Council (FSC), Good Weave, Sustainable Agriculture Network/Rainforest Alliance (SAN/RA), Social Accountability International (SAI), and UTZ Certified, iSeal defines a living wage as "the remuneration received for a standard work week by a worker in a particular place sufficient to afford a decent standard of living for the worker and her or his family. Elements of a decent standard of living include food, water, housing, education, health care, transport, clothing, and other essential needs including provision for unexpected events."[53] iSeal argues that a common methodology is key to better understanding and tracking labor standards, stating that

> our six organizations are collectively working together with Dr. Richard Anker, an international specialist on living wage, to design and test a com-

mon methodology to estimate living wage levels for the areas in which we work. The methodology being developed draws on lessons from pilot projects in various countries. In a nutshell, the living wage is estimated by adding up: the cost of a low cost nutritious diet that is appropriate for food preferences and development level of a country, plus the cost of decent housing in the area, plus other costs for essential needs, which are assessed through a method of extrapolation. A small margin above the total cost is then added to help provide for unforeseen events such as illnesses and accidents to help ensure that these events do not easily throw workers into poverty. This total per capita cost is scaled up to arrive at the cost of a decent standard of living for a typical family and then defrayed over a typical number of full-time equivalent workers per household.[54]

Livable-wage campaigns advocate respect and protection for workers worldwide. While the discrepancies in earnings are huge, it is important to note that, federally, workers in the United States are also not guaranteed a livable wage and that in fact, in most areas of the country, the minimum wage is not a livable one. In 2015, according to the Living Wage Calculator created by Dr. Amy Glasmeier at MIT, the national living wage is $15.12 pre-tax dollars, for a family of four.[55] Single-parent families need to work twice as hard to earn a living wage, according to the Living Wage Calculator, and "a single-mother with two children earning the federal minimum wage of $7.25 per hour needs to work 139 hours per week, more hours than there are in a 5-day week, to earn a living wage."[56] As a result, when many of us are barely getting by, it is difficult for women making substandard wages in the United States to be concerned with the conditions of women in other countries. In other words, it is difficult to work for better wages in China when we don't have the time, resources, or energy to fight for better wages for ourselves. Additionally, making consumer choices along political lines becomes increasingly difficult when our goal is to find the least expensive product to meet our family needs. And, of course, corporations literally bank on this fact.

The U.S. Department of Labor defines a sweatshop as any factory that violates more than one key U.S. labor law, such as paying a minimum wage or paying overtime. UNITE, the Union of Needletrades, Industrial and Textile Employees adds that a sweatshop is any factory that doesn't respect workers' right to organize a union. Other accountability groups, like Global Exchange, argue that sweatshops are also defined as those that don't pay a living wage.[57] Many countries house sweatshop factories to benefit consumers in the United States and supply merchandise to some of our most prized companies—Walmart, Nike, Guess, Disney, the Gap, and Tommy Hilfiger, to name a few. According to the National Labor Committee, women in El Salvador are paid twenty-five cents for every $140 Nike NBA t-shirt they sew, and they are subjected to mandatory pregnancy tests, unsafe drinking water, and surveillance cameras in the bathrooms; Walmart factories in Bangladesh deny women legal maternity leave, often harassing them into quitting their jobs; working sixty to ninety hours a week without overtime, workers in China assemble Disney's children's books earning thirty-five to forty-one cents an hour and are frequently subjected to dangerous working conditions.[58] But foreign countries are not the only home for sweatshop factories—the United States also reaps the benefits of the hard labor of women. Particularly in states that are major points of entry—California and New York are two key examples—the fashion or apparel industry has factories that employ low-wage immigrant labor. Los Angeles, California, for example, is home to more than 43,000 garment workers—mostly Latina and Asian women—who work ten hours or more a day without overtime or a guaranteed minimum wage (not to mention a livable wage) in dangerous and unsanitary conditions.[59] This occurs in a state and a country that are supposed to have safety and wage protections for workers.

The issues of sweatshop labor are pervasive and challenging. On the one hand, there are the extensive problems outlined earlier. But, on the other hand, there is the argument that some work (even poorly paid work in abusive settings) is better than no work. Many argue that multinational corporations provide a source of income for untrained and uneducated, low-wage workers that would not exist should multinationals disappear. Some argue the tenets of capitalism and the "right" to profit at any cost—and assert that in business the bottom line must be the primary focus. Of course, I question how much profit is enough. There's no surprise that governments and corporations are motivated by money. But what we must remember is that both governments and corporations are made up of, and rely upon, people. Their greatest success is not their money, or their prestige and recognition. Their greatest success is their ability to convince people that they exist in a vacuum and that their power lies within their structure and not with people.

Corporations and governments are not the only entities that carry responsibility for the existence of sweatshops and the exploitation of workers. As we buy the message sold to us through advertising, we harm not only ourselves, but the lives of women worldwide. It is a vicious cycle that isolates us from one another globally. We deal daily with the struggles of fitting in and looking cool without knowledge or understanding of the lives of women who make our coveted designs. These struggles are so powerful—the desire to follow the current fad is so overwhelming—that we spend beyond our means, we endanger our bodies to meet a physical ideal, and we play into a globalized system that profits off the desperate struggle for survival of women in one region and the desperate need for popularity of women in another region. The connection among sweatshops, capitalism, and globalization and their relation to body image, self-esteem, advertising, and the beauty industry is that the entire cycle—from production lines to the donning of clothing—profits from the exploitation of women.

But we can stop this pattern and create a new reality. Companies cannot profit if people do not buy their products. Our consumer choices have power. If we make wise choices collectively, we can change the practices of the beauty and garment industries. If we could create a movement where it is "cool" to be socially and globally aware, where we care about where our products come from, and where we look not just at the economic price tag but also at the human price tag, then we could redesign the system. I believe that if enough of us contact our favorite companies and say that we will stop buying from them until they pay a livable wage to their workers worldwide, then companies will eventually begin to do so—not necessarily because of altruism, but because their economic bottom lines will decrease—remember, their success is dependent on our support. In the meantime, we must also support those companies that support unions, fair pay, livable wages, and the advancement of women. Look for union labels on clothing and products. Reference organizations dedicated to fair and equitable working conditions for their recommendations of union- and woman-friendly companies. Consider the health, safety, and equality of workers as you spend your consumer dollars.

There is a fine line between boycott and consumer power. I am reminded of an interview with Naomi Klein, author of *No Logo*, who recounts her travels through Asia researching sweatshop labor issues. She tells of interviews with Filipino women who want their stories told about working in the factories but also share a concern about a boycott of the product line. They fear the loss of jobs if production declines and ask that Naomi bring their plea for improved working conditions and a hope for job protection to the consumers of wealthy nations, whom they see as having the power to change corporate practices.[60] Klein says in her interview, "I felt a tremendous sense of responsibility from the workers because they shared their stories with me. . . . They said to me over and over again, 'please tell people what it is like for us' and at the same time their greatest fear was that I was going to go home and tell people to boycott these companies and that they were all going to lose their jobs. So there is a tremendous uncertainty and confusion about what to do."[61] In response to the World Trade Organization protests in Seattle in 1999, Klein gives us some advice. She says we must "fight genuinely to raise labor standards around the world. . . . Stop just opposing the World Trade Organization and start proposing an alternate vision for globalization which answers these problems, which does propose minimum labor standards."[62] As consumers, we need to contact companies and tell them what we want—we want to buy products that are the result of fair labor practices. We need to tell them that company revenues must be better allocated to provide livable wages for their workers—while still allowing for significant gains for the company's bottom line. We must increase awareness among corporations and consumers and empower people to make a difference.

Consumer activism does work. And the examples are growing. After years of being targeted as the poster child for sweatshop labor and unfair practices, in 2005 Nike became the first major corporation "in the industry to publish a list of factories it works with and a report detailing working conditions and pay."[63] In 2009, United Students Against Sweatshops was formed protesting the use of sweatshop labor in the creation of college logo products. This movement has spread to over 150 colleges and universities in the United States and, today, takes on the garment industry as well as a number of campus equity issues. Seattle's 15 Now campaign won a citywide minimum wage increase: at $15, Seattle is now closer to a living wage. As a result, cities across the U.S. are taking up the fight. The popularity of homemade, direct-sale sites like Etsy, the resurgence of vintage and upcycled clothing stores online and in communities across the country, and the Buy Nothing Day and Giving Tuesday campaigns in response to Black Friday sales are all significant examples of a trend toward conscious consumerism and questioning the true human costs behind cheap and plentiful products.

CHANGING THE IMAGE

As Laura Fraser writes in *Losing It: America's Obsession with Weight and the Industry That Feeds on It*, "we need to resist and change the diet culture for ourselves."[64] Perhaps the largest change we must make is to begin to raise girls to believe in themselves regardless of the images on television, in the movies, and on the pages of magazines. As a culture, we must demand an end to advertising that objectifies women and girls or articles that encourage girls and women to ignore their own needs, dreams, and desires in favor of those of men. Instead of bombarding our girls with their own teen versions of *Cosmo*, we should create more magazines like *New Moon*, which focuses its attention on the empowerment of girls rather than drawing them into a cycle of diet trends and fashion fads. We need to promote the message that women and girls' value lies in themselves, in their capabilities, in their thoughts, in their health, and in their strength. For our girls' and women's health, we must change our messages, teach them to be proud of who they are, help them to find their own strength and beauty, and respect women and girls as they are—because as they are is more than good enough.

SPOTLIGHT ON ACTIVISM

Founded in 1992 by Nancy Gruver, mother of twin daughters, *New Moon* magazine provides a radical alternative to most magazines geared toward young women. *New Moon* emphasizes self-exploration and discovery in an ad-free environment. With a true commitment to girls' voices, *New Moon* worked with twenty girls, ages 8–14, to initially develop the focus and content of the magazine. Today, a fifteen-member Girls Editorial Board continues to advise *New Moon*. Full of fiction, poetry, artwork, science experiments, and cartoons, *New Moon* is a great resource for girls. *New Moon* provides a critical source of information about coming-of-age issues for girls, including a comprehensive look at girls' lives—their hopes, fears, and dreams. Not stopping there, the education within *New Moon* extends beyond our borders, often including stories of girls from around the globe.

In addition to this fabulous magazine, *New Moon* provides curricula, a speakers' bureau, workshops, a book club, a pen-pal program, website, and Adventure trips (dolphin camp in Florida and dog sledding in Minnesota). For more information about *New Moon*, visit the magazine's website at www.newmoon.org.

TAKE ACTION

Getting Started

Read up! Great books are out there to educate, empower, and change the way we view ourselves.

Listen to self-affirming music, poetry, and comedy! Check out Margaret Cho, Ani DiFranco, Alix Olson, Alicia Keys, Pink, India Arie, Beyoncé, Maya Angelou, Lucille Clifton—just to name a few.

Move your body in ways that feel good—dance, run, swim, stretch, do yoga or tai chi.

Eat! Remember that food is not the enemy; it is our fuel. And we need fuel to take care of ourselves and to change the world!

The Next Step

Try subscription card activism; using the abundance of subscription cards in magazines, write a brief message to the magazine. It foots the bill (postage paid!). A couple of my favorite messages—"Stop starvation imagery" and "Feed the models."

Create collage projects—using the advertisements in magazines, cut and paste new messages that are empowering and counter the messages of fashion/beauty advertising.

Be an active and informed consumer—find out the politics of the company behind the product—how much do they pay their workers, is there fair trade involved, do they reinvest into host countries, where are products made, and what are the human rights records of those countries?

Celebrate Buy-Nothing Day the day after Thanksgiving every year—commit to not shopping on the most popular shopping day of the year. Visit www.adbusters.org for more information.

Follow up Buy-Nothing Day with Giving Tuesday . . . donate what you can to feminist nonprofit organizations in your area, nationally, or worldwide.

Getting Out There

Shop alternatively. Shop at locally owned, thrift, or secondhand stores.

Take action—send an email to companies to tell them how their advertising is affecting the health of women and girls. Tell them that you won't buy their product(s) until their advertising features healthy women and girls.

Host groups, house parties, and meetings to discuss body image with other women. Show a film, discuss a book, share your stories.

Cover the mirrors in your home/office/school for twenty-four hours and become conscious of the role a mirror plays in your life—how often do you try to look? What is the response of others who come to your house or are in your school or office? Journal or start a dialogue about your reactions.

Make a celebration out of International No-Diet Day—May 6.

Contact the National Organization for Women Foundation (www.nowfoundation.org) and request Love Your Body Day campaign materials for more facts, actions, and resources.

Host a No-Logo Day on your campus, at your community center, or with your friends or family—commit to wearing logo-free clothing. Set up a table with sweatshop information.

Encourage your campus to use sweatshop-free manufacturers for all university or college clothing. Visit the website of United Students Against Sweatshops, www.usas.org, for more information.

FABULOUS FEMINIST WEB RESOURCES

About Face

www.about-face.org

A San Francisco–based nonprofit promoting positive self-esteem through education, outreach, and activism. Their website has great information and resources.

Adbusters

www.adbusters.org

A magazine and a website, Adbusters is dedicated to looking critically at the role of advertising, consumerism, and media in our lives. A host of a number of campaigns, including Buy Nothing Day; check 'em out.

Anorexia Nervosa and Related Disorders, Inc.

www.anred.com

Provides comprehensive information about eating disorders, including statistics, as well as warning signs and information on treatment, and recovery.

Association for Size Diversity and Health

www.sizediversityandhealth.org

Education, research, and services based on the Health at Every Size principles, dedicated to combating weight discrimination and bias.

Body Positive

www.bodypositive.com

A fabulous website dedicated to helping women change the way they see and relate to their bodies. Their website include resources, message boards, Q&As for body size acceptance, and other great resources for combating negative attitudes about our bodies.

Coalition of Labor Union Women

www.cluw.org

The only organization for union women in the United States, CLUW provides resources and networking for union-based issues.

Coalition to Abolish Slavery and Trafficking (CAST)
www.castla.org
Resources, services, and information about forced labor and slavery. Provides information on case management, advocacy, public education, and training.

Coalition Against Trafficking in Women
www.catwinternational.org
A nongovernmental organization promoting women's human rights. CATW's website includes information about countries throughout the world, with facts and campaign information.

Corporate Watch
www.corpwatch.org
Critical of corporate-led globalization, Corporate Watch provides issue information, activism, and networking.

Eating Disorders Referral and Information Center
www.edreferral.com
Resources and referrals for eating disorders. Their website has a national and international database for therapists focused on eating disorders. While primarily covering Canada and the United States, the site does have referrals for the United Kingdom, Germany, and Australia. It also includes a wide range of information, from definitions of specific eating disorders to information on research and advocacy.

Fat and Feminist: Large Women's Health Experience
www.fwhc.org/health/fatfem.htm
A part of the Feminist Women's Health Center website, Fat and Feminist provides first-person accounts, research information, discussion on size prejudice, and additional resources.

Health At Every Size
www.haescommunity.com
Based on the book Health at Every Size *by Linda Bacon, this website creates an online community centered around the HAES principles of respect, critical awareness, and compassionate self care.*

National Eating Disorders Association
www.haescommunity.com
Information for professionals as well as the general public—education, resources, and treatment referrals. In the United States, call 1-800-931-2237 for more information.

National Organization for Lesbians of Size
www.nolose.org
Size-acceptance resources specifically for the lesbian and queer community. Their website includes information about events, conferences, speakers, and links to supporting organizations.

NOW Foundation Love Your Body Campaign
www.nowfoundation.org
A project of NOW, the Love Your Body Campaign is a nationwide effort to raise awareness about body image, eating disorders, and women's health issues. A great source of information as well as a connection to activism.

The Real Women Project
www.realwomenproject.org
Funded through the Athena Charitable Foundation, the Real Women Project features images of women through art, music, and poetry. The intent of the project is to educate women about their health and self-worth.

UNITE! HERE
www.unitehere.org
Website dedicated to union workers, primarily women. Information about union activity within textile, hotel, and restaurant industries.

United Students Against Sweatshops
www.usas.org
USAS formed in 2009 as a grassroots organization run by youth and students to fight against sweatshop labor and for workers' rights. Chapters exist across the United States.

6

KNOCK 'EM UP . . . KNOCK 'EM DOWN

"Monica" gave birth at seventeen. The pregnancy was wanted, celebrated, and shared with her partner. She knew about the politics of abortion, pregnancy, and women's health. She had been paying attention. So when Monica got pregnant she decided to activate her choice by choosing to become a parent. She thought that by making the decision to have a baby, she was making the decision most supported in our culture. However, from the moment of her first prenatal care appointment, she felt ignored and mistreated. Monica had done the research, had come prepared with questions, and attempted to be an advocate for herself. But, throughout what proved to be a difficult pregnancy and birth, her questions and needs went unmet. Monica looks back at this time with a certainty that she received this treatment solely because of her age; being a "teen mom" carried with it a stigma of mistake and irresponsibility. Monica was one of my students, and, unfortunately, her story is all too common.

This chapter looks at the health of girls and women. It is important to recognize that not all bodies are the same. Some women menstruate, some do not. Some women will have pregnancies, some will not. Sometimes this is based on our choices, sometimes based on our biology. We do not have to have the same experiences to create space in the movement to talk about menstruation, pregnancy, abortion, birth. We create this space because our bodies are politicized. Women's reproduction is politicized. There are many who continue to exert control and dominance over women's bodies, personally and politically. To address this, to counter this, is a political act. You don't have to have ever had a pregnancy, an abortion, or a birth to care about the political battle that rages around women's bodies.

In the movement today a conflict has arisen debating whether or not you have to have a vagina to be a woman. Let me be clear from the start, biology does not necessarily make you a woman. While some continue to debate this, I do not. Trans women are women. Some of what I discuss in this chapter will relate to trans bodies, much won't. And that has to be ok, because, again, not all women's bodies are the same. Addressing the issues and challenges of trans bodies need not be perceived as exclusionary to cis bodies, nor should discussing the issues and challenges of cis bodies be perceived as exclusionary to trans bodies. That said, I do not deny that trans exclusion is happening in the movement. We have to continue to make space for all experiences and to work for equity for all. Doing social justice work requires that we embrace all injustices as our own. This means that we take up the fight for trans health and access to affordable hormone treatments and gender affirmation surgeries, with the same commitment that we fight for affordable and accessible birth control, safe and legal abortion, and comprehensive sex education. This means that we make the connections between economic justice and reproduction, between sexuality and oppression, between racism and incarceration—that we unpack the intersections of our lives and the impact of socio-political oppression on our bodies.

Many women, and many trans men, face specific issues about our bodies—menstruation, birth control, pregnancy, breast cancer, menopause. As such, we need to make sure that the health care we receive is designed with our bodies in mind. For women, that means women-centered health care. Women-centered health care is health care for women that puts the needs of women's bodies at the center of treatment. Such a system values the legitimacy of our experiences, provides full disclosure of medical risks, and respects the choices that we make. Indeed, today's health care for most Americans, if you have access, is arguably better than it's ever been. Technology has allowed us to extend our lives, to cure diseases, and to greatly improve our chances when we do get sick. As women, we are beneficiaries of this improved system; however, there are still advances to be made, and there are still obstacles to receiving the best care.

PUTTING WOMEN AT THE CENTER

What would a health care system that had women at the center look like? It seems common sense that the more information we have, the more likely we are to make decisions that benefit our lives, and the less fearful, disengaged, and dependent we are. The principles of women-centered health care are these: put women at the center of their experiences; reclaim the knowledge that used to be passed down between generations of women; believe in our experiences and their legitimacy; demand full disclosure of information to clients; respect the choices we make.

I remember my first gynecological exam. I was fifteen, and the gynecologist told me that I had a tipped uterus. I was too afraid to ask what this meant. I thought that I had been born wrong and that I would never be able to have babies—or at least, bizarrely, somehow develop a limp. For years, I walked around feeling deficient and scared. Not until I went to a Feminist Women's Health Center, one that provides women-centered health care, did I learn how misguided I was. I thank them because they changed the relationship I have with my body. A tipped uterus is common, no biggie: the uterus is just tipped back toward the back of the pelvis, away from the belly; it is usually not painful, and it doesn't mean you can't conceive or give birth.[1]

This is one example, and a fairly innocuous one at that, of what many other girls and women often face in the doctor's office or in the hospital operating room. A more disturbing story might involve the unnecessary hysterectomies that many women still have each year—reports find that approximately one in five hysterectomies are medically unnecessary.[2] Yet, hundreds of thousands are performed in the United States annually.[3] Another example is the continued and systematic gender bias in medical research and funding.[4]

What we need is a women's health agenda. While there certainly are some groups working toward this goal—some of which I will highlight later—we need a broad approach to women's health that is women-centered. A women's health agenda, for example, questions why men who have health insurance can get prescription coverage for Viagra (and Levitra, Cialis, and the other "male enhancement" products on the market), but women face an ongoing political battle for birth control coverage. A women-centered health movement might also question why women's health concerns are consistently unfunded or underfunded or why women are less likely to appear in medical trials. A women-centered health movement might also see the wisdom in midwifery, a tradition of women helping women to birth babies that dates back centuries. And, even for those who choose to have their babies delivered in modern hospitals, as many of us do, this movement would still recognize and value our right to make that choice. A woman-centered health movement might recognize the diversities of bodies and confront the one-size, one-gender fits all model. A women-centered health movement is about allowing women to be in control of the choices that affect our bodies.

This chapter focuses on women's health and women's bodies. I want to make it clear that this women's health agenda contains a number of issues we've got to learn about and fight for. At the same time, there is perhaps no issue more essential to women's bodies than the right to control our reproduction—from birth control to abortion to adoption and pregnancy. Central to much of this debate is the *Roe v. Wade* decision, since it guarantees women the right to privacy, essentially allowing them to decide for themselves what to do if they become pregnant. Since so much of the past forty-five years has been spent fighting for and against this decision, and since the decision still seems imperiled as the Supreme Court balance is always in flux, I will spend a good deal of this chapter discussing "the politics of choice." But, as essential as this issue is to the feminist movement, it's important to stress that the concerns of women's health encompass more than just this issue. In this chapter we'll look at the concept of Reproductive Justice, so powerfully and critically put forth by Loretta Ross and the SisterSong organization. Reproductive Justice requires us to move beyond a limited "choice" framework that focuses solely on abortion rights to a political discussion about the self-determination of all women in their bodies, including the right to control reproduction, as well as freedom from police brutality, the right to education, and a focus on economic justice. So for those women (and anyone else) who do not consider themselves pro-choice, there is still much here to fight for.

TAKE A GOOD LOOK

We don't have to go very far back to find the origins of the modern feminist health movement. In 1971, the Feminist Women's Health Centers were founded by a group of Los Angeles women who wanted to know more about their bodies and their reproductive selves. At a time when pregnancy tests and yeast infection treatments were available only at physicians' offices and when libraries and bookstores were void of women's health books, the Feminist Women's Health Center provided a source of information and a place for women to gather to share experiences about their bodies, health, and lives.[5] They helped women across the country and around the world set up "self-help groups," where women came together to share information, learn from one another, and practice cervical self-exam. Yes, basically a group of women hangin' out and looking at their vaginas—despite the efforts of Eve Ensler to bring vaginas into fashion, this still may sound a bit weird to people today—but it was a real revelation to women then (and still is today!). The cervical self-exam was a way to gain control of one's body at a time when this domain belonged more to women's doctors and sexual partners. The practice continues to put women in touch with themselves and to assist in their awareness of their bodies—which returns our power to us. The Feminist Women's Health Centers' self-help is about understanding how our bodies work through our eyes; it is about making our bodily knowledge available and legitimate. Perhaps this is the first step in freeing ourselves from dependence on a medical system that does not value us. So, if you haven't done so, grab a mirror, and take a good look.

Vaginal and Cervical Self-Examination

Vaginal and cervical self-examination is one of the most useful health tools a woman can have. It enables us to see a vital part of our anatomy that is hidden from plain view—the vagina and cervix (the neck of the womb). By using a speculum, you can observe changes in your cervix and its secretions, the menstrual cycle, and indications of fertility; you can identify and treat common vaginal conditions such as yeast, trichomonas, or bacterial infections (which often cause itching or discharge); and you can learn what your cervix looks like day by day, rather than depending on a physician to look once a year to pronounce what is normal for you.

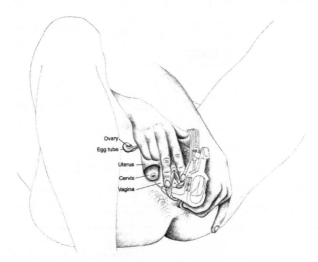

To insert a plastic speculum, spread the inner lips of the clitoris with two fingers of one hand, hold the bills of the speculum tightly together with the thumb and index finger of the other, and guide it into the vaginal canal. You can use a water-soluble jelly or just plain water to make insertion smoother. This woman is inserting her speculum with the handles upright, but some women prefer to insert it sideways initially. Inserting the speculum with the handles down is strictly for the doctor's convenience, and it requires that a woman put her feet into stirrups at the end of an exam table.

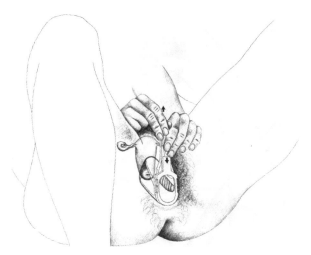

When the handles of the speculum are pinched together, they force the bills open, stretching the vaginal walls and revealing the cervix. With the handles held tightly together, the short handle slides down and the long handle slides up. When there is a sharp click the speculum is locked into place.

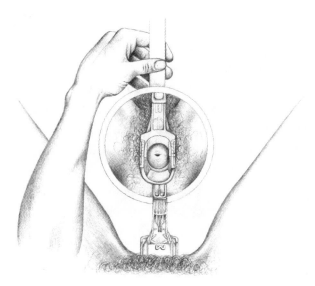

With the speculum locked, both hands are free to hold a mirror and a flashlight or gooseneck lamp. If a flashlight is used, shine the beam into the mirror, and it will, in turn, be reflected into the vagina, illuminating the vaginal walls and the cervix. The cervix won't always pop instantly into view. Sometimes you have to try several times. If it stubbornly refuses to appear, you can move around or jump up and down a few times. Sometimes it is also helpful to move to a firmer surface, like the floor or a tabletop. When the cervix is visible, you can see a rounded or flattened knob, between the size of a quarter and a fifty-cent piece, like a fat doughnut with a hole or slit in it. The hole, called the cervical os, is where the menstrual blood, other uterine secretions, and babies come out. Your cervix might be pink and smooth, or it might have a few reddish blemishes. It can also be uneven, rough, or splotchy. In any case, the only time to worry is when abnormal cells are found in a Pap smear.

* Material adapted from *A New View of A Woman's Body*, Federation of Feminist Women's Health Centers, Feminist Health Press, Los Angeles, CA. Suzann Gage created these beautiful illustrations, pp. 22–24. Reprinted with permission.

Beyond getting to know one's own vagina, a women-centered health agenda might also start at the beginning of our young lives and recognize the different ways that we are treated and taught to understand our own bodies. Little boys are often encouraged to be baseball players; little girls are encouraged to be fairy princesses. Little boys are encouraged to use their bodies in physical ways, whereas little girls are encouraged to dress their bodies in different clothes. When a little boy gets dirty, some say, "that's just a boy being a boy," but when a little girl does the same, she is a "tomboy" or "not acting like a nice little girl." While some of these tendencies may be biological, there is no doubting that society encourages these stereotypes. (Some might even say that this is how patriarchy continues itself.) Thankfully, there are now sports leagues for both boys and girls, but there is still no doubting that there are many more athletic opportunities for boys than for girls and that, overall, boys are encouraged to be more physical and athletic than girls.

These bodily differences all but erupt at puberty. From the start, we are divided in gender-specific groups to see separate films about our changing bodies. Many of us struggle to pay attention during the coming-of-age video that highlights young girls that we barely recognize, while our curiosity wonders what the boys are learning about us—from someone else. Still others are placed into a gender group with which we don't identify, and struggle to figure out who we are and where we fit when only two genders are presented. We are both envious and fearful of the girls who begin menstruation before us—wanting to both be them and avoid the situation altogether. Very little if anything is shared ahead of time—as with most of our "education," we swap stories with our friends, trying to sort out this mess called *womanhood*. And then . . . the day—the day we see blood. We are indoctrinated into this new club, but usually with very little celebration. And our modern ritual begins—pads versus tampons, Midol versus heating pad—we learn the tortures of "the curse." We are bombarded with messages of fear—fear of someone knowing, fear of odor, fear of bloating, fear of leakage, fear of staining, fear of pain, fear, fear, fear. We are told that we need protection—but from what? Ourselves, our menstruating selves. The Solution: Deodorize, minimize, and hide the fact that we are women. Though this "secret" of womanhood is something that only women share as a rite of passage and though it may give us a certain sense of bonding (though the bonding over an "emergency" tampon gets you only so far), ultimately, this is a shameful secret to be kept, even from other women, in public. Even if we may want to, it is no wonder that we don't embrace and celebrate our femaleness; the messages that we should be ashamed are too strong.

We usually learn that menstruation and our cyclic bodily functions are disgusting. Just as quickly, we learn to judge these bodies harshly, and from another's point of view. As Emily Martin writes in *The Woman in the Body: A Cultural Analysis of Reproduction*:

> But because women are aware that in our general cultural view menstruation is dirty, they are still stuck with the "hassle": most centrally no one must ever see you dealing with the mechanics of keeping up with the disgusting mess, and you must never fail to keep the disgusting mess from showing on your clothes, furniture, or the floor.[6]

As a result, I argue that we gradually become disconnected from our bodies, particularly female bodies. And it is also no wonder that we are so disconnected—between the lack of adequate education and the widely endorsed negative attitudes about our bodies, our menstruation, and our sexuality—women learn early on to ignore, underemphasize, or keep quiet about the functions of our bodies. As Martin writes, ultimately, women are taught to see bodily functions such as menstruation, birth, and menopause as happening to them; they become an object to be dealt with and manipulated by the medical field.[7]

If we are to create a women-centered health agenda, we must recognize and appreciate the differentness of our bodies, perhaps even celebrate our female bodies. In addition to the Feminist Women's Health Centers, organizations like the Boston Women's Health Collective and the National Women's Health Network advocate for women's health so that we may have research that represents us and information that is accessible and comprehensible. Organizations like Good Vibrations and Babes in Toyland offer women a positive image and support for our sexuality. Authors like Christiane Northrup, Dorothy Roberts, Inga Muscio, Roxane Gay, Jessamyn Stanley, Geneen Roth, Melanie Klein, Eve Ensler, Jes Baker, and Marilyn Wann encourage us to embrace and celebrate our bodies. It is from each of these that we find resources and support for a women-centered approach to our health and wellness. Or, as Eve Ensler has said, "I love the word *vagina*."

SUGAR AND SPICE AND EVERYTHING NICE

In a sea of glamorized sexuality, young women today are left with conflicting messages about themselves—to be sexy but not too sexy, to be available but not too available. Good girl vs. slut. Short skirts. High heels. Sweet talk. Naughty whispers. He wants me. He wants me not. He loves me. He loves me not.

Tremendous pressure is placed on young women around sexuality and sexual activity. We see heterosexual sex everywhere—in movies, television shows, commercials, billboards, and magazines. We're even starting to see some "sex-positive" images of gay men and lesbians, though they're often seen less as sexual and more as just funny (think *Will & Grace*, *Modern Family*, or *Ellen*). And, yet, we often leave young people without adequate knowledge or resources to empower themselves to make decisions that are best for them or to protect themselves from possible negative results of uneducated actions. We are in the midst of a long battle surrounding sex education in our schools. The way young people actually live their lives often gets lost in this debate. Sex education is inconsistent; we leave individual school districts to decide what is to be taught. Our federal government is often embroiled over national crusades to limit sex education to abstinence-only-until-heterosexual-marriage programs, even while denying a true conversation about abstinence. To say "just don't have sex" without explaining the true definition of abstinence or teaching negotiation skills or providing a "back-up" plan (if abstinence does not remain the choice) is, in my not-so-humble opinion, a crime. Those who force this approach are responsible for unintended pregnancies, HIV infections, the spread of sexually transmitted infections (STIs), and the sexual disempowerment of young people.

> Abstinence means forgoing, or limiting, sexual activity to prevent the sharing of bodily fluids (i.e., semen, vaginal secretions, and blood) that can cause pregnancy or spread sexually transmitted diseases.

IGNORANCE IS BLISS?

There is no uniform approach to teaching about sex and sexuality in our public schools. Twenty-four U.S. states and the District of Columbia do require some sort of education—either sex education or education on HIV/AIDS and STIs—though only thirteen states require that this information be medically accurate and only eight states require the information to be culturally appropriate and unbiased.[8] What does exist is almost always decided upon at the local level, allowing community politics to dictate the depth of education and creating a lack of consistent education nationwide. More and more, however, we see school districts gravitating toward abstinence education, with 76 percent of public and private high schools enforcing a sex education policy that promotes abstinence.[9] While under the Obama administration, we saw a significant shift, at least in federal funding, away from abstinence-only education, the Trump administration has many of us concerned. Conservatives have long supported an agenda of abstinence-until-marriage and purity programs. Further damaging is the conservative agenda to demonize LGBTIQ+ peoples. In fact, four U.S. states currently require that only negative information be given on sexual orientation.[10] Despite the fact that the majority of parents—some 75 percent—do want their children to receive comprehensive sex education, on topics including contraceptive and condom use, sexually transmitted infections, safer sex practices, and even abortion and sexuality education,[11] conservative politicians continue to enact rules and regulations that deny access to accurate and inclusive sexual information.

Despite having patterns of sexual activity like their counterparts in other developed countries, U.S. teens have higher pregnancy, birth, and abortion rates and higher rates of sexually transmitted infections.[12] The Guttmacher Institute found this to be largely a result of the fact that U.S. teens are less likely to use contraceptives and more likely to have shorter relationships and more partners.[13] Additionally, teens in other developed countries receive more social support and have better access to contraceptive services and comprehensive sex education.

Social attitudes in the United States regarding teen sexuality differ significantly from those prevalent in other developed countries. In its report "Sex Education: Needs, Programs and Policies," the Guttmacher Institute writes:

> There is evidence that in many developed countries with low levels of teenage pregnancy, childbearing and STDs, adults tend to be more accepting of sexual activity among teenagers than are adults in the United States. However, adults in these countries also give clear and unambiguous messages that sex should occur within committed relationships and that sexually active teenagers are expected to take steps to protect themselves and their partners from pregnancy and STDs.
>
> Moreover, while these societies may be more accepting of teenage sex than the United States, they are, in fact, less accepting of teenage parenthood. Strong societal messages convey that childbearing should occur only in adulthood, which is considered to be when young people have completed their education, are employed and are living in stable relationships. Societal supports exist to help young people with the transition to adulthood, through vocational training, education and job placement services, and childcare. As a result, teenagers have positive incentives to delay childbearing.[14]

Better information, better resources, and better attitudes from adults— sounds about right. Not only have we created a culture that refuses to drop antiquated attitudes about sex, but we have so politicized sex that our teens lack resources that could literally save their lives.

In the meantime, our culture condemns young women who become pregnant. Recent high-profile cases of teens hiding pregnancies or giving birth silently in basements or public bathroom stalls and the highly dramatized images of these girls being hauled off to jail are indicative of the contradiction in which young women live their lives in this culture. Young women often have sex to find love and approval, but this comes with very little if any self-definition and little understanding of how their reproductive bodies work. Young women often have few places to turn for this information, with marginal access to birth control to prevent

Emergency Contraception, sometimes referred to as the "morning-after pill" or "Plan B," has been a key area of focus of activism, especially for young women today. Often confused with RU-486, the abortion pill, emergency contraception is *not* an abortion, but rather an effective and important form of birth control. Used up to seventy-two hours after unprotected intercourse, emergency contraception contains the same hormone as that used in birth control pills and works to prevent a pregnancy by stopping the release of the egg, preventing fertilization or preventing the egg from implanting in the uterus. Emergency contraception is up to 95 percent effective if used within the first twenty-four hours after unprotected intercourse. Emergency contraception is a safety-net method in case a birth control method fails, the couple has not used birth control, or in cases of rape. EC is incredibly safe, in fact statistically safer than aspirin. It should be noted that emergency contraception does not protect against sexually transmitted infections, including HIV/AIDS. In 2013, after significant effort, activists were finally able to achieve the goal of having EC approved by the FDA for sale over-the-counter. This is significant, as we know that the earlier you take EC the more effective it is. However, approval has not yet led to accessibility, as states continue to restrict access by refusing to dispense, allowing consciousness clause objections for pharmacists, or denying Medicaid coverage for EC in state family planning coverage. As this nation continues to debate health care access, funding access, and family planning measures, activists need to continue to put pressure on legislators to secure access and affordability of emergency contraception.

pregnancy and little or no access to abortion once they are pregnant. And let's be clear: the burden falls on the young woman—very little attention is given to the young man who helped to create this situation.

We need to provide adequate information and resources, to teach girls to embrace and honor their bodies, to empower them to discover their sexuality on their own terms and not through peer and social pressure (and we must not discourage or penalize girls who do embrace their sexuality). We also need to create a dialogue and a reality where girls can get their questions answered and get the support they need in any situation without shame and blame. Providing this information, resources, and dialogue is what a feminist health agenda is all about.

STICK AND STONES

Murderer! Baby Killer! Sinner! shouted a group of white men crowding the sidewalk across the street from the clinic. Rocks were hurled through the air toward my head, coming from behind the oversized signs of bloody miscarriages claiming to be the results of abortion. I heard women's voices close to my ear, fervently thanking me for putting my body between them and these fanatical men who did not know them. The men did not know me, either. They did not know that I babysat through my teen years, that I love children, and that I will later have two of my own. They did not know that I fight as hard for women to get birth control services, adoption services, and prenatal care as I do for abortion care. They also did not know, or did not care, that women from all walks of life come to this health center for care that is women-centered, so that they might better understand their bodies and make choices in a supportive environment that is free from blame and shame. They did not care about women who were denied services in other health facilities because they did not have insurance or enough money, or because they were drug addicted but trying to care for themselves when no one else would, and came here to this amazing non-profit women's health center. They did not care as they yelled, chanted, and threw sticks and stones at the women entering the health center.

My first day escorting at the Chico Feminist Women's Health Center, in 1992, was eye opening, to say the least. I volunteered to be there because I believe that women should be safe when accessing a legal option. I volunteered because the stories of women dying in back-alley abortions haunted me. I volunteered because I believe in women and I trust them to make choices that are best for them in their lives. And I volunteered because the Feminist Women's Health Center changed my life, and I wanted to make sure that other women had access to the same care.

The thought that anyone else could interfere in decisions I make about my body both infuriates and frightens me. If I don't have the right to choose over my own body, then I do not belong to myself. Shawna, 30, white, heterosexual, California

The attack on abortion is so great that we are constantly reminded about the importance of protecting a woman's right to choose. From the lack of education women receive about their bodies, to the lack of funding and access to needed services, to the dangerous and debilitating acts aimed at those who provide services and staff at the health centers to which women turn—we face the reality that legal abortion and health information are not readily available to women. Approximately 90 percent of counties across the United States do not have an abortion provider.[15] Religious hospitals and health service organizations are quickly buying out medical practices, health plans, and hospitals, making abortion and contraceptive care even more difficult to obtain. Unfortunately, attempts to win legislative protection have failed, to be replaced with legislation targeted at reducing women's right to choose. Additionally, conservatives remain determined to appoint circuit judges and Supreme Court justices who do not support abortion rights.

Acts of violence continue to plague our reproductive health care— threats, harassment, bombings, and murders are a reality for many providers. The Nuremberg Files—a website that spewed false accusations about abortion, posted personal information about anyone connected to abortion care (i.e., advocates, providers, activists, escorts, health workers), and ran video of clinic entrances—served as very real harassment and threat to abortion providers. The website was repeatedly challenged in the courts, appeared and disappeared multiple times under different web addresses, and was ruled as "constituting a threat of violence" in *Planned Parenthood v. American Coalition of Life Activists*. The site was ordered to be taken down, but then reappeared after appeal. Otis O'Neal Horsley Jr., the site's founder, died in 2015, and the site seems to have finally disappeared, but similar harassment continues. National campaigns, like 40 Days for Life, target health centers twice a year, busing in anti-choice extremists to harass, intimidate, and at a minimum, annoy women and their partners coming to health centers for services. And in the White House, anti-choice activists once again have a great supporter in Donald Trump, who never seemed to care about abortion until taking the presidency. He now touts extreme anti-choice positions, amplified through his vice president Mike Pence. Pence ardently argues, and has a long voting history, against abortion funding, against embryonic stem cell research, against funding family planning education, and has worked to constitutionally declare personhood to fetuses and make harming a fetus a criminal offense. It's no surprise that NARAL Pro-Choice America has given Pence a 0% rating for his congressional voting history. As we have seen with previous anti-choice presidents, the impact of their appointees is long, and specifically with regard to U.S. Supreme Court nominees, this impact is lifelong.

> Being from a third world country, Peru, I know what other women are living. I have a good idea what it was like before Roe v. Wade *because it's still like that in my country. I know how Bush's global gag rule affected women, because it's happening in my country.* Deborah, 25, Peruvian-Hispanic, Massachusetts

As with his conservative predecessors, Trump reinstated the global gag rule immediately upon entering office, thus defunding family planning education and services around the globe. The global gag rule is a perfect example of how women's bodies are political volley. It has become almost tradition to reinstate or overturn the global gag rule within the first twenty-four hours in office as president. This begs the very important question of why it is allowable to play ping pong with the often desperate realities of women's reproductive lives around the globe. Women's access to reproductive health education and services should not be dependent upon the political affiliation of the men elected U.S. president.

Officially titled the Mexico City Policy, the global gag rule mandates that "no U.S. family planning assistance can be provided to foreign NGOs that use funding from any other source to: perform abortions in cases other than a threat to the woman's life, rape, or incest; provide counseling and referral for abortion; or lobby to make abortion legal or more available in their country" (The Global Gag Rule Impact Project, www.globalgagrule.org). This policy affects countries even where abortion is legal. There is no evidence that the gag rule has reduced the number of abortions worldwide, but research has shown that, in addition to limiting free speech, it has negatively and with devastating effect impacted family planning and reproductive health services in developing countries.

Today, we have multiple generations that came of age, or are coming of age, knowing some degree of reproductive freedom. This is a blessing and a curse; on the one hand, we have freedom of choice, but, on the other hand, we have the luxury of believing that abortion is not an issue that we need to fight for. The result is a generation that largely takes legality, and the availability, of abortion for granted. Fortunately, among these younger generations there are also numerous activists who do understand the fragility of choice in today's politics. And their activism is palpable in local communities, as well as on the national scene—as evidenced by the millions who marched, the day following Trump's inauguration, in Washington, DC, all over

I believe that being an abortion provider and working toward safe, effective contraception for any and every woman is how I can be the most help for today.
Sherry, 34, medical student, California

the country, and indeed the world. And while the Women's March recognized a threat far greater than just abortion, the understanding of autonomy over one's body in every way is essential to self-determination.

Whether we are disengaged from the politics of abortion or on the front lines of the abortion battle, whether we have adequate access to abortion care or are without the money, the transportation, the legal right, or a provider within reach, whether we are fighting for the right to have children while on welfare or in prison or fighting the abuse of sterilization, the fight to make choices for ourselves and about our bodies belongs to each of us.

THE POLITICS OF ABORTION

Abortion is a hugely controversial issue in our society. Who should decide? What should be legal? Who should have access? Is abortion murder? When does life begin? All very important questions to sort out—personally but also politically. On a personal level, it is essential to explore these issues because it comes down to choice—and the right for you to make yours. Finding out where you stand on these issues is the pathway to deciding what you might choose when facing an unintended pregnancy. This is also true for men; while I believe that women should have the final decision in these cases, men can more effectively volunteer their voices regarding pregnancy if they know where they stand before having sex and if they communicate with their sexual partners. Given the political environment of the day, it is also important to address these questions on the public front as we have seen a decades-long battle to secure a woman's right to choose—a battle that is far from over. While I would argue that abortion is a personal decision and one that should belong to women and whomever they choose to include in their decision-making process, there is no argument about the reality that abortion is a significant political matter in our society today. We'll come back to the political challenges facing abortion rights in the United States—truly unique in the world—and I will also detail the history of abortion. But first I think that it is important to understand the context of abortion in women's lives today in order to fully understand what is at stake.

WHY DO WOMEN HAVE ABORTIONS?

I have worked with the Feminist Women's Health Centers in Northern California (now the Women's Health Specialists)[16] since 1992. I have escorted; I have been an advocate, a health worker, a health educator, and a manager. I serve on the board of directors. I have talked with many women who volunteered to share their stories with me—stories about how they got pregnant, the role of the guy in their decision to have an abortion, their religion, family, work, school, and futures. They shared the many reasons behind their decision for abortion—from being too young to being too old; from financial concerns to health concerns; from fear to freedom. The reality is that the reasons why women choose abortion are as diverse and unique as the women themselves.

Some studies, however, have given us a framework for exploring the general reasons behind a woman's choice for abortion. The Guttmacher Institute found that "on average, women give at least four reasons for choosing abortion: three-fourths of women cite concern for or responsibility to other individuals; three-fourths say they cannot afford a child; three-fourths say that having a baby would interfere with work, school or the ability to care for dependents; and half say they do not want to be a single parent or are having problems with their husband or partner."[17] Indeed, these are common reasons behind a woman's choice of abortion. Other reasons include fear of disappointing a parent, physical or sexual abuse at home or in an intimate relationship, and rape and sexual assault. These are important reasons to recognize; not only are they issues that we must address in order to ensure safety to women and girls, but we must also appreciate the realities in which we live. Should we compound the tragic reality of abuse with a pregnancy that results from this abuse? Should women be forced to give birth to the biological offspring of a family member? A rapist? It is important to note that some women do continue with pregnancies that come from abuse and rape. It is important to support and respect that choice. But it is also important to respect and protect a woman's right to choose not to continue that pregnancy. Only the individual knows what she can handle, and my point is that we need to respect her choice and not force her to make one that fulfills someone else's agenda. These are appalling but real situations that must be remembered when exploring legal and physical access to abortion.

On this note, we must continue to shut down the pundits and legislators that disregard women's experiences and spread false information in their quest to control the lives and bodies of women. We cannot excuse legislators, like Todd Akin (R-Mo) who falsely and outrageously argued, in 2012, that "if it's a legitimate rape, the female body has ways to try to shut that whole thing down."[18] I don't know what is more offensive—his lack of basic anatomical and reproductive knowledge or his premise that some rapes are legitimate and others are not. Thanks to activism, Akin did not win reelection that year. Unfortunately, Akin is not the only one who made such assertions. Similarly, Representative Paul Ryan (R-WI), Representative Trent Franks (R-Ariz), Representative Henry Aldridge (R-NC), and Representative Stephen Friend (R-PA), all, in one way or another, ignore science and disregard women's experiences to make the case to limit abortion.

WHO ARE THE WOMEN WHO HAVE ABORTIONS?

The anti-choice movement would like to paint a picture of women who have abortions as irresponsible, lazy, and promiscuous. But the reality is that all "types" of woman are equally likely to have an abortion: women with one partner, women with multiple partners, religious women, women of all ethnicities, women of different ages, married women, single women, straight women, bisexual women, lesbian women—and even women who argue against abortion rights. In my work with a women's health center, I helped to provide abortion services to a woman who frequently stood on our sidewalks in protest of abortion. She returned to the sidewalk the following week, signs of protest in her hand, after her safe, legal, non-judgmental procedure. Additionally, I have had friends who have argued vehemently against abortion, but who, upon discovering they were pregnant, chose abortion as the only option for them. One friend told me, on the drive home from her safe and legal abortion, that she was glad that it had been there for her but didn't think abortion should be legal.

I don't tell these stories to judge these women, but rather as a wake-up call. Situations that we never dreamed of can occur that ultimately lead us to abortion. Almost half of all pregnancies among American women are unintended—and four in ten of those unintended pregnancies are terminated by abortion.[19] Contrary to popular myth, very few women use abortion as a method of birth control—in fact, the National Abortion Federation, a group of providers and researchers, found that "half of all women getting abortions report that contraception was used during the month they became pregnant."[20] Further, the Guttmacher Institute found that "fifty-one percent of women having abortions used a contraceptive method during the month they became pregnant."[21] Abortion is not the enemy, nor are the women who have them. Abortion is a health issue and a reality.

One of the things that I have learned in the years of working in reproductive health care is that women will always need access to abortion. We know this from our history, and our current reality is our confirmation. Let's be clear—not all women will have abortions, but those who do not want to be pregnant—whatever their reasons—will find a way not to be. Women's stories from around the world prove that, regardless of legality, safety, resources, culture, religion, fear, and risk, women who want an abortion will find a way. The question is not whether women will have abortions but whether they will be safe in doing so. I believe that when we have the capability, the know-how, and the resources for abortion services, we have an obligation to make sure that women are safe. Abortion is about life and death—but not in the sense the opposition would like us to believe. The difference between illegal abortion and safe, legal, accessible abortion is whether women survive. Abortion, despite its controversy, is a medically safe and simple procedure. Unfortunately, the politics surrounding abortion—particularly the goal of making abortion illegal—is what makes abortion unsafe.

THE SAFETY OF ABORTION

Abortion in the first trimester (less than thirteen weeks' gestation) is safer than a tonsillectomy, an appendectomy, or a shot of penicillin.[22] Ninety-seven percent of women who have aspiration abortions in the first trimester report no complications.[23] Early medication-based abortions, limited to under nine weeks' gestation, have a complication rate of less than 0.5 percent.[24] Further, despite anti-choice assertions, abortion in the first trimester has no impact on future fertility, nor is there a link to an increase in breast cancer. The risk of abortion lies less within the practice of abortion than within the politics of abortion. Globally, where abortion is illegal, unsafe abortion remains a leading cause of death for women.[25] From the declining number of providers (we saw an 11 percent decline in the number of providers between 1996 and 2000[26] and another three percent decline between 2011 and 2014, along with a six percent decline of clinics providing abortion services during this same time period[27]) to the political environment in this country, access has become a key issue impacting the safety of abortion. In 2014, 90 percent of counties in the United States had no abortion provider, and 39 percent of American women lived in these counties.[28] Anti-choice activists have hindered medical research as well as access to clinic services. They fought the release of RU-486, or medication/nonsurgical abortion, despite the low complication rate and even though the medication has been used successfully for years in Europe. They continue to fight for legislation that would limit and restrict a woman's right to choose. They picket clinic entrances and badger staff and clients. And some within the anti-choice movement are violent terrorists who stalk, harass, and even murder doctors and clinic staff. They harass the children and family members of providers and have even been known to poison pets. What makes abortion unsafe is the fact that women have to travel extended distances, cross violent protest lines, and confront a culture of shame that far too often silences them.

THE FIGHT FOR YOUNG WOMEN

The debate around teen access to abortion is brutal; in most cases, it is conducted in the absence of teens themselves, who are rarely included in decision-making or policymaking positions about reproductive health care, who are generally not included in the dialogue about teen sexuality and pregnancy, and who are not able to cast a vote regarding initiatives or propositions or for the officials who are charged with representing them. And yet, they are directly impacted by the laws and regulations that are put in place without their voice.

Minors' access is perhaps one of the most politically and socially controversial aspects of the abortion debate. Most voters support the inclusion of some parental-involvement provisions in the law—I think because they believe that it will *guarantee* that their teen will talk to them when faced with an unintended pregnancy. Honestly, emotion aside for a moment, is it possible to enforce legislation that demands that teens talk to parents? Think about it for a minute. My reaction is that it's impossible to demand this. (Fortunately, however, 61 percent of teens report that they would willingly discuss an unintended pregnancy with their parent(s).[29]) When looking at this debate, I believe that we are obligated to see the bigger picture and not focus just upon our own family. We must think of those teens who do not believe that they can turn to their parent(s). Whether abuse is involved or fear of disappointing a parent, if she does not believe that she is safe in confiding in a parent, a teen will not. Like women who sought illegal abortions in the years prior to *Roe v. Wade*, these young women will also seek the termination of a pregnancy in any way they can. And in states where there is a parental-notification or parental-consent requirement, young women will be forced into self-inducement or "back-alley" abortions. Despite the availability of legal and safe abortion in this country, young women are dying, or seriously harming themselves. Most notable to this reality was the death of Becky Bell, in 1988. Becky died, at age seventeen, from complications following an illegal abortion. She was a teen who lived in a parental-consent state. Her parents, who prior to her death supported parental-consent laws, bravely traveled the country to tell their daughter's story and to encourage other parents to oppose laws restricting minors' access to abortion. In many ways, Becky has become the symbol of the fight for minors' access. But Becky is not the only teen who turned to desperate measures when confronted with an unintended pregnancy. I have spoken with young women who have thrown themselves down stairs, taken baseball bats to their abdomens, intentionally gotten into car accidents—all with the desperate hope of inducing a miscarriage. Is this the reality that we want for our youth? As long as we continue to allow restrictions to minors' access to abortion (and contraceptive) care, this is the reality they will live with.

Many of my peers are not aware of the political climate and threats that are being made to women's rights, particularly with reproductive freedom. Diane, 23, Caucasian, heterosexual, Michigan

Generally, parental-notification laws require a health provider to notify a young woman's parent of her intent to have an abortion, and parental-consent laws require permission from a parent before a teen can access abortion services. In most cases, a "judicial bypass" option is available that allows a teen to go before a judge to request permission for access to abortion services. But this option hardly seems an *option* when courts are difficult and intimidating to traverse, judges are biased, teens have to leave school to go to court, leaving them subject to calls home for absenteeism, and when confidentiality is compromised.

FAKE CLINICS: CRISIS PREGNANCY CENTERS

Crisis Pregnancy Centers, CPCs, are fake clinics that prey on vulnerable women who fear that they may be unintentionally pregnant. CPCs are called any number of things . . . A Woman's Friend, Choices, and Pregnancy Resources to name a few. Many of these centers have required women to watch anti-abortion films with false and misleading information before they can receive their pregnancy test results. Some of these centers have intentionally given women false negative results with the strategy of delaying her knowledge of her own pregnancy, particularly in states with bans on later term abortions. CPCs do not give abortion referrals; some refuse women birth control information. Most are religiously-based and well-funded through anti-choice, religious organizations. CPCs are commonly found near high school and college campuses and often visit free speech areas of those campuses. Generally, CPCs are not medically licensed and many of the volunteers at CPCs can also be found picketing in front of legitimate health centers that do provide abortion services.

The fact that CPCs intentionally give misleading information has been documented in several states. This was found to be so problematic that in 2015 California enacted a law, the Reproductive FACT Act (AB 775), that essentially requires "truth in advertising." The California law requires centers to notify clients of reproductive health services available through the state, including abortion. The law also requires clinics to have a doctor on staff, or they must notify the client that they are not a licensed health clinic. The Ninth Circuit Court of Appeals unanimously upheld the California law. However, anti-choice activists challenged the decision and the case went to the U.S. Supreme Court. The U.S. Supreme Court heard the case in 2018, in *National Institute of Family and Life Advocates v. Becerra*, unfortunately ruling against the state of California. In his dissenting opinion, Justice Breyer argued that the Court acted inconsistently. Citing an earlier case, Justice Breyer asked, "If a state can lawfully require a doctor to tell a woman seeking an abortion about adoption services, why should it not be able, as here, to require a medical counselor to tell a woman seeking prenatal care or other reproductive health care about childbirth and abortion services?"[30] This decision will likely have broader impacts than just in California, as other states, Illinois and Hawaii, have similar laws in place.

In his statement in support of the Reproductive FACT Act, California Attorney General Becerra stated, "Information is power, and all women should have access to the information they need when making personal health care decisions. The Reproductive FACT Act ensures that women in California receive accurate information about their health care options, including whether a facility is a licensed medical provider. The California Department of Justice will do everything necessary to protect women's health care rights."[31]

A BRIEF HISTORY OF ABORTION IN THE UNITED STATES

Abortion in the United States was not always the political firecracker that it is today. Not to romanticize the past, but there was once a time when women's health was in women's hands—including all aspects of reproductive care, from abortion to prenatal care, pregnancy to birth, infertility to birth control. Prior to the mid-1800s, women worked in community with one another, familiar with the use of herbs and massage and knowledgeable in the cycles of the female body. Women would visit women healers, including midwives, to receive assistance with infertility, the prevention of pregnancy, support during a pregnancy and/or a birth, or for assistance in terminating a pregnancy when needed. To the general public, abortion was really a nonissue. Throughout history, abortion was not controversial; for example, abortion was readily available and used in the Roman Empire; there are no references to, or provisions against, induced abortion in the Christian Bible or the Jewish Talmud; and Catholic canon law found early abortion legally unimportant.[32] Initially, American legal opinion followed suit, but, as women's health moved more into the realm of male-controlled science, knowledge and control were taken away from women. The science of women's health, or obstetrics and gynecology, emerged, replacing women healers with male "experts." In order to become these self-proclaimed experts, male doctors practiced surgical procedures on slave and immigrant women without consent or anesthesia.[33] They also created a campaign—the witch trials—to exterminate women healers and thereby eliminate their abilities and to scare other women away from woman-controlled knowledge and health care.[34] With the eradication of women healers, men began to take over healing and medicine—first in Europe and then in the United States. As Barbara Ehrenreich and Deirdre English, authors of *Witches, Midwives and Nurses: A History of Women Healers*, ask,

> The question is not so much how women got "left out" of medicine and left with nursing, but how did these categories arise at all? To put it another way: How did one particular set of healers, who happened to be male, white and middle class, manage to oust all the competing folk healers, midwives and other practitioners who had dominated the American medical scene in the early 1800s?[35]

The answer, according to Ehrenreich and English, is the class and sex struggles of the nineteenth century. These struggles led to the rise of a medical profession that considered women, and women's health, subservient to men. And, as G. J. Barker-Benfield writes in *The Horrors of the Half-Known Life*, "one of the casualties of the male drive to take control of women was the midwife."[36] With the loss of the midwife came the loss of woman-centered health care and knowledge, the loss of woman's control over her body, and the politicizing of women's bodies, which served as a means to control women and to maintain male—specifically white male—power.

Nowhere do we see greater evidence of this than in the drive to control women's reproductive lives. Men's takeover of medicine in the 1800s gave rise to a growing "right to life," or antiabortion, movement, in the 1900s.[37] Despite the fact that early-nineteenth-century America had "no statute laws governing abortion" and only minimal regulation of abortion after "quickening" (that is, when a pregnant woman begins to feel fetal movement), by 1900, every state had passed some sort of law restricting abortion at all stages of pregnancy.[38] Although provisions existed for the preservation of the woman's life, these restrictions were the beginning of a far-reaching and contemptible politic regarding abortion, which we continue to combat today.

Further, scholars argue an inherent racism to laws restricting abortion access. The fear was that white women may be dodging their duties as wife and mother, thus negatively impacting the growth of a white nation. Loretta Ross and Rickie Solinger write, in their book *Reproductive Justice: An Introduction,*

> While laws, policies, and brutal practices degraded enslaved and Native women, they ennobled free white women in contrast. According to law and cultural norms, the white mother was the fundamental creative symbol of the white nation: dependent but dignified, innocent and pious but wise, a person of deep sentiment but also judicious. She was tethered to the home while shaping the destiny of the nation by raising citizen-sons and future mothers of the Republic. Prescriptively, and in distinction to the African American mother, the white mother could, due to her whiteness, choose her husband and the father of her children. Her whiteness allowed her to manage and protect her own family. Her embodied, intimate whiteness—her alleged "chaste" sexuality, together with her fecund reproductive capacity—amounted to the nation's most precious resource. The nineteenth-century laws against contraception and abortion expressed the importance of the white mother's role in making the white nation and the government's interest in protecting her fertility.[39]

Racism continues to play a significant role in access to reproductive health services and the rights over one's body. White women did, and continue to, have privileges that women of color are denied. Our experiences vary significantly due to race and class; that can't be ignored. Nor can the fact that communities of color more harshly feel the consequences. The commonality that we share is that female bodies confront restrictions for the benefit of maintaining the power structure.

Kristen Luker, author of *Abortion and the Politics of Motherhood,* writes that "many cultural themes and social struggles lie behind the transition from an abortion climate that was remarkably open and unrestricted to one that restricted abortions (at least in principle) to those necessary to save the life of the mother."[40] As the United States shifted from an agriculture-based society to an urban one and with the rise of immigration, abortion became a central theme in women's health and politics. Change in the status of women that paralleled the demographic shift from rural to urban life, along with changing social values and "strains between rural and urban dwellers; between native-born 'Yankees' and immigrants; between the masses and the elites; and possibly between men and women"[41] all contributed to the growing politic of prohibiting abortion. Like Ehrenreich and English, Luker cites the rise of male physicians as a main influence leading to restrictive abortion laws. She writes,

> The most visible interest group agitating for more restrictive abortion laws was composed of elite or "regular" physicians, who actively petitioned state legislatures to pass anti-abortion laws and undertook through popular writings a campaign to change public opinion on abortion. The efforts of these physicians were probably the single most important influence in bringing about nineteenth-century anti-abortion laws.[42]

She goes on to argue that these same physicians viewed the issue of abortion through a political and social lens that continues to influence the debate today. Abortion became increasingly difficult to obtain throughout the early and mid-1900s, further impacting the political debate about women's lives while simultaneously endangering women, as back-alley butchers, who posed as doctors, took advantage of the situation.

It is impossible to know how many abortions occurred prior to legalization, or to fully understand the impact of illegal abortion on the lives of women prior to *Roe v. Wade*, the landmark 1973 U.S. Supreme Court decision that legalized abortion in the first trimester. Statistics were not often tracked, and fear of prosecution kept many women and practitioners from reporting abortion. Additionally, the cause of death for women who had had botched abortions was often misreported. Poor and low-income women suffered the most during these times, since they lacked the financial resources to obtain private and less dangerous (albeit illegal) abortions in the United States or to travel to other countries for safer abortion procedures. For poor women, the price of abortion often included danger, disease, unsanitary conditions, rape and sexual assault, and death. Patricia Miller's book *The Worst of Times* details accounts of such illegal abortion. In one story, a woman tells of her abortion in 1952. She recalls, "He made me have sex with him before he would do the abortion. My husband never knew that. He would have been wild if he had known. This abortion was expensive in lots of ways."[43] One Pennsylvania coroner, in comparing abortion death rates before and after *Roe v. Wade*, said, "In the coroner's office we would see three or four deaths a year from illegal abortions . . . the deaths stopped overnight in 1973, and I never saw another abortion death in all the eighteen years after that until I retired. That ought to tell people something about keeping abortion legal."[44]

The *Roe* decision is fundamental to abortion rights in this country, and a decision that we must protect. But legalization did not end the attack on abortion. Today, we continue to fight a daily battle against the chipping away of abortion rights and reproductive rights in general— from the debate about when life begins to the battles over judicial nominees and the court system to the language we use and the fight for a greater recognition and protection of all women's reproductive health care needs.

WOMANHOOD VS. FETUSHOOD

While the debate between which to value—woman or fetus—is long in our history of abortion rights in this country, over the last decade and a half, we have seen an interesting shift in the language used to frame the debate. Where once the term "unborn children" was central among anti-choice Republicans and zealots and was frequently used in debates, campaigns, and propaganda, we now see this phrase commonly used as well on soap operas and television shows and during news reports.

Not only does such language reframe the debate so that the pregnancy is valued over the rights of the woman, it is also now influencing policy. Nowhere did we see this more than in the public pronouncements of the G. W. Bush administration, which put forth and supported a number of policy proposals that define fetuses as people. While the Bush era is over, many of these policies persist and continue to impact the daily lives of women. Now with Trump in office, the anti-choice movement has a new ally, as well as the many anti-choice Congress members who continue to assert an anti-choice agenda—from the Unborn Victims of Violence Act to medical coverage for the "unborn" to the so-called Partial Birth Abortion Ban Act, which equates late-term abortion with "infanticide." What is important to know about the so-called partial-birth procedure is that, medically speaking, it does not exist. Rather, the terminology is central to the anti-choice movement's goal of fooling people into envisioning a baby that is brutally murdered by heartless women and abortion providers. This personification of the fetus shifts the focus away from women and their experience, thus allowing the political debate about abortion to exist in the absence of women. As a result, anti-choice advocates have a powerful tool in arguing against abortion rights for women. Unfortunately, theirs has been a very successful campaign; G. W. Bush signed into law the Unborn Victims of Violence Act in 2004 and, as of 2017, "partial-birth abortion ban" acts have passed in nineteen states[45] and forty-three states have some type of limitation based on gestational age.[46] Similar federal legislation was vetoed twice by President Bill Clinton, but President Bush signed a federal version in October 2003, making it the first federal ban on abortion in the United States. The Partial-Birth Abortion Ban was challenged in the courts, making it to the U.S. Supreme Court in 2007. In a 5–4 vote, the *Gonzales vs. Carhart* decision, the Court ruled that the statute was not unconstitutional, thus upholding the so-called partial-birth abortion ban.

Make no mistake: the ultimate goal of political conservatives is to overturn *Roe v. Wade*. Their tactics include opposition to sex education in public schools, opposition to comprehensive reproductive health care options, opposition to state or federal funding for reproductive health services, and a complete ban on abortion services. They conjure false images in the minds of the American public and gain support for banning abortion in all circumstances by slowly chipping away at reproductive health care rights, access, and education. The intent of the radical right has always been a source of concern, but the movement's infiltration into popular culture is even more worrisome. As our media adopt the language of the political right and project this politic onto the American public, women face a greater challenge in remaining central to the discussion about abortion. Increasingly lost are our voices and our stories, since claiming to have had an abortion is seen as shameful—a dirty secret—replaced now with images and discussions of the "unborn." The result is greater shame and blame targeted at women, the eventual loss of abortion rights, and the devastating return to back-alley butchers.

THE ROLE OF THE COURTS

Another critical area of concern related to women's reproductive rights is the courts. We continue to witness an intense fight over judicial nominees, one whose outcome will continue to impact us for many generations to come. With a Republican-controlled Congress and White House, we see a pattern of nominating extreme ideologues to high appointive positions, particularly to the federal Court of Appeals (district courts or circuit courts) and to the U.S. Supreme Court. These court appointments are lifetime positions, and it doesn't take much to imagine the impact that this pattern will have on women's rights, reproductive rights, civil rights, and LGBTIQ+ rights. Fortunately, we had a bit of a reprieve under President Obama who, among many District and Appeals court appointments, also appointed U.S. Supreme Court Justices Sotomayor and Kagan. Both Sotomayor and Kagan have strong commitments to equity and justice. Obama's final court nominee, however, was unjustly blocked by congressional Republicans in his final year in office, leaving Trump to appoint Judge Neil Gorsuch. Gorsuch, a legal conservative, was a hotly debated nominee whose appointment was only gained through the Republicans employing the "nuclear option" to end debate and pass his nomination by simple majority. Among other concerns, there is fair evidence to assume that Gorsuch will apply personhood to fetuses, thus ruling against most, if not all, abortion cases that may come before the Court, including challenges to *Roe v. Wade*. In 2018, despite multiple sexual assault and harassment allegations, Trump's nominee Judge Brett Kavanaugh was confirmed to the U.S. Supreme Court with a 50–48 vote in the Senate. Kavanaugh's confirmation garnered outrage by many throughout the country, as once again the "old white boy" network prevailed. In addition to these concerns, many feminists are worried about Kavanaugh's positions on abortion, gun control, voting rights, presidential executive power, and his overall lack of judicial demeanor shown during the hearings.

The Supreme Court is critically important, because Supreme Court justices have the power to influence every aspect of our lives with their decisions, from the right to privacy (including abortion) to the right to free speech. As activists, it is important to watch what nominations, appointments, and cases come before the Court. Currently, with the appointments of Gorsuch and Kavanaugh, the Court once again swings to the conservative, impacting abortion rights as well as LGBTIQ+ and many other civil rights. Additionally, it is important that we not ignore the significance of the U.S. Court of Appeals, which, at the bare minimum, decides which cases go on to the Supreme Court. Under G. W. Bush, we saw the appointments of Judges Carolyn Kuhl, Charles Pickering, Priscilla Owen, D. Brooks Smith, and Miguel Estrada, who were just a few in a long line of Bush nominees that are disconcerting to women's rights activists. These nominees have opposed the use of buffer zones to protect health centers, limited minors' access to abortion, and supported bans on abortion practices. They are evidence of the agenda among conservatives to pack the courts with judges who do not support women's reproductive rights. Indeed, Trump has, as of this writing, successfully appointed two such judges. In contrast, the feminist movement is fighting for judges who uphold the Constitution and continue to protect women's right to privacy and their right to safe abortion. We must have courts that represent and protect the people, not courts that carry out the will of a few powerful politicians.

KEY SUPREME COURT CASES

A very brief overview of the key cases that impact reproductive health in this nation. I encourage you to research these further.

1965: *Griswold v. Connecticut* established a constitutional right to privacy for married couples seeking birth control.

1972: *Eisenstadt v. Baird* extended the right to privacy provision established in *Griswold* to unmarried couples.

1973: *Roe v. Wade*—the landmark case that used the right to privacy to essentially legalize abortion (in the first trimester) throughout the country.

1975: *Bigelow v. Virginia*—the Court ruled that states could not ban abortion providers from advertising.

1976: *Planned Parenthood of Central Missouri v. Danforth*—the Court ruled unconstitutional a Missouri state that required spousal and parental (if under 18) consent for abortion.

1976 and 1979: *Bellotti v. Baird*—argued twice and ruled on after its 1979 hearing. The Court upheld the *Danforth* decision invalidating state laws requiring parental consent for minors seeking abortion.

1977–1980: *Maher v. Roe, Beal v. Doe, Poelker v. Doe,* and *Harris v. McRae* each addressed public funding for abortion; ultimately the Court ruled that the federal government had no obligation to fund abortion (the Hyde Amendment, a legislative act, continues to reaffirm that no federal funding is used for abortion care).

1986: *Thornburgh v. American College of Obstetricians & Gynecologists*— the Court struck down a Pennsylvania law requiring a state-scripted speech designed to discourage a woman from getting an abortion.

1986: *NOW v. Scheidler*—The National Organization for Women used the RICO (Racketeer-Influenced and Corrupt Organizations) Act and antitrust laws to fight anti-choice terrorists like Joseph Scheidler.

1989: *Webster v. Reproductive Health Services* upheld a Missouri state ban on using public employees or services for abortion services; particularly significant as some U.S. Supreme Court Justices called *Roe* into question.

1991: *Rust v. Sullivan*—this ruling upheld what is known as the "gag rule," a federal regulation that prohibits abortion referrals from federally funding family planning service agencies.

1992: *Planned Parenthood v. Casey*—this case significantly weakened *Roe* by upholding a number of restrictions such as waiting periods and parental consent.

1997: *Schenck v. Pro-Choice Network of Western New York*—the Court upheld a fixed fifteen-foot buffer zone around clinic entrances and driveways; they did not extend this as a floating buffer zone around cars or individuals entering clinics.

2000: *Stenberg v. Carhart*—the Court struck down a Nebraska ban on the so-called "partial-birth abortion" procedure.

2001: *Ferguson v. City of Charleston*—the Court held that states were not permitted via the Fourth Amendment to drug test pregnant women seeking prenatal care in a public hospital, without warrant or reasonable suspicion.

2007: *Gonzales v. Carhart* and *Gonzales v. Planned Parenthood Federation of America, Inc. (Carhart II)*—the Court upheld the Partial-Birth Abortion Ban Act of 2003, which was signed into law by G. W. Bush and limits some abortion procedures. Note that, medically speaking, there is no such procedure as "partial-birth abortion."

2018: *National Institute of Family and Life Advocates v. Becerra*—free speech case challenging California's FACT Act requiring Crisis Pregnancy Centers to provide accurate information about reproductive health services and to disclose if they are not medically licensed. The Court ruled against Becerra and the State of California.

PRO-CHOICE IS ABOUT YOUR CHOICE

Let's look at language—"pro-choice" versus so-called "pro-life." Since entering the movement to protect safe, legal, and accessible abortion for women, I have been on a campaign to change the way we talk about abortion politics in the United States. "Pro-choice" is exactly that—making a personal choice about abortion. Pro-choice encompasses both those who choose abortion and those who do not. Pro-choice is about exercising your ability to evaluate options in the context of your individual life— after all, who better to make decisions in your life, to know the intimate details of your life, than you? But "pro-life" does not accurately reflect the politics of that side of the debate. The "pro-life" movement argues against abortion—often under any circumstances, including rape and incest. They place value on a potential life as opposed to a woman's life.

Particularly saddening about the politicization of these terms is the polarization that can occur among women themselves. Through the misrepresentation and manipulation of the "pro-choice" position as one that does not support having children, some women who have, or desire to have, children of their own may feel that they cannot be "pro-choice." The politics of this debate has mistakenly pitted women against one another, when we ought to be standing together in support of healthy, wanted, funded pregnancies and children. And, indeed, you can be pro-choice and be committed to the health, safety, and rights of children.

Additionally, the tactics used by the "pro-life" movement often contradict the movement's name—with clinic violence, doctor and clinic worker murders, harassment, stalking, fire bombing, and anthrax and butyric acid attacks among the tactics its adherents have used. The National Abortion Federation (NAF) first began collecting data on anti-abortion violence in 1977. They continue to be the primary source of information, as they work with providers directly. Between 1977 and 2016, NAF found over 340,000 incidents of violence against abortion providers, including 11 murders, 26 attempted murders, 42 bombings, 186 arsons, 1,643 cases of vandalism, 100 butyric acid attacks, 583 cases of stalking, 69,191 incidents of hate email/internet harassment, and 252,470 incidents of picketing.[47] To be fair, this violence represents only a fraction of this movement's activities, but, nonetheless, the statistics are staggering and affect the lives of women every day. And as I wrote this, a news alert popped up on my phone that Fox's *The Five* will now move to the coveted airtime previously held by Bill O'Reilly. O'Reilly has blissfully been removed by Fox following repeated sexual harassment claims. However, *The Five*'s co-host Greg Gutfeld said that he has "a problem saying that you are pro-life but you respect the other side," arguing that this makes you a coward. Instead, in a bizarre and offensive comparison, Gutfeld made linkages between abortion and slavery and argued that if you are "pro-life and you believe [abortion] is murder, you should be willing to fight for it . . . you should be able to start a war if you believe in this that strongly."[48]

Noting all of this, I think that it is critical to revisit the language of this abortion movement. This movement is about choice, having one and not having one. Consequently, I refer to the "pro-life" movement as the "anti-choice" movement. Anti-choice activists believe that women are not capable of making a difficult and complicated choice. Ironically, many anti-choice activists are men who will never become pregnant and who therefore will never have to make this choice.

Additionally, the language of "choice" does not always represent the greater concerns of reproductive health. I see abortion as one part of women's health care—and I think that it should be treated as such and destigmatized. I also think, in line with a reproductive justice framework, the issues extend beyond choice, to those of access. We'll get further into this conversation in a bit. Unfortunately, the politics of abortion have created a steady threat to abortion rights, causing activists to focus their attention on this single issue. Whether or not this result was intentional, I believe that it might be one of the most effective tactics of the anti-choice movement, in that other, equally important health issues have taken a back seat to abortion and the issue has divided women within the movement. And whenever we are divided, we lose strength.

It is critical to protect and respect women's right to choose—and it is particularly urgent that we put a stop to the attack on abortion rights, abortion providers, and the women who choose and need abortion. But abortion is only one part of women's health. It is not the whole story. We must also fight for the overall health of all women.

MORE THAN ABORTION

One of my greatest frustrations about the abortion rights debate is that the fight to protect a woman's right to choose has diverted attention from the other, equally important issues surrounding reproductive rights. I think that one of the most successful elements of the anti-choice campaign has been its ability to divide women on the issues of reproductive health by creating a threat-based need to constantly defend a woman's right to abortion. The relentless attack on abortion has created a focus and a consciousness among mainstream women's rights organizations so that they spend their energy on abortion, often prioritizing abortion over the range of issues that makes up "reproductive freedom." There is a legitimate threat to the legal right to abortion, but there are also other reproductive issues that have long been neglected. One such issue is the critical fight to protect women from unnecessary medical treatments without their consent; sterilization, hysterectomies, and episiotomies are just a few of the common procedures that have been performed on women without informed consent—and which have become so common that consent is often assumed.

In fact, reproductive health incorporates a wide variety of health-care issues for women. From menstruation to menopause, from sexuality to birth control, from pregnancy to infertility, from abortion to adoption, from breast health to osteoporosis, women face these issues daily. The feminist movement is dedicated to educating women, incorporating them into research, and empowering them to make informed decisions for themselves. But the focus on abortion has diverted many resources and energies from these other important health issues. This diversion has served as a major source of division among women activists. Notably, women of color have voiced their frustration over the lack of attention given to the critical issue of forced sterilization that exists in epidemic proportions.

Dorothy Roberts, author of *Killing the Black Body: Race, Reproduction and the Meaning of Liberty*, details numerous accounts of such abuses— including "the practice of sterilizing Southern Black women through trickery or deceit," surgeries performed for "training purposes," lack of adequate education and explanation prior to medical procedures, sterilization emphasized over information about other birth control methods, the performance of hysterectomy in place of abortion, and the lack of accurate documentation of such procedures in medical records.[49] Women of color have long fought to bring these and other issues to the forefront of society and to the agenda of the feminist movement. However, these issues have far too often taken a back seat to issues championed by white women, furthering the divide among activists. Roberts describes the divide between women of color and white women in the feminist movement, writing that "the disparate experiences of women of color and white women led to a clash of agendas concerning sterilization."[50] The fight of white women to gain access to voluntary sterilization and other birth control methods undervalued the fight of women of color to end forced sterilization. Roberts writes, "There is nothing contradictory about advocating women's freedom to use birth control while opposing coercive birth control practices. The focus on the interests of white privileged women led to a myopic vision of reproductive rights."[51]

Unfortunately, this limited vision continues to impact the debate and fight for reproductive health rights—including all issues related to women's reproductive health care. Organizations like SisterSong and its founder, Loretta Ross, have effectively reframed much of the reproductive rights discussion, utilizing a justice framework. Recognizing that women of color, indigenous women, and trans people have been doing this work for generations, the term "Reproductive Justice" was first coined in 1994 following the International Conference on Population and Development in Cairo. SisterSong defines Reproductive Justice as "the human right to maintain personal bodily autonomy, have children, not have children, and parent the children we have in safe and sustainable communities."[52] Reproductive Justice combines reproductive rights with social justice, making a very important argument that Reproductive Justice is a human right and as such must be protected by governments. Reproductive Justice is about abortion, but so much more. It is about access, information, resources, dignity, freedom from violence interpersonally and in our larger communities, and economic justice. Reproductive Justice argues a critical analysis and deconstruction of power, addressing the intersections of our identities, and bringing those most marginalized to the center of discussion and policymaking.[53] Loretta Ross and Rickie Solinger write in their book, *Reproductive Justice: An Introduction*, "Reproductive justice is based on the understanding that the impacts of race, class, gender, and sexual identity oppressions are not additive but integrative."[54]

> Reproductive rights needs to include the rights of queers to reproduce and to have legal guardianship of their kids. Noemi, 28, white and Jewish, queer, California

Similarly, the issues of lesbian and queer women are neglected in health care discussions that are heterosexually based. Much emphasis is placed on pregnancy prevention and female-male relationships. As a result, lesbians are often marginalized in the health community. Lesbians and trans women face a number of critical barriers to access—including

---

Lesbian and gay adoption is complex. State laws vary from state to state. In many cases, courts determine the rights of same-sex couples to adopt. The Human Rights Campaign (www.hrc.org) has comprehensive information about laws and regulations impacting the lesbian, gay, bisexual, and transgender community, including state-by-state regulations on adoption.

For supportive, nondiscriminatory, feminist adoption services, contact Adoption Choices at http://www.womenshealthspecialists.org/adoption/adoption-Choices.shtml or call (530) 891-0302. Birthparents can call (800) 607-9200 toll-free for more information.

structural, financial, personal, and cultural barriers. Homophobia, transphobia, and a heterosexual norm, combined with the lack of sensitivity and education among health care providers, further limit the LGBTIQ+ community's access to health care. Political battles regarding sexuality education, sexual orientation, gender identity, gender reaffirmation surgery, marriage equality, rights to adoption, and parental rights further marginalize the LGBTIQ+ community, seriously undermining access to services and education.

TAKING BACK THE DEBATE

In order for this movement to continue and to be successful, we must take back the debate. We need to confront the stereotypes about women's health, combat the negative imagery in our media, broaden our discussion and policy work regarding women's health, and empower women to have respect for and pride in their bodies. Far too often, our society sends the message that women are unable to consider their options, evaluate their lives, and make decisions for themselves. Whether we are looking at abortion care or prenatal care, whether a woman is considering adoption or infertility treatments, hospital or home births, medical doctors or midwives, we must ensure that women have access to needed services. Politically and economically, we have not made women's health a priority. Despite the increase in health care coverage for women under the Affordable Care Act, women still have less access to health care. Approximately 11 percent of women were still uninsured in 2015, with women of color, undocumented women, and single mothers at the greatest risk.[55] Uninsured women, of course, have less access to quality care and are more likely to forgo preventative health care due to costs. Women, whether insured or not, continue to pay more than men in out-of-pocket medical costs, primarily due to contraception and other reproductive health costs. As long as health care is a political bargaining chip, women will continue to lose.

We must take back the women's health agenda. No longer should the radical conservative right control the discussion of women's bodies, nor should extremists control women's access to services. The feminist health movement began because women were not receiving the information and services they deserved. A feminist health agenda says that all women have the right to health care and health information that is supportive, respectful, and nonjudgmental. We have to say "no more" to limitations on treatment that are based on race, economics, class, sexual orientation, or age. No more to forced sterilization. No more to the denial of reproductive health information and services for young women. It is not enough to fight for women's rights to abortion or other reproductive health care options. We must also fight for women's freedom to make these choices—from abortion, to birthing, to adoption, to the decision not to have children—without shame or blame. Women must have access to all their health information, from education about their bodies, to funding and support, to participation in decisions about what to research and fund. We can stand collectively and send the message that women will fight back, that we will not stand for limitations on our health care options and services, that our sexuality is ours, and that decisions about our bodies belong to us.

SPOTLIGHT ON ACTIVISM

The Beautiful Cervix Project has my grassroots, feminist, body-loving self so happy! The Beautiful Cervix Project is an online blog and photo gallery that encourages women to know their bodies, specifically their cervixes, by sharing photos and information about cervixes. In a culture that continues to tell women and girls that their bodies are dirty, that their bodies do not belong fully to themselves, and that discourages self-exploration and self-acceptance, the Beautiful Cervix Project is radical. The site shares photos to show the large range of what is "normal," which is particularly important as women and girls are so often left without adequate information about their bodies. The site shares information about charting changes in one's cycle, shares resources like where to order your own speculum kit, and creates an online community for women to ask questions and share stories. The site creator welcomes people to the page, explaining, "We hope The Beautiful Cervix Project inspires our readers' curiosity to observe and appreciate what is normal for each one of us as we track the subtle changes in our bodies throughout our cycles." I hope your curiosity is piqued; check out the site! www.beautifulcervix.com

TAKE ACTION

Getting Started

Know the facts! There is a successful slam campaign against abortion. It is our responsibility to set the record straight and to dispel the myths about abortion.

Discuss contraceptive choices and sexual histories with your sexual partners before you have sex. What you don't know could hurt you.

Carry condoms for you and your friends when you go out for the evening. There's no shame in being protected.

Visit the Guttmacher Institute's website to see how your state meets the need for birth control services, sex education programs, and abortion care.

The Next Step

Take part in a fundraising walk (for breast cancer, MS, heart disease, domestic violence, etc.); most major cities host walks throughout the year.

Write your local school board in support of open and honest sex education in our public schools.

Refuse to support companies (local and national) that don't support women's reproductive health options—for example, only after intense activist pressure did Walmart agree to provide emergency contraception pills in its pharmacies, and Hobby Lobby continues to try to block its female employees' access to birth control.

Write to your health care insurer questioning its practice of covering contraceptive products for women.

Call or e-mail your local, state, and federal representatives when a hearing, a bill, or a nomination comes up regarding reproductive rights.

Getting Out There

Research if and where Crisis Pregnancy Centers exist in your community and spread the word.

Hold a V-Day event, such as a benefit production of *The Vagina Monologues*; see www.vday. org.

Volunteer for your local women's health center.

Become a clinic escort. Contact local feminist organizations for more information or work with local clinics to start your own escort program.

FABULOUS FEMINIST WEB RESOURCES

Guttmacher Institute

www.guttmacher.org

Great source for statistics and fact sheets about reproductive health care issues.

Babes in Toyland

www.babeland.com

Operated by women, this site is plush with sex education and plenty of fun toys.

Betty Dodson

www.bettydodson.com

The mother of sex education and empowerment in sexuality. Her site is full of great information.

Black Women's Health Imperative

www.blackwomenshealth.org

Founded in 1983 by Byllye Avery, the Black Women's Health Imperative, previously the National Black Women's Health Project, serves as an important resource for education, leadership training, advocacy, and research on African American women's health issues.

Boston Women's Health Collective

www.ourbodiesourselves.org

The authors of the feminist health classic Our Bodies, Ourselves *and a number of other important books with a woman-centered approach to health information. Their website includes a wealth of women's health information and resources.*

Catholics for Free Choice

www.cath4choice.org

Information and resources for Catholics who support a woman's right to choose.

Center for Excellence for Transgender Health

www.transhealth.ucsf.edu

Based at UC San Francisco, the Center for Excellence for Transgender Health hosts direct services, educational resources and programs, and research.

Feminist Women's Health Centers
www.fwhc.org
Women-centered health care information and services nationwide.

Good Vibrations
www.goodvibes.com
A great store in Berkeley and San Francisco—and online! Toys, books, education for sex and sexuality. Will make you comfortable the moment you walk in the door. Staff is readily available and helpful.

Lesbian Health Research Center
https://lgbt.ucsf.edu
Affiliated with UC San Francisco, the Lesbian Health Research Center provides comprehensive health information and research geared toward lesbians, bisexual women, and transgender individuals. Housed with the UCSF LGBT Resource Center.

Medical Students for Choice
www.ms4c.org
An international organization for medical students interested in learning about and providing abortion services. Great source of information and support for student leaders.

National Abortion Federation
www.pro-choice.org
An organization made up of abortion providers. Their site provides statistical information and internship and job opportunities.

National Abortion Rights Action League
www.naralprochoiceamerica.org
NARAL Pro-Choice America is an advocacy organization working to protect abortion rights. Their site contains updated legislative information, along with NARAL action campaigns.

National Asian Pacific American Women's Forum
www.napawf.org
Organization focusing on immigrant rights, Reproductive Justice, and economic justice efforts.

National Latina Institute for Reproductive Health
www.latinainstitute.org
"The mission of NLIRH is to ensure the fundamental human right to reproductive health for Latinas, their families, and their communities through public education, policy advocacy, and community mobilization."

National Organization for Women
www.now.org
A national nonprofit organization fighting for women's equality. Their site includes information on a host of women's rights issues, including abortion and reproductive rights. Can also locate local chapters, action, and find contact information to get involved.

Physicians for Reproductive Choice and Health
www.prch.org
An organization for physicians who want to participate in providing universal reproductive health care.

Planned Parenthood
www.plannedparenthood.org
Provides a variety of reproductive health care services for women and men. Their site includes health information, as well as political action updates.

Pro-Choice Public Education Project
www.protectchoice.org
"The Pro-Choice Public Education Project (PEP) is a collaborative project of the country's leading national pro-choice organizations dedicated to empowering this new generation of pro-choice activists and supporters.

With the input of young pro-choice leaders, PEP puts choice on the radar screens of today's young women, educates them about threats to reproductive rights, and provides them with tools for action."

Scarleteen

www.scarleteen.com

A fun, contemporary site with sex education geared toward teens.

Sistersong—Women of Color Reproductive Health Collective

www.SisterSong.net

Site includes information, resources, and events geared toward the reproductive health care needs and activism of women of color.

Unite for Reproductive & Gender Equity (URGE)

www.urge.org

Previously Choice USA, founded by Gloria Steinem. A youth leadership organization that focuses on abortion, parenting, sex, and civic engagement.

Women's Health Specialists

www.womenshealthspecialists.org

A member of the Federation of Feminist Women's Health Centers, Women's Health Specialists provides reproductive health care information and services to women and men in northern California. Also provides resources for cervical self-exam. Adoption Choices is a program of Women's Health Specialists.

Young Survival Coalition

www.youngsurvival.org

The only international, nonprofit organization dedicated to the concerns of women with breast cancer under the age of forty. Their website has advocacy, action, and educational information about breast self-exams and breast cancer.

7

FIGHTING BACK

It's dark as she enters the parking garage. No one is around. She is walking in high heels to her car. The camera scans the garage, and the viewer sees the dreaded but expected shadow lurking in the background. She notices, too. Distinctly male in his shadowed size, he begins to slowly follow her. She picks up her step, her high heels quickly clicking against the cement. His speed increases, too. Suddenly, he is gaining on her. She begins to run, toward what we are not sure. He is running. She is running. We're on the edges of our seats watching this unfold. Suddenly, she falls. We scream, "Get up! Get up! Run!," knowing it is only a matter of moments before this stranger is upon her—to do the unspeakable violence that we hear about everyday.

Why is this story played out over and over? Why is this scene so common in the media and in our minds? Why don't we hear more stories about women who fight back? Instead of this ever-so-typical garage scene where the woman runs and falls and becomes a victim, why don't we see her turn around and yell, "Get the fuck away from me!" Why aren't there more movies about girls who kick ass? Why aren't we our own superheroes? Why don't we hear more real-life stories of women who defend themselves—like the South Philadelphia high school girls who ran down the twenty-five-year-old man who had been exposing himself in front of their high school campus and beat the crap out of him until the police arrived?[1] Why don't we hear more stories of the countless women who fight back in the streets, on our campuses, and in our homes? Why isn't the lead news story about the woman who apprehended her attacker and not about the woman who was brutally raped and murdered? More important, why are news accounts of women who are brutally violated so commonplace? Why isn't the storyline about the shock of the nation—shock at the fact that violence against a woman occurred in the first place? And why don't we live in a culture where we wouldn't think to show images of women victimized in movies for entertainment and that those who dared to do so would be shunned by audiences and the Academy Awards alike (as opposed to being recognized with the highest Hollywood honors)? Why don't we learn the history of women warriors? Perhaps, if they knew these stories, more girls and women would know their strength, believe in their worth, and

---

Women Are Warriors

Women have always been warriors—from Greek and Roman times to the modern day, across the globe and in every culture. We have fought in wars, we have been spies, we have volunteered, we have served as nurses, we have been prisoners of war, we have died in battle, and occasionally we have been recognized as heroes alongside men. Women fought in the American Revolution—like Margaret Corbin, who took over her husband's cannon in the Battle of Fort Washington. She was the first woman in U.S. history to be awarded a disability pension for being wounded during military service. Disguised as men, women served on both sides of the conflict during the War of 1812 and during the Civil War. Dr. Mary Walker received the Congressional Medal of Honor for her service with the Union Army. Harriet Tubman served as a nurse, spy, and scout for the Union Army during the Civil War. Women served as nurses in the army in World War I, and those who were not nurses enlisted in the Marines and the Navy. Edith Cavell and Mata Hari were both prisoners of war, and both were executed as spies during World War I. Virginia Hall was awarded America's Distinguished Service Cross after eluding the Nazis for years while working for the French and the United States as a spy. Women served in World War II, in Vietnam, in the Persian Gulf, and, most recently, in Iraq. Many women have served, and many have given their lives in the line of duty. But, as with most areas of history, women's contributions and sacrifices in the armed forces have largely been ignored.

What would it be like for little girls if they grew up knowing their history as fighters? I wonder how this knowledge would have impacted our self-esteem when it came time to defend ourselves—physically but also emotionally. We need to reclaim our history as warriors, respect the fight within us, at the same time we seek peaceful resolution. We need to recognize and respect that women fight everyday for safety, self-determination, and freedom.

not internalize fear-based assumptions about their ability and safety. And maybe more men would learn to appreciate and respect women's strength. A reach? Perhaps. But this vision requires us to imagine a society that does not yet exist.

I know that we currently live in a culture where many women are afraid to fight back, where most women are taught that we can't fight back, and where some are even disempowered and believe that we are not worth fighting for. We live in a culture where, on a conscious, semi-conscious, or unconscious level, men are encouraged to see women as property and believe that we exist for their amusement and convenience. Think Hooters, Playboy, Miss America. We live in a culture where rape and gender-based violence is condoned—either actively or by inaction. But we must realize that we create this reality. Our movies, news media, and television shows create a culture of fear for women and desensitize men (and women) to the realities of violence against women. And so we watch the actor-police officer step over the rape victim to get to the "real" story; we watch women slapped and shoved and pushed and punched in music videos; we see images of brutalized women on the pages of our magazines to sell products; we see images of male dominance and control in advertising; image after image inundates us, the viewer, until we believe that violence against women is insignificant or, worse, that such violence is entertainment—*just part of the story line.*

Violence against women is real. It is not entertainment. In the United States, every nine seconds a woman is beaten or assaulted.[2] Nearly one in two women will experience sexual violence, other than rape, in their lifetime.[3] And one in five women will experience rape.[4] One in four women will experience severe physical violence at the hands of an intimate partner.[5] An estimated one in three women will experience sexual harassment at work.[6] Fifty-six percent of girls in grades 7–12 experi-

> Vi·o·lence *n.* an unjust or unwarranted exertion of force or power.

ence sexual harassment at school, and 52 percent experience sexual harassment on some form of social media or online.[7] Women experience sexual harassment, sexual assault, rape, dating violence, domestic abuse, street harassment, sexual trafficking, and many other heinous acts of violence. Many of us survive. But, tragically, many of us do not.

INTIMATE PARTNER VIOLENCE

We are taught the magic of love. We believe that love will be enough. We believe that *we* will be enough. Intimate partner violence—whether in a dating, live-in, marriage, or partner relationship—is devastating. The person who hurts us is the person who is supposed to love us. The fairy tale of falling in love and living happily ever after can go desperately wrong. And for one out of every four women, it does.[8] Intimate partner violence—also referred to as domestic violence, spousal abuse, battering, or courtship or dating violence—is the intimidation, assault, battery, or verbal or sexual abuse perpetrated by one intimate partner against another. Intimate partner violence occurs in both heterosexual and LGBTIQ+ relationships, among married and unmarried couples, and across all economic and racial lines. Gender, however, does seem to make a difference in the statistics about intimate partner violence. While men are victims and survivors of intimate partner violence, women represent the vast majority of those being violated. A National Intimate Partner and Sexual Violence Survey conducted by the Centers for Disease Control found that women are disproportionately impacted by intimate partner violence and frequently experience multiple forms, including rape, physical violence, and stalking.[9] Women living in poverty, women of color, and trans

> I have often heard jokes and comments regarding women and "their place" in school, my workplace and in social circles. Some people may say it is only a joke or tell me to lighten up, and I constantly find myself fighting these comments. I feel that even though someone may be joking, it is creating an acceptance of these issues, without challenging them, which I see as contributing to the problem. Christine, white, heterosexual, Massachusetts

women are at greatest risk.[10] Intimate partner violence consists of a number of abusive behaviors, including:[11]

Physical abuse: Hitting, shoving, slapping, punching, and so on—any physical violence or force inflicted upon a partner.

Sexual abuse: Any unwanted sexual behavior. Though legal at one time, marital rape is now illegal in all fifty states. Rape is a key form of violation in dating relationships.

Mental/emotional abuse: Also referred to as psychological or verbal abuse, the breaking down of a person's self-esteem, often through derogatory and demeaning comments that serve to keep the abused individual in the relationship. Individuals are broken down and come to believe that they are worth nothing and that no one will ever love them. Among the LGBTIQ+ community, this can also take the form of threatening to "out" someone to their family, job, or community.

Financial abuse: Tight control over financial resources by controlling bank accounts, allotting a strict allowance, and making the abused individual account for every penny spent. When these "regulations" are violated, the victim is likely to be physically or emotionally attacked.

Legal abuse: Withholding alimony or child support payments, hiding financial assets, dragging out custody hearings or legal proceedings, fighting for custody just to avoid making child support payments to control the victim's whereabouts.

Communal abuse: Also referred to as "spiritual abuse." This category encompasses activities such as prohibiting one's partner from attending social activities, such as churchgoing; visiting friends or family; or participating in a social club. This tactic isolates the abused individual from potential sources of help and support.

Intimate partner violence often occurs in a cycle that is perpetuated until the abused individual either leaves the relationship or dies.[12] As with any cycle, it is difficult to determine which stage begins first, and certainly individuals begin this cycle in different places, but for explana-

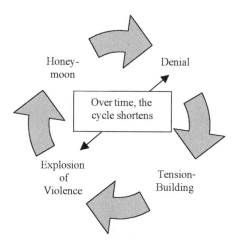

tory purposes let's begin with the "walking on eggshells," or *tension-building*, stage. In this stage, the abused individual is unsure when the physical abuse will occur but is certain that physical abuse is imminent. They feel as if they are "walking on eggshells," waiting for the abuse to occur. One strategy for dealing with this stage is to attempt to make everything "perfect" to prevent the explosion from the abusive partner. Unfortunately, this is only a temporary band-aid, because perfection is impossible, and eventually the abusive partner will abuse. Another way to handle this stage is to provoke abuse in order to get the attack out of the way. Many who have never lived in an abusive relationship have a hard time understanding this response, but provoking violence can be the only form of control an abused individual may have. This strategy can be as simple as controlling when the abuse occurs to avoid an explosion in front of children or to allow bruises to heal sufficiently that they can be covered with make-up before a family member is scheduled to visit. It is important to note that the best solution is to leave the relationship, but it is equally important to understand that everything is a process, and gaining control in any aspect of your life is an important step to taking back your life.

The next stage is the *explosion-of-violence* stage. Fairly self-explanatory, it is the stage of physical abuse—slapping, hitting, punching, beating, or sexual abuse. Physical abuse can take many different forms and can inflict bodily damage ranging from bruising to death. Every year more than one in three women, and one in four men, are raped, physically assaulted, and/or stalked every year by an intimate partner.[13] Though the actual numbers are difficult to account for, the National Intimate Partner and Sexual Violence Survey estimates that twenty people per minute experience violence at the hands of an intimate partner in the United States, and 27 percent of women and 12 percent of men report short- or long-term impacts, such as post-traumatic stress disorder and injury.[14] Sadly, these figures are likely an underestimate as thousands of others are often prohibited from seeking or too embarrassed or fearful to seek medical treatment. In fact, only an estimated 34 percent of survivors of intimate partner violence receive medical care for their injuries.[15] Physical violence is known to rise during a woman's pregnancy, with an estimated 324,000 women annually experiencing intimate partner violence while pregnant.[16] Women are far more likely than men to be murdered as a result of intimate partner violence, accounting for two out of three victims killed by an intimate partner.[17] Women of color, trans women, and women living in poverty are at the greatest risk for intimate partner homicide.

> It is inexcusable that this war on women continues on a daily basis in our country and around the world . . . until we can protect half our citizens, give them the right to protect and feel safe in their bodies—I find all other issues to be secondary. Julia, 24, Hispanic/Caucasian, bisexual, California

Following the explosion of violence is the *honeymoon* stage, perhaps the most dangerous stage because it creates a false picture of the relationship, often leading the abused individual into believing that all is well. The honeymoon stage is the make-up stage—the flowers and candy, the "I'm sorry and will never do it again" stage. Bruises and breaks are healing, our abusers are sweet and kind and vulnerable, we're told they can't live without us, we believe our love will make them better . . . excuses are believed, and we head right into the next stage.

The *denial* stage is the key to perpetuating the cycle of abuse. During the denial stage, the abused individual is convinced that the violence is isolated and not part of a cycle. It is during this stage that excuses replace questions and we make the ultimate decision to stay. A common question arises: why do we stay? Women stay in abusive relationships for a wide array of reasons: love, fear, religious and cultural beliefs, low self-esteem, isolation, self-blame, for the children, as a response to pressure from family or friends, embarrassment, shame, a belief that no one will help, economic dependency, a belief that the abuser will change, and opposition to divorce, among other reasons. And, as with many life events, it takes a catalyst to propel us to leave the situation—a near-death experience, a threat to a child. In absence of this experience, we continue through the cycle. Over time, the cycle shortens until we ricochet between denial and the explosion-of-violence stage. This continues until someone leaves or someone gets killed.

TEENS AND INTIMATE PARTNER VIOLENCE

Intimate partner violence is increasingly prevalent among teenagers. The National Coalition Against Domestic Violence reports that nearly 1.5 million U.S. high school students are physically abused by an intimate partner, with 20.9 percent of females and 13.4 percent of males reporting such abuse.[18] Only about a third of teens report this abuse, leaving them with fewer resources, support, and potential interventions. Teens who are, or have been, in an abusive dating relationship are significantly more likely to attempt suicide. The National Coalition Against Domestic Violence reports, "50% of youth reporting dating violence and rape also reported attempting suicide. This is compared to 12.5% of non-abused girls and 5.4% of non-abused boys."[19] Many explanations can be offered to better understand teen dating violence—the imagery of violence against women in our media, violence in the home modeled to young adults, lack of education and empowerment training, and attitudes about violence against women perpetrated throughout our society.

Some studies point to the use of heavy alcohol or drug use, the presence of sexually aggressive peers, male acceptance of dating violence, traditional sex roles, negative attitudes about relationships, and the prevalence of rape myths.[20] Whatever the reason, young people are at risk.

SEX TRAFFICKING

We tend to think of sex trafficking as something that only occurs in other parts of the world. While sex trafficking is certainly an international issue, it would be a mistake to ignore what is happening immediately in our communities. People of all genders, ages, and ethnicities are trafficked. However, making up 96 percent of those trafficked worldwide,[21] women and girls are disproportionately at risk. As with other forms of trafficking, sex trafficking is a form of slavery. People are trafficked through abduction, threat, violence, coercion, and manipulation. In 2017, the National Center for Missing and Exploited Children reported that of the nearly 25,000 runaway children in the United States, one in seven were victims of child sex trafficking.[22] A history of molestation and sexual abuse, which may be the reason for running away, make a child particularly at risk for trafficking. A U.S. Department of Health and Human Services study found that the average age that a young woman in the U.S. is trafficked for sex is twelve to fourteen years old.[23] A reality that we don't often recognize or focus upon is the prevalence of "boyfriend pimps" who create a dynamic that feels like love and protection to a young woman who is desperately seeking someone to care for her. That sense of love and protection can lead to her doing anything her "boyfriend" wants, including prostitution and the recruitment of other women into this system. This dynamic can make it particularly challenging to address trafficking; when you feel more provided for then you were in your life outside of trafficking, it can be hard to convince young women to leave their boyfriend pimp.

To end sex trafficking we must raise awareness, recognize that trafficking is modern-day slavery, address the issue of demand, sanction companies that provide sex tourism as bonuses to business men, pass anti-trafficking legislation domestically as well as through global initiatives, acknowledge that not all sex work is forced and coerced, provide resources to better enable someone to thrive outside trafficking, and collaborate across community organizations, law enforcement, and with sex workers and survivors of trafficking to create solutions and effectively address the issue.

> Rape: Forced sexual intercourse, which includes both psychological coercion and physical force. Forced sexual intercourse means penetration by the offender(s). Includes attempted rapes, male as well as female victims, and both heterosexual and same-sex rape. Attempted rape includes verbal threats of rape.
> Sexual assault: A wide range of victimizations, separate from rape or attempted rape. These crimes include attacks or attempted attacks generally involving unwanted sexual contact between victim and offender. Sexual assaults may or may not involve force and include such things as grabbing or fondling. It also includes verbal threats.
> (Definitions come from the Bureau of Justice Statistics, Department of Justice.)

RAPE AND SEXUAL ASSAULT

Rape. Just the word itself invokes a kind of fear that is truly gender-specific. While it is true that men are raped, women live with the constant reminder that they are at risk. A 2014 U.S. Department of Justice report confirmed that women, particularly between the ages of 18–24, are most likely to experience sexual violence, including rape.[24] Rape is a kind of abuse that is so specific, so violating, that it thrives off our fear and insecurity and strips us of our dignity and our freedom. The myths and misconceptions surrounding rape are further violating in that they create a culture of blame and responsibility targeted at women. Some of the most prevalent myths about rape include these:

Rape is part of men's biological nature (they need to "spread their
seed").

Men cannot control their sexual desires/arousal.

Rape is sex.

Women provoke rape by the clothes they wear, their make-up, the way
they act—all "victim-blaming" myths.

Rapists are always strangers.

Rape occurs only when a woman is alone.

Rape occurs only at night.

Rape doesn't occur in the safety of your own home.

Rape cannot occur in intimate relationships (or with someone that you
have previously had sex with).

The truth, of course, is that rape has nothing to do with sex and everything to do with power, control, and violence. Women don't cause rape;
rapists do. Marriage and intimate relationships do not guarantee inti-
macy, security, or protection and far too often are the source of violence.
And, despite the myths, 75 to 80 percent of the time, a woman knows
her rapist.[25] In fact, a number of different categories for understanding
rape exist:

Stranger rape—The most recognized type of rape and the one that most
believe to present the majority of risk. In reality, stranger rape accounts
for only about 20–25 percent of all rapes that occur. Yet, this is the type
of rape that is most represented in our media—the dark stranger in the
bushes awaiting his victim and ready to pounce. The threat of stranger rape
is often at the heart of self-defense programs and cautionary advisories for
women as they traverse their worlds.

Acquaintance rape—Rape committed by anyone that the victim knows—a
boyfriend, a work colleague, a schoolmate. Acquaintance rape accounts
for 75 to 80 percent of all rapes. Date rape, particularly common on
high school and college campuses, has become the subject of a great
deal of criticism, misconception, and debate. Survivors of acquaintance

rape are often not believed by others because they knew, or were involved with, the perpetrator. As a result, acquaintance rape is seriously
underreported.[26]

Spousal rape, or intimate partner rape—Rape that occurs within the con-
fines of marriage, domestic partnerships, or intimate relationship.

Substance-related rape—Rape that occurs while the victim is under the influence of alcohol or drugs. While this type of rape can occur when drinking
or drug use is consensual, U.S. federal code now determines that sex under
the influence is not consensual.[27] In the 1990s and early 2000s, a great deal
of attention was given to the prevalence of so-called date-rape drugs like
Rohypnol and GHB (gamma-hydroxybutyrate), which had led to an increase in substance-related rape, particularly on college campuses. Initially
marketed as a short-term treatment for insomnia, Rohypnol (commonly
referred to as "rophies") was often used in the United States as a date-rape
drug. Rophies dissolve quickly in a drink and take effect within thirty minutes. Combined with alcohol, rophies can cause "blackouts," with memory
loss and decrease in defenses. Because the drug has no taste, odor, or visual
residue, attackers can slip it into a drink and violate someone with little or
no resistance. Gamma-hydroxybutyrate, or GHB, is another form of date-
rape drug. GHB has a sedative and euphoric effect and has been referred to
as "liquid ecstasy" and "Easy Lay." Like Rohypnol, GHB has been used in a
number of sexual assaults; however, both drugs have become less common
today due to even easier access to over-the-counter medications. Common
antihistamines and cold medicines, like Benadryl, particularly in combination with alcohol, create a sedative effect and have become a preferred
drug for many perpetrators. The most common substance used in date and
acquaintance rape remains alcohol.

Multiple-assailant rape—Also referred to as "gang rape." This type of rape
occurs when there is more than one attacker. Professor Peggy Reeves
Sanday's *Fraternity Gang Rape* details her extensive research on multiple-
assailant rape on college campuses. She focuses upon sexual aggression as
part of the definition of masculinity, stating that "sexual aggression is the
means by which some men display masculinity and induct younger men

into masculine power roles."[28] This type of male aggression is supported through peer acceptance and the practice of blaming the victim. Sanday writes, "By blaming the victim for provoking their own sexual aggression, men control and define acceptable and unacceptable female sexual behavior through the agency of fear."[29] While her work emphasizes behavior among members of college fraternities, Sanday notes that "gang rape" is also prevalent among "many other exclusively male contexts at colleges and universities in the United States, such as organized sports."[30] Activist, educator, and author Tony Porter's powerful 2010 TED Talk describes how the expectations of masculinity are often rooted in violence. He describes a gang rape situation, of a neighborhood girl, used to initiate boys into manhood. He discusses the pressure of the "collective socialization of men," which leads to the creation of a "man box," narrowly defining masculinity in terms of aggression, violence, and no show of vulnerability. Boys and men are taught to see women as having less value, to see them as property, leading to objectification and ultimately then to violence against women.[31] Thus gang rape is used to signify manhood.

Corrective rape—Specifically targeting the LGBTIQ+ community. This extreme form of homophobia and transphobia is done in an attempt to punish and "correct" someone who is gay or transgender.

Clearly, women have more to fear from the men they know than from strangers. Unfortunately, many believe the opposite and can be duped into keeping their defenses high in public while lowering them in private situations. Additionally, these misconceptions can cause others to distrust women's accounts of date and acquaintance rape. Rape myths have far too often been used against women—leading to the assumption that rape between acquaintances is somehow *just the result of a miscommunication*, a misunderstanding.

Because of these misconceptions about rape, the response women receive after the rape can feel like a second violation, adding to the trauma of the initial attack. From family and friends to police and the courts, women confront an intense blame-the-victim mentality that asks them to account for the behavior that left them "vulnerable" to rape. More energy is spent on dissecting women's behavior and clothing than on locating and prosecuting the attackers. While coping with her rape, the woman's sense that she is somehow at fault is confirmed by questions like, Why were you at that bar? Why were you drinking? Were you being "flirtatious"? Were you wearing a short skirt?

WHY WOMEN GET BLAMED

Why do we blame women for being raped? I think that there are many reasons, but the strongest have to do with the culture surrounding women's sexuality and male entitlement and the need to create a sense of security, false though it may be. The first reason, I believe, is deeply rooted in history. As Estelle Freedman recounts in her excellent history of feminism, *No Turning Back*, rape didn't exist as a category in patriarchal societies prior to the 1800s, but was seen as a "theft of virginity," a category that applied only to those women who had not yet married and/or women who were virgins. The crime was actually considered to be one against her father or her promised husband and not against the woman herself.[32] In addition, rape has also been viewed historically as a crime against family property. This not only meant that a woman had no personal recourse for sexual violation, but also laid the foundation for the concept of male entitlement to women's bodies—especially as property. Men were not legally accountable for acts against their own personal property. Marital rape was not recognized as a crime in the United States until 1976 and was not considered a crime in all fifty U.S. states until 1993—how do you rape something that you own?[33] Indeed, for generations, to some extent, women have been viewed as men's property, creating a very unbalanced power dynamic.

In recent years, while we have instituted laws to protect women, we have also perpetuated a victim-blaming culture as means to check women's sexuality. Perhaps one of the most effective ways in which we restrict women's sexuality is through categorizing and labeling. In *Slut! Grow-*

ing Up Female with a Bad Reputation, Leora Tanenbaum discusses the power of the "slut" label. She writes that

> girls who are singled out for being "sluts" are by no means a monolithic group. And contrary to what most people think of when they visualize a "slut," many have no more sexual experience than their peers do, and some have no sexual experience at all. Whether or not a girl is targeted because of her sexual behavior, the effect is nonetheless to police her sexuality.[34]

This "policing" is a powerful influence over female adolescent sexuality, one that deeply impacts young women's exploration and self-definition. As a result, young women spend a tremendous amount of energy trying to adhere to teenage sexual norms and avoid the "slut" label. But the unfortunate reality is that young women have little control over whether they are labeled sluts.

Tanenbaum identifies multiple reasons that girls are labeled sluts, including being outsiders, developing breasts earlier than other girls, suffering from revenge, or being the victim of abuse or rape. The slut label is particularly powerful in response to rape; as Tanenbaum writes, "the 'slut' reputation protects rapists because it makes the victims believe that they are partly to blame."[35] In other words, the slut label carries with it the assumption of consent. As a slut, it is presumed, the girl in question wants sex with anyone, anytime, and that consequently she did something to "ask for it" or "led him on" and therefore is to blame.

Another reason women get blamed is that this creates a false sense of security. I find this particularly to be the case when it comes to acquaintance or date rape. Society at large does not want to believe women who are raped by a date or acquaintance. Instead, assertions that the attack resulted from a miscommunication, derogatory assumptions about women's sexuality, the slut myth, or accusations of morning-after regret are used to justify this type of rape. I believe that these justifications reflect fear. Often, it is believed that if a specific behavior or behaviors can be identified, then we can ensure our own safety. In other words, if the woman who was raped drank too much, then we can avoid rape by not drinking. If she wore "provocative" clothing, then we can prevent rape by rejecting similar clothing. But there is no justification for the perpetration of violence. Recognizing that rape is out of our control is scary, for what do we do then? We want to date, we want to have sex, but how do we prevent violence? Are men the enemy? But what happens to our quest for a man if men become the enemy? And what becomes of us if we pursue dating relationships? Are we at risk, as well? Not if the rape was her fault; then we are safe. This line of reasoning doesn't have to be so all-or-nothing; not all men are rapists or enemies, and aligning ourselves with other women for the protection of all women doesn't have to mean deciding to have girlfriends but no boyfriends. Instead, we could create a world where women are valued. If we collectively stood together, we could change the consciousness of what it means to be female. We could define ourselves independent of our male counterparts, where our sexuality is ours regardless of whether or not we choose to have sex with men. We could take back control over our own sexuality so that we are no longer forced to feel shame or be seen in terms of male desire. While this may not eradicate violence against women, it can expand existing supportive and safe communities for women, where we address the realities of rape, work to end violence, and feel free from shame and blame.

According to the National Crime Victimization Survey, conducted by the Department of Justice Bureau of Justice Statistics, about two out of every three rapes go unreported.[36] While trust is increasing in law enforcement's ability to effectively and sensitively handle rape cases (thanks in large part to the activism and training of the sexual-assault awareness and prevention movement), experts in the field with whom I have spoken confirm that the number of women who go directly to the police following their rape is still very low. While the rate at which rape is reported may have gone up in the past few years, factors such as poverty, racism, marriage, gender identity, or military service can drastically impact the rate of reporting. Women understandably fear that no one will believe them, that their personal sexual history will be used against them, that they will lose friends, and that their family will blame them. In date or acquaintance rape, women question whether their behavior led to or caused the rape. They question whether what happened could even be called rape. Was it their fault? Unfortunately, instead of standing together with women speaking out against violence, some women have taken center stage on this issue—loudly sending the message that women are to blame. Katie Roiphe's book, *The Morning After*, made headlines (thanks to a great deal of support from the conservative right) when she claimed that date rape couldn't exist because, to her knowledge, none of her friends had been raped. In a 1993 *New York Times* magazine article based upon her book, Roiphe stated, "If I was really standing in the middle of an 'epidemic,' a 'crisis'—if 25 percent of my women friends were really being raped—wouldn't I know it?"[37] Throughout her book, Roiphe misrepresents statistics and research on date rape and dismisses the realities and secrecy surrounding rape—what makes her think that her friends would tell her they had been raped? While we have heard little from Roiphe in recent years, I reference her work because it presents an important debate that we continue to engage in today. Similarly, the author Camille Paglia has created a tone that blames women and demonizes our sexuality with comments like "if you're advertising, you better put out," implying that we are obligated to provide sex and that men are justified in taking it.[38] It's the classic message to women that our appearance and behavior are designed to illicit responses from men and not to serve ourselves. In other words, our actions are viewed in the context of men and not independent of them. While the views of Roiphe and Paglia may have received a lot of press at the time, suggesting the increasing influence of the right on the media, the research on rape does not support their views. Are the millions of women who claim to have been date raped all wrong?

Attitudes like Paglia and Roiphe have real consequences. In the 1970s, feminists coined the term "rape culture" and, among feminist circles, we have recently seen a revival of the term and its understanding. Rape culture refers to the way we collectively view rape. For example, onesies for infants that say "lock up your daughters" or t-shirts targeted at teenagers that say "it's not rape, it's a snuggle with a struggle." Rape culture is about music lyrics, advertising, so-called jokes, and about how the media report on rape and sexual assault. The 2012 Stuebenville High School rape case garnered national attention when, in a rare occurrence, the rape of an unconscious female high school student did go to court. But rather than demonstrating support for the brave, young woman who stood up for herself, the community, social media, and mainstream news outlets sympathized with the perpetrators. Perhaps most outrageous was the reporting of CNN's Poppy Harlow who, following conviction with a mandated minimum sentence, stated it was "incredibly difficult, even for an outsider like me, to watch what happened as these two young men that had such promising futures, star football players, very good students, literally watched as they believed their lives fell apart . . . when that sentence came down."[39] Sadly, Harlow was not the only sympathetic reporter. And the Steubenville case was hardly unique. Attitudes dismissing the legitimacy and horror of rape are widespread. In 2012, Fox News's Liz Trotta asserted that women in the military should expect to be raped and argued that the U.S. government paid too much attention to women who were "raped too much."[40] By means of explanation, a Montana prosecutor told the mother of a five-year-old rape survivor that "boys will be boys."[41] In 2012, when asked about an abortion exception if pregnancy resulted from rape, Representative Todd Akin, a Republican from Missouri who opposed such an exception, questioned the legitimacy of rape, saying, "If it's a legitimate rape, the female body has ways to try to shut that whole thing down."[42] Virginia Senator Dick Black argued that a woman can't be raped by her husband because she shares the same bed with him, wearing a "nightie" and all! Despite public outrage, Santa Clara County Superior Court Judge Aaron Persky ignored prosecutor requests and sentenced former Stanford University swimmer Brock Turner to a minimal six-month sentence for sexually assaulting an unconscious woman. In defense of his ruling, Judge Persky said, "A prison sentence would have a severe impact on him."[43] Yup, but being raped, in public, and while unconscious has no impact. Perhaps the most outrageous example is that, in 2016, Donald Trump won the U.S. presidency despite being caught saying, "I better use some Tic Tacs just in case I start kissing her. You know, I'm automatically attracted to beautiful—I just start kissing them. It's like a magnet. Just kiss. I don't even wait. And when you're a star, they let you do it. You can do anything." He then followed with, "Grab 'em by the pussy. You can do anything."[44] This is our president, folks! He is this despicable, certainly, but that enough people did not believe that misogyny, sexual assault, and blatant sexism (not to mention racism, ableism, sizism, and homophobia) are deal breakers . . . well, that is a whole other problem.

The feminist community has led the way in trying to end rape and to help those who have been raped. Education, crisis lines and centers, and the enactment of new laws and regulations have all been part of the effort. Community organizations, federal programs, and tribal efforts have all made inroads in changing the consciousness around vio-

Rape Kits

Rape kits, or sexual assault evidence kits, consist of DNA evidence that is gathered from a survivor of rape. These kits can be an essential tool in prosecuting a rape crime, and preventing future attacks. Rape kits have a history of being undervalued and underfunded, but in 2014, President Obama included dedicated funding in his budget proposal. In 2015 and 2016, the federal government granted support to test backlogs of rape evidentiary. The 2013 reauthorization of the Violence Against Women Act (VAWA) included the Sexual Assault Forensic Evidence Registry (SAFER) Act, which addresses ongoing funding issues for rape kit testing. According to the organization End the Backlog, in 2017 eighteen rape kit reform laws and four resolutions were successfully enacted across nineteen states in the U.S. Activism is making a difference. We need to support these efforts and push for additional measures to ensure that all rape kits are tested and logged into a national database. Check out EndTheBacklog.org for ways to take action.

lence against women and have led the way to establishing important and needed programs and services. Any institution of higher education that receives federal funds is required to provide some form of sexual-assault awareness program (the extent to which this occurs is dependent on the campus; usually, student activists rather than administrators head these efforts). While this is a success story of activism

I'm a man against rape and I'm a man who sees that my fellow males have a responsibility to do something. Rishi, 20, Indian, Chicago, hetero-flexible/queer

creating change and addressing needs, the ideal success story would be the end of the need for any of these programs because sexual violence no longer exists. But, until that day comes, college campuses; community centers; churches, temples, synagogues, and mosques; apartment complexes; coffee houses; salons; health centers; and bookstores can all serve as great vehicles for spreading information about rape resources. We must also remember that the fight for essential services continues. A Rape Crisis Center report, conducted by the National Alliance to End Sexual Violence who polled rape crisis centers nationally, found that more than a third of centers have a wait list. Despite this, almost 75 percent of rape crisis centers lost local, state, and federal funding in 2013.[45]

Supporting and providing resources to rape survivors is a critical piece of feminist activism, but if we want rape to end, we have to target rapists. While I absolutely believe that we should continue to support education, shelters, and self-defense, I also think that we need to expose rapists. Why not shame them instead of shaming women? We need to stop blaming women for rape and using women's sexuality against them. We must stop the message that what we wear, say, or do invites sexual abuse. Let's place blame on the perpetrators and not on those who are abused.

The California legislature made history when, in 2014, it became the first state to pass legislation clearly defining consent. Senate Bill 967, commonly referred to as the "Yes Means Yes" bill, changed education code, now requiring an affirmative consent standard. Among other elements, this bill requires state colleges and universities to establish protocols and trainings that change the focus of rape education and services away from the controversial "no means no" approach, which has often served to put the responsibility of rape on the victim/survivor. Did she say no? How many times? Did her clothing send a different message than no? If she didn't clearly say no, then whose fault is the attack? Maybe this is just morning-after guilt? You know the drill. You've heard this before. Rape culture allows for, even promotes, ambiguity around rape. So much so that studies repeatedly tell us that most women blame themselves for being raped. SB 967 is a step to change this, clarifying that consent can't be given if asleep or under the influence. Consent cannot be assumed through lack of protest, silence, or lack of resistance. Consent must be affirmative and ongoing. SB 967 is the result of much statewide activism, written in consultation with rape prevention organizations. This bill is changing conversations. Campuses across the state are rewriting protocols and procedures, creating consent marketing campaigns, and partnering with local rape crisis organizations.

MEN, VIOLENCE, AND FEMINISM

This fight does not belong to only women. Men must step up and change the consciousness of other men. In January 2015, *Newsweek* reported that nearly a third of college males would have "intentions to force a woman to have sexual intercourse" if "nobody would ever know and there wouldn't be any consequences."[46] Despite this, many of these same men do not consider themselves rapists: "only 13.6 percent admit to having 'any intentions to rape a woman' under these same circumstances."[47] These attitudes, along with the realities of male-perpetrated violence, make it no surprise that many women fear men and the rape that they could enact. In my classes, I ask my male students to be aware of women's responses to them on the street. I ask them to observe the body language of women and their behaviors. They usually come back shocked to learn that women avert their eyes, switch their purses to their opposite arm, change the side of the street they are walking on, or hurry their step. We also discuss the often joked-about notion that women go to the bathroom in pairs, and expose the lessons that many girls grow up learning—that the bathroom is a potentially dangerous place. I have my female students call out examples of messages they have received about "how to stay safe"; for example, carry your keys in your fingers, park under a light, use the buddy system, don't go to nighttime gym classes, avoid evening classes on campus, and pretend to talk on your phone. This is an eye-opening exercise for my male students because while men fear violence from other men, they rarely fear it from women. And if they don't see themselves as perpetrators, they rarely believe that others would. To see the reaction of women who don't know them, or don't know them well, can serve as a wakeup call regarding their role in violence against women. It is not enough to be nonviolent yourself; men must take an active role in challenging rape culture and ending rape and sexual assault.

Fortunately, some men are heeding this call. There are great men and male-led organizations working to realize true political, social, and economic equality between women and men. One such man is Jackson Katz.[48] His film series *Tough Guise* suggests that while we learn violence and ideas of masculinity from many sources, one powerful source is the media. From video games to wrestling to the movie screens, we see a masculinity defined for boys and men that reinforces and supports violence as integral to this definition and to the real-life behavior of men. And, in fact, as cited by Jackson Katz in his work:

- 86% of armed robberies are committed by men.
- 77% of aggravated assaults are committed by men.
- 87% of stalkers are men.
- 86% of domestic violence incidents resulting in physical injury are perpetrated by men.
- 99% of rapes are committed by men.
- Men commit approximately 90% of murders.
- And over the past 30 years, 61 of the last 62 mass shootings have been committed by men.[49]

I fear that violence, specifically male-perpetrated violence, has become so commonplace that it is largely accepted. As a culture, we make excuses for male temper, we flock to violent movies for entertainment, we watch rape scenes on prime-time television without a flinch, we buy *Grand Theft Auto III*[50] and other video games for boys' birthdays—and what this all contributes to is an overall desensitization to violence—particularly violence against women. Jackson Katz addresses this concern well in stating:

> The reality is that messages that link being a man with being violent, controlling and intimidating are everywhere in the culture—from gun magazines, sports and wrestling, to romantic comedies and talk radio—as well as in the more obvious places like video games and television. If we want to deal seriously with reducing violence, we have to turn away from thinking about violence as "kids imitating violence," and focus instead on the incredible diversity of ways that we as a society are actively constructing violent masculinity as a cultural norm; not as something unusual or unexpected, but as one of the ways that boys become men.[51]

Katz eloquently outlines the challenges of masculinity in today's American society. From the violent actions of boys to the trivializing of the importance of violence by adults, violent masculinity undermines the quest for true equality and creates a greater barrier to raising boys into nonviolent men.

Violence prevention is a key area of activism for feminist men. In Canada, the White Ribbon Campaign: Men Working to End Men's Violence Against Women has grown into the largest worldwide effort of men working to end violence. Founded in 1991, this volunteer organization pledges "never to commit, condone nor remain silent about violence against women."[52] The White Ribbon Campaign encourages men and boys to wear ribbons for one to two weeks starting November 25—the International Day for the Eradication of Violence Against Women. The campaign brings awareness to the prevalence of violence against women and the role that men can play in eradicating such violence. Additionally, in the United States, Men Stopping Rape programs at college campuses are working with already existing women's centers and women's organizations to address the epidemic of date rape.

The work of Jackson Katz and of organizations like the White Ribbon Campaign and Men Stopping Rape has made significant inroads in deconstructing the attitudes of masculinity, confronting the realities of male violence, and fostering respectful and egalitarian relationships between women and men. Men must stand up against the harmful attitudes of their peers toward women. Men can speak out and actively work to change the cult of masculinity that embraces and promotes violence against women. Malcolm X used to be asked by white people, What can I do to end racism? He would tell them to go back and talk to other white people to try to change their ideas about racism. Similarly, men need to talk to other men about their behavior and attitudes toward women. Rape will not end when women stop wearing short skirts; it will end when men stop overpowering and violating women. This is not to say that women have no role in changing ideas about rape or that they are only powerless victims, but it is to recognize that without men's involvement and change, the violations will only continue. Real change requires all of us to make it happen.

Addressing violent masculinity also includes addressing violence against men, as 93 percent of rape against men is perpetrated by men.[53] Rape is about overpowering someone, exerting dominance, and taking control. The code of masculinity often requires men to be able to do just this. As both Jackson Katz and Tony Porter have discussed in their work, there is nothing worse for men than to be equated to being female, or female-like. In his TED Talk, Tony Porter relays a story of asking a young male how he would feel being compared to a girl. The story is very telling. He said:

> I can remember speaking to a 12-year-old boy, a football player, and I
> asked him, I said, "How would you feel if, in front of all the players, your

coach told you you were playing like a girl?" Now I expected him to say something like, I'd be sad; I'd be mad; I'd be angry, or something like that. No, the boy said to me—the boy said to me, "It would destroy me." And I said to myself, "God, if it would destroy him to be called a girl, what are we then teaching him about girls?"[54]

In traditional masculinity, women and girls are lesser. Any exception to this threatens manhood. What happens, then, to men who challenge, or reject, traditional masculinity? What about the men who appear more feminine or are gender non-conforming? Does calling these men "sissy" or "pussy" push them back into the "man box"? If name-calling isn't enough, is the threat of rape? The act of rape? In confronting our derogatory cultural attitudes about women, we also must question the limited notions of masculinity, and see the inherent connection between the two.

SEXUAL HARASSMENT

Sexual harassment in our schools, on our jobs, and in our communities is intended to intimidate and threaten. Sexual harassment is a power trip, allowing the harasser to exert control over another. There are two main types of sexual harassment, *quid pro quo* and *hostile environment*. Quid pro quo is a Latin term that means "this for that" and, when used in reference to sexual harassment, refers to a situation where "a person's submission to or rejection of sexual advances is used as the basis for employment decisions about him or her, or submission to sexual advances is made a condition of his or her employment."[55] Individuals can often find themselves in a no-win situation, forced to choose between keeping a job and dealing with unwanted sexual advances. A hostile environment occurs when "sexual conduct or gender-based hostility is sufficiently severe or pervasive that it creates an intimidating, hostile, or offensive work environment."[56] Making comments, sending inappropriate e-mails, displaying pornographic pictures, touching, and grabbing are all examples of actions that make a workplace a hostile environment. I know of one case where a male superior sent e-mails of women's breasts to a female worker. When she opened the e-mail (which came titled as work-related), the breasts grew until they exploded. Cases of sexual harassment can also take on more extreme elements in which women's lives are put in danger. For example, a friend of mine is a scientist and fre-

They tell me I should expect sexual harassment and get used to it because I am working a man's job.
Allegra, 30, equipment operator, California

quently works in remote locations. She had a supervisor who pulled a gun on her out in the field after she rejected his advances. She survived and did go through the process of reporting him, but her fear was not diminished. Unfortunately, despite the severity of sexual harassment, many people are fearful to come forward about this abuse. As with the other types of violence against women, they fear not being believed, they fear that the abuse will escalate, and, in the case of workplace harassment, they fear losing their jobs.

SEXUAL HARASSMENT IN THE WORKPLACE

According to the National Women's Law Center, nearly a quarter of women have experienced sexual harassment at work.[57] No industry is immune, but women in traditionally male dominated fields are most likely to experience harassment, likely in retaliation for them breaking a norm. Seventy to ninety percent of those who experience harassment do not report,[58] citing reasons ranging from fear of retaliation to fear that they will not be believed, that they will receive no support, or that they will lose their jobs.

While women are most likely to experience sexual harassment, people of all genders deal with workplace sexual harassment. Sexual harassment occurs between an employee and supervisor, as well as among co-workers. A *Huffington Post* poll reported that one in five women reported being harassed by a boss, and one in four reported being harassed by a co-worker.[59] Men also report sexual harassment, according to the same *Huffington Post* poll, with 6 percent reporting harassment from a boss and 14 percent by a co-worker.[60] While reports specific to sexual harassment are hard to determine, we do know that gay, lesbian, and bisexual workers are disproportionately affected, with 40 percent experiencing discrimination and harassment due to sexual orientation.[61] Further, some 97 percent of transgender workers report experiencing harassment and discrimination due to their gender identity.[62]

SEXUAL HARASSMENT AT SCHOOL

Sexual harassment is not limited to just the workplace. The American Association of University Women estimates that nearly half of students surveyed in the 2010–11 school year experienced sexual harassment at school.[63] From experience, I can tell you that harassment in the classroom is humiliating, frightening, and disempowering. Peer-to-peer sexual harassment is the most common and consists of physical and/ or nonphysical abuse. Verbal harassment is the most common type, but physical harassment is all too common as well. Cyber harassment is increasing, with some 30 percent of students experiencing harassment via social media sites, e-mail, and text. Regardless of whether in person or online, girls are significantly more likely to be sexually harassed than boys and harassment against girls is far more likely to include physical harassment. Harassment due to one's presumed sexual orientation is also prevalent, with 18 percent of students, in equal numbers of boys and girls, reporting negatively being called gay or lesbian.[64] Harassment in any situation is difficult and damaging, but, when it comes from a teacher, a whole new element of abuse is introduced. The abuse of power and trust can make a student feel even more unsafe and isolated. Adults—and certainly teachers—are touted as being there to protect and educate students. When you move out of the peer situation and sexual harassment is perpetrated by teachers, it becomes that much more difficult to speak up and have others believe you.

Increasingly, sexual harassment is being normalized. Despite discomfort and even fear, students say that harassment is just part of their day to day. Women students frequently report that sexual harassment is just "the price for being female." Students have come to expect comments, "jokes," and cat-calling as they walk to class or work in group projects. Over the years, the feminist movement has named it, and raised awareness about sexual harassment, but among many younger people, the prevalence of sexual harassment is commonplace. Many feel that they have little choice in how to handle harassment, and find little support among school administrators in addressing harassment. We need to support trainings, speak-outs, resources, educational materials, and a safe place to talk about harassment. We need to counter the dismissive myth that harassment is a harmless joke or worse, a compliment. We need comprehensive and uniform nationwide training for teachers and administrators about the signs and symptoms of sexual harassment and about the services available to its victims. And, while sexual harassment in education is prohibited under Title IX of the Education Amendments of 1972, we must dedicate the resources necessary and institutionalize a commitment to enforcing this provision.

> *Sexual harassment straight out of college has left me reelin' in the truth that objectification of women is the fearful reaction of threatened men.* Amanda, 27, botanist, California

> **Ho·mo·pho·bi·a** *n.* unreasoning fear of or antipathy toward homosexuals and homosexuality.

POWER, GENDER, AND HOMOPHOBIA

Violence within the LGBTIQ+ communities is much the same as violence among heterosexuals. There are similar rates of occurrence, and the types of violence perpetrated are similar, as well. An added power dynamic, however, is the threat to "out" the abused individual to family, friends, or workplace colleagues. This threat serves to keep an individual in an abusive relationship for fear that the abuser will retaliate by revealing the victim's sexuality. Homophobia is present throughout our society, within our workplaces and our families. "Coming out" as lesbian, gay, queer, or trans is often a significant event, bringing with it fear of being ostracized by family, friends, and co-workers. Institutional homophobia works to control an abused individual by creating a fear (and, far too often, a reality) that the person will not be believed, that resources for help are limited, that the person will not be accepted in shelters or group programs, and that service environments will be hostile toward the person's sexuality. Additionally, there is often an added pressure to protect the LGBTIQ+ community by not exposing intimate partner violence. The queer community is under such scrutiny that its members fear that exposure of violence within same-sex relationships will reinforce the accusation that homosexuality is immoral.

Social attitudes have influenced legal and structural realities for same-sex couples. For example, in the positive, the 2013 reauthorization of the Violence Against Women Act extended protections to same-sex couples: prohibiting shelters from turning away people based on sexual orientation, funding organizations that specifically serve the LGBTIQ+ community, and allowing state use of federal funds to better respond to same-sex intimate partner violence. On the other hand, the battle over the legal definition of marriage left many same-sex couples fighting for basic protections in cases of domestic violence. With the June 26, 2015, U.S. Supreme Court ruling in *Obergefell vs. Hodges*, legalizing same-sex marriage, one would assume that the same rights regarding intimate partner violence for opposite sex couples would now extend to same-sex couples. While this has been argued, many states continue to question the reach of *Obergefell vs. Hodges*. In backlash to the Supreme Court ruling, conscious objection, religious freedom, and otherwise anti-LGBTIQ+ bills have been, and are being, introduced throughout numerous states. These bills call into question the legitimacy of rights for LGBTIQ+ couples, not to mention rights for intersex and gender non-conforming folks. And this threatens resources and services for LGBTIQ+ folks seeking assistance as survivors of intimate partner violence. Challenges to legal protection, combined with the social stigma, leaves many same-sex partners without resources and protection to fight violence in their lives.

All people, regardless of sexual or gender identity, should be guaranteed the right to safety. The fact that domestic or intimate partner violence exists in same-sex relationships is not evidence that same-sex relationships are wrong. The same standard applied to heterosexual relationships would certainly create controversy. The sad tragedy is that abuse happens in all relationships. To create a healthy world, we need to recognize the prevalence of abuse, confront its stereotypes, identify signs and symptoms, and provide resources, services, and education to all. Additionally, we need to guarantee partners in same-sex relationships the same protections under the law that are available to heterosexuals. Further, we need to eradicate homophobia so that sexual orientation does not serve to further victimize individuals who are fighting for their security.

GLOBAL VIOLENCE

Millions of women around the globe live with violence in their lives—across socioeconomic and educational classes, across cultural and religious lines, and in every region of the world. From intimate partner violence, to rape, to sexual trafficking, to child abuse, to female genital mutilation, violence is a reality known to women worldwide. And violence against women, anywhere in the world, is about control, power, and the devaluing of women. Violence during wartime, violence against refugee women, and abuses of women in prison occur in manners perpetuated, condoned, and ignored by local governments. And the international community is only recently recognizing and taking action to end these abuses.

VIOLENCE AGAINST WOMEN AROUND THE GLOBE

An estimated 200 million women and girls have undergone female genital mutilation across thirty countries.[65] Female genital mutilation is a procedure that removes a varying degree of female genitalia, usually including the clitoris and some portion of the vulva—with an additional estimated two million girls at risk annually.

An estimated 117 million girls who would otherwise be expected to be alive are "missing" from various populations, mostly in Asia, largely as a result of sex-selective abortions, infanticide, or neglect.[66] Global son preference combined with technologies that allow for prenatal sex selection have led to significant sex ratio imbalances, with an estimated 110 to 120 male births per 100 female births in many countries. In some regions, this ratio reaches 120 to 130 male births per 100 female births. Further, female infanticide, the killing of female children, also continues.[67]

Across the globe, more than 700 million women were child brides (married under the age of eighteen). Of these, more than one in three were married before the age of fifteen.[68]

In India, despite the 1961 Anti-Dowry Act and India's ratification of CEDAW in 1993, over 8,600 women died at the hands of their husband and in-laws in dowry-related deaths in 2011, an increase from previous years.[69]

Two hundred seventy-six girls were taken from their school in Nigeria on April 14, 2014. The radical extremist group, Boko Haram, which objects to the educating of girls, stole these girls and subjected them to rape, forced marriage, sexual slavery, stoning, and suicide bombings. The hashtag #BringBackOurGirls brought international attention to the abduction.

Films like *Bordertown* and *Señorita Extraviada/Missing Young Woman* have brought attention to the missing women of the City of Juarez, Mexico. A 2011 Amnesty International statement on Mexico reports that more than 300 young women have been murdered in Juarez.[70]

In Pakistan, the number of "honor killings" continues to rise, with over 1,100 deaths reported in 2016.[71] Honor killings are enacted to restore honor to male members of a family by killing a woman who has been accused of wrongdoing.

Laws exist throughout the Middle East and Africa to protect a rapist from prosecution if he chooses to marry his victim, thereby "restoring honor" to a rape survivor and her family.

Rape is systematically used as a weapon of war all over the world. In Chiapas, Bosnia and Herzegovina, the Democratic Republic of Congo, Kuwait, Haiti, and Colombia, soldiers from both sides of a conflict gang-rape women and girls.[72] A UN Commission on Human Rights estimated that between 250,000 and 500,000 women were raped during the Rwandan Genocide.[73]

In parts of Afghanistan, Iraq, Iran, Malaysia, Indonesia, Saudi Arabia, Pakistan, Somalia, and the Sudan, women who commit adultery, or are accused of such, are stoned to death.

Based on data from the European Union, 34 percent of women with a disability or health issue report physical or sexual violence by a partner. This is compared to 19 percent of women without a health problem or disability.[74]

Women and girls account for 70 percent of global human trafficking. Girls represent two out of every three children trafficked annually.[75]

According to the United Nations International Labour Organization, 40 million people are victims of modern-day slavery; of those, 25 million are victims of forced labor and 15 million are victims of forced marriage. Women and girls comprise 71 percent of those forced into slavery.[76]

Awareness is rising about global violence against women—thanks to the many grassroots efforts of activists around the globe. From community marketplaces to prostitution outreach, from local organizing to nationwide commissions, women work to challenge traditional gender roles and practices, to create and maintain services, and to educate the world's political system to work to eradicate all discrimination against women. When a 1999 court overturned a 1998 rape conviction in Italy, ruling that rape could not occur because the woman was wearing jeans and would need to participate in their removal, thus giving consent, women throughout Italy and the world responded. Female lawmakers wore jeans to Parliament in Rome in protest—and Jeans for Justice was born. Jeans for Justice is an international campaign in which women wear jeans to work, protesting not just the Italian ruling but general attitudes about rape and violence against women. Women in Thailand, Nepal, and the Philippines are working to increase education and access to jobs to end the sexual trafficking of women and girls. Women throughout the developing world are attempting to unionize their labor in an attempt to have more control over their own wages and working conditions. The Asante market women in Ghana, West Africa, have taken control of the central market place, controlling trade and commerce, thereby giving women greater financial independence. Following the 2014 abduction of girls by the Boko Haram, Obiageli Ezekwesili created the phrase that led to the hashtag #BringBackOurGirls, showing just how effective social media can be in creating awareness and igniting global outrage. In the United States, the Coalition to Abolish Slavery and Trafficking (CAST) has established the first shelter for survivors of trafficking in the United States.

Incorporating crisis and transition services, the CAST shelter embraces a holistic approach to wellness, providing garden and art therapy and teaching computer and job training skills. Still noteworthy, and on a global scale, women from around the world came together in Beijing in 1995 to reconfirm CEDAW (Convention on the Elimination of All Forms of Discrimination Against Women) and set forth an agenda for the self-determination of women worldwide. Since then, many nations have taken action to end violence against women. A number of countries, including Austria, Belarus, Mexico, and Hungary, have criminalized sexual violence against women by their husbands. The Philippines initiated a program to combat trafficking in women and children. And Tanzania has enacted laws criminalizing female genital mutilation.[77] And in 2014, kicked off by a powerful speech from Emma Watson, the United Nations created a dynamic global campaign called HeForShe. HeForShe boldly embraces feminism and draws men and boys into the campaign to end violence and promote gender equity. While abuses continue and the amount of violence against women is staggering, we can find hope in the fact that we join our sisters throughout the world to fight back.

I came across an issue of Time *magazine in 1995 about how rape was used as a war tool in the civil war in Yugoslavia. I started doing more research on female genital mutilation, forced sterilizations in China, and the illegal trafficking of young girls in Thailand for prostitution and I started to realize that in the world over, the attitude towards women is destructive, oppressive and unacceptable. This point has been particularly brought home over the years as women I know have been victims of domestic violence, rape and molestation, and I started to realize how much violence is directed at women both in my own life and at women around the world. Lisa, 25, Indo-American, straight, Connecticut*

FIGHTING BACK

Fighting back is about more than physically fighting our attacker. It is about fighting back against violence on every level—fighting for recognition, fighting so that violence against women will be taken seriously, fighting for legislative provisions that will protect women and punish perpetrators (and not the other way around), fighting that our law enforcement and our courts do not re-victimize women in their pursuit for justice, fighting to hold men accountable—both as those who perpetrate violence and as those who stand by in a culture that allows this violence—fighting to change the consciousness of our global culture, fighting to ensure that rape continues to be recognized and treated as a

The sexual assaults and the coercive, abusive marriage I survived led me to the decision to reclaim my life and the lives of other women. Sharon, 33, Asian/White, California, bisexual

violation of human rights whether or not it occurs during wartime, and fighting to create a social and political no-tolerance policy about violence.

The epidemic of violence against women is so vast and so pervasive that it is nearly unspeakable. But, fortunately, women are speaking. We are speaking out and saying NO MORE. Events like Take Back the Night exist for just that purpose—to create a safe venue for women to tell their stories, band together, and, for at least one day, take back the night. Take Back the Night originated in England, in 1877; the first Take Back the Night march and rally in the United States took place in San Francisco in 1978 to bring awareness to and to protest violence against women. This San Francisco march followed the first feminist conference on pornography and brought together more than ten thousand people who gathered to march in the streets, protesting the harms of pornography.[78] Today, Take Back the Night events focus on sexual violence in all forms and occur throughout the world in hundreds of communities. Often associated with Take Back the Night, the Clothesline Project further raises awareness about violence against women through the artistic display of multicolored t-shirts on a clothesline. Started in 1990 by a small group of women in Massachusetts, the Clothesline Project serves to educate about intimate violence while honoring both victims and survivors. Today it is estimated that more than five hundred projects exist nationally and internationally, with between fifty thousand and sixty thousand shirts created.[79] Often building from the energy of Take Back the Night events,

Slut Walks have started throughout the globe. First taking place in Canada in 2011, Slut Walk is a transnational movement calling for the end to rape culture. In 2017, social media was flooded with women's stories of harassment and assault under the #MeToo hashtag, giving voice to often silenced realities that far too many women, across race, ethnicity, sexualities, and class, have experienced. #MeToo ignited a vital conversation about abuses from high-powered men and the women they target, and showed that even those women who we think have a charmed life have been subjected to humiliation, coercion, threat, and violence. But we need not forget the women most vulnerable due to class, race, sexuality, and gender identity. #MeToo argued that women have told their stories for far too long and that #TimesUp—men must also take a stand and we must effectively change the culture of abuse and silence that disproportionately affects the safety and wellbeing of women and girls.

Grassroots activism is the cornerstone that serves as the foundation for political change. Not only do events like Take Back the Night and Slut Walk create a safe place to heal; they also raise awareness about societal and governmental responsibility. It was from grassroots activism that we achieved legislative action, for example, the Violence Against Women Act (VAWA) in 1994, and helped win its reauthorization in 1998, 2000, 2005, and 2013. Despite wide opposition from congressional Republicans, the 2013 reauthorization of VAWA required all federally funded hospitals, domestic violence shelters, and service agencies to "implement inclusive policies that include and affirm gender identity, gender expression, and sexual orientation and ban discrimination."[80] Reauthorization in 2013 also clarified, expanded, and supported sovereign power of prosecution within Native American tribes; strengthened survivor immigrant rights and resources; and increased reporting requirements and expanded educational resources at colleges and universities. While VAWA is not the cure-all for intimate partner violence, it is a strong start to prioritizing funding, resources, and education to end violence against women. Administered by the Department of Health and Human Services and the Department of Justice, VAWA includes grants for survivors' shelters; a National Domestic Violence 24-hour hotline (1.800.799.SAFE / 1.800.787.3224 TTY); outreach to runaway, homeless youth; programs to reduce sexual assault; and coordinated community programs. VAWA also addresses issues related to trafficking, battered immigrant women, dating violence, services for disabled women, services for elderly women, and transitional housing. But we're not done yet. It is important that we elect representatives who will continue to support and expand VAWA until the violence stops.

A world free of violence against women benefits EVERYONE. Nicole, 25, biracial, heterosexual, Connecticut

Indeed, efforts throughout the world are under way to end violence against women—from the international campaign for CEDAW to local outreach, education, and crisis programs. College campuses have widely taken up the issue of rape and dating violence, hosting Clothesline Projects, Take Back the Night rallies, dorm outreach programs, Men Stopping Rape projects, and V-Day activities. We continue to raise awareness in our communities, to support our local shelters and hotlines, and to raise money through walk-a-thons and charity events. We continue to fight for the support of the Violence Against Women Act in Congress and for federal funding for and prioritizing of programs to end gender-based violence. We can all be part of this fight; whether we are on the floor of our legislatures making policy or talking to a friend or family member who is in an abusive relationship, we can make a difference. We must change the consciousness of this culture to end violence. Remember, no act is too small. We never know whose life we are helping with our activism.

SPOTLIGHT ON ACTIVISM

Documentary filmmaker Hind Bensari chose to take on the issue of forced marriage following rape in her native Morocco. Morocco's practice of marrying a rape victim to her rapist is rooted in a belief of restoring "honor" to the woman and her family. Bensari wanted to better understand this practice. Following the suicide of a sixteen-year-old girl who killed herself after being forced to marry her rapist, Bensari left her home in London to return to Morocco with her camera and lots of questions. Bensari challenges the idea that rape is a women's issue and argues that it is a societal issue. In a 2013 TED Talk, she said that she wanted to understand the social attitudes around forced marriage and interviewed 14–19 year olds, believing they would speak from the heart. She found that what they spoke of was determinism, which she describes as a self-reproducing system that believes that things are as they are because they have always been that way. She hoped in creating the film *475: Break the Silence* that people would see the possibility of change. Bensari took the film to the Moroccan parliament and pushed for it to air on national television. In January 2014, the Moroccan parliament overturned Article 475, the penal code that allowed rapists to avoid prosecution if they married their underaged victim. In her TED Talk, Hind Bensari says, "Things are never just the way they are. They are what we let them be." Indeed.

TAKE ACTION

Getting Started

Take a feminist self-defense class. Get to know your own power.

Call out rape culture. Raise awareness around jokes, clothing, movies, and music that perpetuate rape myths.

Contact the Rape, Abuse, and Incest National Network (www.rainn.org) and request materials about violence against women to hand out to your friends or in your community.

Take educational materials about date-rape drugs to your local clubs and bars, and ask the management if you can put them up in bathrooms (best if you go during the day, before they are busy with the club scene). Pass out materials at the clubs during club hours.

Support rape-kit funding—contact your legislators to support increased funding.

Counter the myths about gender-based violence. Speak up.

Educate yourself about global acts of violence against women (see Fabulous Feminist Web Resources for online resources).

The Next Step

Donate clothes, books, and household goods to a local domestic abuse shelter. Many cell-phone vendors now take donations of old phones to support domestic violence centers.

Participate in your local Take Back the Night or Slut Walk event. Bring a friend.

Talk to your friends about violence. Reach out to those whom you suspect are dealing with abuse in their lives. Let them know that they are not alone, that they are not to blame, and that resources are available.

Get involved with campaigns to end violence against women worldwide. See Fabulous Feminist Web Resources for online resources.

Getting Out There

Host an informational forum at your school, at a local bookstore, at a coffee house. Invite a speaker from your local shelter to facilitate.

Start a Clothesline Project on your campus or in your community. Visit www.clothes-lineproject.org for more information.

Support the V-Day campaign. Bring a performance of *The Vagina Monologues* to your campus or community. Participate in a local performance.

Request that your high school or college institute a consent-based sexual conduct policy.

Call on your state legislators to pass legislation that requires consent-based policies and protocols be instituted at public educational institutions. See California's SB 967 for an example.

Volunteer at a local domestic abuse shelter.

Volunteer for a rape crisis line. Volunteer to be an on-call language interpreter.

Take Action for Men

Don't rape.

Join the fight to end violence against women.

Talk to your friends.

Speak out.

Confront rape culture.

Pay attention.

Deconstruct the myths of masculinity.

Commit to living a nonviolent life.

Recognize and support November 25, the International Day for the Eradication of Violence Against Women, and support the White Ribbon Campaign. See www.whiteribbon.ca for more information.

Give money to domestic-violence and sexual-assault prevention organizations.

FIGHTING BACK: FILM RESOURCES

The Accused (1988)

Bastard Out of Carolina (1996)

Beloved (1998)

Bordertown (2007)

Boys Don't Cry (1999)

Brave Miss World (2013)

The Burning Bed (1984)

The Color Purple (1985)

Crimes of the Heart (1986)

The Crying Game (1992)

Date Rape Backlash: Media and the Denial of Rape (1994)

Defending Our Lives (1993)

Double Jeopardy (1999)

Dreamworld (1991) and *Dreamworlds II* (1995)

Enough (2002)

Fear (1996)

Free CeCe! (2016)

Freeway (1996)

Fried Green Tomatoes (1991)

Girlfight (2000)

Girl Rising (2013)

Girls Town (1996)

Half the Sky (2012)

Honor Diaries (2013)

The Hunting Ground (2015)

I Am a Girl (2013)

It's a Girl! (2012)

The Joy Luck Club (1993)

Kiss the Girls (1997)

The Long Kiss Goodnight (1996)

Monster (2003)

North Country (2005)

Once Were Warriors (1994)

Precious (2009)

Señorita Extraviada/Missing Young Woman (2001)

Sleeping with the Enemy (1991)

Thelma and Louise (1991)

Tough Guise (1999) & *Tough Guise 2* (2013)

The Vagina Monologues with Eve Ensler (2002)

What's Love Got to Do with It? (1993)

Where the Heart Is (2000)

FABULOUS FEMINIST WEB RESOURCES

American Women's Self Defense Association

www.awsda.org

Dedicated to ending violence against women, AWSDA provides a central place for information, referrals, training, and resources for self-defense.

Amnesty International

www.amnesty.org

An international campaign working for human rights and peace. Their website includes a wealth of information, including information on campaigns to end violence against women, protect refugee rights, end torture, and control arms.

California Coalition Against Sexual Assault

www.calcasa.org

A coalition of sexual rape crisis and prevention centers throughout California.

Young Women's Freedom Center

www.youngwomenfree.org

Formally the Center for Young Women's Development, the Young Women's Freedom Center is dedicated to improving the lives of cis and trans women of color, who are affected by the juvenile justice system and/or the underground street economy.

The Clothesline Project

www.clotheslineproject.org

Information about the Clothesline Project, including history and starting a project locally.

Coalition to Abolish Slavery and Trafficking

www.castla.org

Resources, services, and information about forced labor and slavery. Provides case management, advocacy, public education, and training.

Equality Now
www.equalitynow.org
International campaigns to end violence against women, including female genital mutilation, trafficking, rape, and domestic violence.

Feminist Majority
www.feminist.org
National and international information, resources, and activism. The Feminist Majority website is a great source of information on how to get involved and make a difference in the lives of women worldwide.

Hollaback
www.ihollaback.org
Focused on street harassment, online harassment, and gender justice, Hollaback invites people to share their stories to create support and community. Hollaback provides information, resources, and trainings.

Jackson Katz
www.jacksonkatz.com
Official site for Jackson Katz and his work. Includes antiviolence education and resources specifically for men.

Know Your IX
knowyourix.org
Great source of information on Title IX provisions against sexual violence at high schools and colleges.

Maiti Nepal
www.maitinepal.org
Information on working to protect Nepalese girls from prostitution, sex trafficking, domestic violence, child labor, and torture.

National Coalition Against Domestic Violence
www.ncadv.org
Education and resources about domestic violence; includes information about starting a domestic violence shelter in your area.

National Coalition of Anti-Violence Programs

www.avp.org

National advocacy for local GLBT communities. Their website includes information and resources for programs around the nation. It also includes reports on hate crimes and domestic violence.

National Organization for Men Against Sexism

www.nomas.org

Pro-feminist, gay-affirmative, antiracist organization dedicated to enhancing men's lives.

National Sexual Violence Resource Center

www.nsvrc.org

A collection of resources and referral regarding sexual violence; includes statistics, information, and resources for state, community, and tribal programs.

The Network

www.tnlr.org

English- and Spanish-language website providing information and resources about domestic violence against the LGBTIQ+ community.

NYC Alliance Against Sexual Assault

www.nycagainstrape.org

Based in New York City, website provides resources and referrals for area services. Also includes extensive library, research, fact sheets, and information about training programs.

Rape, Abuse and Incest National Network

www.rainn.org

Comprehensive resources, statistics, research, and program information.

Revolutionary Association of the Women of Afghanistan

www.rawa.org

The oldest sociopolitical organization of Afghan women fighting for justice.

Street Harassment Project (NYC)

www.streetharassmentproject.org

In response to the harassment of fifty-six women in New York's Central Park, the Street Harassment Project meets weekly to work to end harassment of women in public places. It hosts workshops and street theater to raise awareness about and to stop street harassment.

The Survivor Project

www.survivorproject.org

Information and resources for intersex and trans survivors of domestic and sexual violence. Their website also provides great resources regarding language, definitions, and building allies for the trans community.

VAW Net

www.vawnet.org

A network of referrals and resources for gender-based violence programs, research, and projects on the Internet.

V-Day—Stop Violence Against Women

www.vday.org

The Vagina Monologues' *V-Day Campaign, working to eradicate violence against women around the globe.*

White Ribbon Campaign

www.whiteribbon.ca

Canadian-based organization of men working to end men's violence against women.

Women for Women International

www.womenforwomen.org

International program working to aid women in war-torn regions in the world. Program provides financial and emotional support, vocational training, and micro-credit loans and financial assistance and works to promote women's rights.

8

LEADING THE WAY

When I first wrote *Fight Like a Girl*, I made the argument that women needed to be at the tables of decision-making. I still firmly believe this. We know, and evidence shows, that when women are present the conversation is more holistic. In the decade since *Fight* was first released, we have witnessed the historic run of Hillary Rodham Clinton, the first woman to earn a major party nomination in a presidential election; the heroic fight of Malala Yousafzai to champion education for girls; and the election of Danica Roem, the first openly transgender woman to serve in any U.S. state legislature. These and many other gains are to be celebrated, but we need to also recognize that there has been little overall movement in the numbers of representation for women in leadership positions. We need to continue to fight for a seat at the table, or as Shirley Chisholm once argued, "If they don't give you a seat at the table, bring a folding chair." We must also advocate for, insist upon, and settle for no less than feminist leadership—regardless of the gender of the person in the seat.

> Feminism is not a static thing. It should be changing with every day. Listen and learn to the people who came before but do not be afraid to move forward with what you've learned. Jay, 22, genderqueer/trans, Doukhobor, Canada

Leadership takes many forms and exists in many venues. Being elected to local, state, or national office is key, but so too is leadership in our local communities and schools. Working in community centers, in campus task forces, or as individuals, young people are making change everywhere. Whether we are working on body image, violence prevention, Reproductive Justice, clean air, economic justice, or free trade, young women are fighting for a better world. Some of us call ourselves feminists, while others do not. Some of us belong to long-established organizations, while others are forging a new path. Some of us work within the system, some of us work outside it—and sometimes we do both. While not all are active, there is a strong presence of young women—young people—who are plugged in. Most recently, we witnessed the invigoration of high school students around the country, as they took a collective stand against school shootings. Protesting in their cities, at their state legislative houses, and in Congress, high school students spoke out and demanded change in the laws that govern gun safety in this country. Collectively they organized a march and rally, "the March for Our Lives," in cities around the nation. Despite criticism, threat of expulsion, and arrest, these students continue to enact their right to protest. Every generation gets accused of being apathetic, and yet every generation has contributed something significant to the fight for social justice. As Vivien Labaton and Dawn Lundy Martin write in their anthology, *The Fire This Time: Young Activists and the New Feminism*, "young feminists are not only creating new organizations, new models of organizing, and new forms of cultural work but re-envisioning the world in which we live, and placing a renewed feminism at its center."[1]

WOMEN WHO HAVE MADE A DIFFERENCE

Abigail Adams wrote her now-famous letter to her husband, John Adams, asking him to "remember the ladies" while writing the Declaration of Independence, 1776.

Judith Sargent Stevens Murray advocated for equal education for women and men in *On the Equality of the Sexes*, published in 1790.

Emma Hart Willard founded Troy Female Seminary, the first endowed school for girls, 1821.

The first women's rights convention in the United States took place in Seneca Falls, New York, where the Declaration of Sentiments was written, calling for equal rights for women, 1848.

The first four-year college for women, Mount Holyoke College, in Massachusetts, was founded by **Mary Lyon**, 1837.

Harriet Tubman, in the 1850s, ran the Underground Railroad to help slaves escape.

Sojourner Truth delivered her famous "Ain't I a Woman" speech in Akron, Ohio, 1851.

The American Equal Rights Association, advocating for universal suffrage, was formed by **Elizabeth Cady Stanton** and **Susan B. Anthony**, 1866.

In 1870, abolitionist, suffragist, dress reformer, and the only women to receive the Medal of Honor **Dr. Mary Edwards Walker** was arrested in New Orleans for dressing like a man.

Victoria Woodhull was the first woman to campaign for the U.S. presidency, 1872.

Ida B. Wells created a national antilynching campaign, 1892.

Charlotte Perkins Gilman first published *The Yellow Wallpaper*, 1892.

Hannah Greenbaum Soloman founded the National Council for Jewish Women (NCJW), 1893.

The National Association of Colored Women (NACW) was formed by **Mary Church Terrell, Ida B. Wells-Barnett, Margaret Murray Washington, Fanny Jackson Coppin, Frances Ellen Watkins Harper, Charlotte Forten Grimké,** and **Harriet Tubman,** 1896.

Marie Curie was the first woman to win the Nobel Prize for physics, 1903.

Maggie Lena Walker, the first woman bank founder and president, founded St. Luke Penny Savings Bank in 1903 and served as its president until 1930.

Mary McLeod Bethune started a school for African American girls in Florida with $1.50, 1904.

Lois Weber, the first female movie director, began directing in 1913.

Jeannette Rankin, of Montana, was the first woman to serve in the U.S. House of Representatives, 1916.

Alice Paul and other members of the National Women's Party first proposed, and drafted, the Equal Rights Amendment, 1923.

Amelia Earhart was the first woman to fly solo across the Atlantic Ocean, 1932.

Frances Perkins became the first woman to hold a Cabinet position in U.S. politics when she was appointed Secretary of Labor by Franklin D. Roosevelt, 1932.

The National Council of Negro Women was founded by **Mary McLeod Bethune,** who also became the organization's president, 1935.

Eleanor Roosevelt was the first U.S. delegate to the United Nations, 1945–1951.

Alice Coachman was the first black woman to win an Olympic gold medal for the high jump, 1948.

Rosa Parks touched off the Montgomery, Alabama, bus boycotts when she refused to sit in the back of the bus, 1955–56.

Daughters of Bilitis, the first lesbian rights organization in the United States, was founded by **Del Martin** and **Phyllis Lyon,** 1955.

Jerrie Cobb was the first female astronaut candidate for NASA, 1959.

Wilma Rudolph was the first woman to win three gold medals in a single Olympiad, 1960 (Rudolph had had polio as a child and was told that she would never walk).

Delores Huerta co-founded the United Farm Workers to advocate for farm workers' rights, 1962.

Patsy Takemoto Mink, Democrat of Hawaii, was the first Asian/Pacific Islander woman elected to the House; she served from 1965 through 1977 and was re-elected in 1990 and 1992.

Largely in response to the exclusion of women from the National Conference on the Status of Women, **Betty Friedan, Catherine Conroy, Inka O'Hanrahan, Rosalind Loring, Mary Eastwood, Dorothy Haener, Pauli Murray,** and **Kay Clarenbach** formed the National Organization for Women in 1966.

Shirley Chisholm, Democrat of New York, became the first black woman U.S. representative in 1968. She ran for U.S. president in 1972, becoming the first woman and the first African American to seek the nomination of the Democratic Party.

The Feminist Women's Health Center was founded in Los Angeles by **Carol Downer** and **Lorraine Rothman** in an effort to create women-centered health care, 1971.

In 1969, a young lawyer in Texas took on a pro bono case to fight for one woman's right to abortion. The case went to the Supreme Court in 1971. It was *Roe v. Wade*, and **Sarah Weddington** was the attorney. On January 22, 1973, women won the right to an abortion in the first trimester.

Aileen Hernandez, a labor organizer and a black feminist activist, became NOW's second national president, 1971.

Ms. magazine was founded by **Gloria Steinem** and **Pat Carbine**, 1972.

The first woman producer to win an Oscar was **Julia Phillips**, who won for *The Sting*, 1974.

Julia B. Robinson was the first mathematician to be elected to the National Academy of Science, 1976.

Sarah Caldwell was the first woman to conduct the orchestra at the Metropolitan Opera; Beverly Sills refused to sing until Caldwell was allowed to conduct, 1976.

Bette Nesmith Graham, a single mother who had not finished high school and who was working as a secretary, invented Liquid Paper ("white-out"). In 1979, she sold her invention to Gillette for $47.5 million, plus royalties.

The National Women's History Project was founded, 1980.

In 1980, **Audre Lorde**, **Barbara Smith**, and **Cherrie Moraga** co-founded Kitchen Table Press, the first U.S. women of color publishing house.

Maya Lin, a twenty-one-year-old Chinese-American architectural design student, won the competition for the design of the Vietnam Veterans Memorial in Washington, DC, 1981.

Sally Ride was the first female American astronaut to go into space, 1983.

Alice Walker was awarded a Pulitzer Prize for her novel *The Color Purple*, 1983.

Geraldine Ferraro was the first woman to run on a national political party ticket for vice president, 1984.

The **Guerrilla Girls** was founded by a group of anonymous women with the goal of bringing recognition to women artists, 1984.

Emily's List was founded by **Ellen Malcolm**. Emily's List gives money to Democratic, pro-choice, women political candidates, 1985.

Wilma Mankiller was the first female chief of the Cherokee Nation, 1987.

In 1987, **Kimberlé Williams Crenshaw** published a paper on, and introduced, the theory of intersectionality.

Toni Morrison received the Pulitzer Prize for *Beloved* in 1988 and became the first black woman to win the Nobel Prize in Literature in 1993.

Ileana Ros-Lehtinen, Republican of Florida, became the first Cuban American (male or female) and the first Hispanic woman to be elected to the U.S. Congress, 1989.

The first woman to wear pants on the U.S. House floor was **Susan Molinari**, a Republican from New York, 1990.

Sylvia Rhone, CEO of East West Records, became the first woman and the first African American woman to head her own record label, 1990.

Anita Hill testified before the Senate Judiciary Committee, bringing sexual harassment to national awareness as she confronted her harasser, Supreme Court nominee (now Justice) Clarence Thomas, 1991.

Nydia Velazquez, Democrat of New York, was the first Puerto Rican congresswoman, 1992.

Dr. Mae Jemison was the first black female astronaut to successfully complete a space shuttle mission, 1992.

Rebecca Walker founded the Third Wave Direct Action Corporation in 1992, which later became the Third Wave Foundation.

Carol Moseley-Braun, Democrat of Illinois, was the first woman of color to serve in the U.S. Senate, elected in 1992. She later ran for president of the United States, 2004.

Lucille Roybal-Allard, Democrat of California, was the first Mexican American congresswoman, elected 1993.

Dr. Joycelyn Elders, former U.S. surgeon general, dared to speak about masturbation at the United Nations World AIDS Day 1994 conference. She was fired the following week.

Andi Zeisler and **Lisa Jervis** founded *Bitch* magazine, in 1996.

Lilith Fair, an international women's music festival that critics said would never happen, was created by **Sarah McLachlan**, 1997.

At just fifteen years of age, Shelby Knox took a stand against the abstinence-only curriculum at her school in Lubbock, Texas, prompting the creation of a PBS documentary film, *The Education of Shelby Knox*, by the filmmakers **Marion Lipschultz** and **Rose Rosenblatt**.

In 2004, sisters **Jessica and Vanessa Valenti** founded *Feministing*, an online blog that brings young feminist voices to the public discourse on society and politics today.

Katie Couric became the first solo network anchorwoman when she joined CBS in 2006.

Tarana Burke coined the hashtag #MeToo to raise awareness of sexual abuse and assault in 2006.

From 2007–2011, **Nancy Pelosi**, Democrat of California, served as the first woman House Speaker, and thus the highest ranking woman in politics in U.S. history.

Barbara Lee, Democratic Representative from California to the U.S. House of Representatives, was the sole voice against the vote for "authorization of use of force" following the attack of 9–11.

Alicia Garza, **Patrisse Cullors**, and **Opal Tometi** created the Black Lives Matter movement in 2013.

Malala Yousafza became the youngest Nobel Peace Prize Laureate, in 2014, for her efforts to fight for girls' access to education.

Danica Roem became the first openly transgender women to be elected and serve in any U.S. State Legislature in 2018.

In 2018, **Deb Haaland** and **Sharice Davids** became the first Native American women to be elected to the U.S. Congress. **Rashida Tlaib** and **Ilhan Oman** became the first Muslim women elected to the U.S. Congress. **Alexandria Ocasio-Cortez** became the youngest woman ever elected to Congress.

CHALLENGES WE FACE

Throughout this book, I have highlighted the many issues we face as women, both in society and within the movement itself. If our voices are to impact the decisions of a society, we must achieve equal repre-

sentation. No longer can we stand for government without equal representation; nor can we allow business, media, military, religion, or education to exist without fair representation for women.

What you say matters. Stand up, shout it out. Rachel, 26, Caucasian/American, heterosexual, Nebraska

Our safety and health cannot be negotiable. Accessible and comprehensive health care, health research, funding, and services that meet all women's needs—at every stage of her life—are what we need. Women must have economic justice. Our relationships need to be by choice and not dictated by government. Our sexuality must belong solely to ourselves—in definition and in practice. And we need to be taught from the earliest stages that we are valuable, powerful, beautiful beings. Some would say this is too much to ask for, but I argue that it is the bare minimum for a safe, healthy, equitable society. I also argue that it is worth the fight. But, as we have learned from our past, this fight is neither a quick nor an easy one. Those who have taken up the challenge in the past risked, and lost, a great deal. Far too many never lived to see their work realized. But they fought, not just for themselves, but for the vision of a better world for all. Now it is our turn. Phyllis Chesler tells us in her book *Letters to a Young Feminist,* "Know that you too may be punished for fighting back, whether you do so alone or with others. But know that if you persevere, you may improve the fate of future generations."[2] Many of us have stepped up to the challenge; we work every day to make sure women and girls, and people of all genders, have a fair chance at a life of quality and equality. Still others must join us, for freedom and justice are not yet fully realized. We must practice cultural humility in our organizing and our discussions. We must insist on partnership over hierarchy. The fight for social justice must be intersectional. We must integrate and honor the multiple identities that make up our movement. This must inform our politics and our efforts. As Audre Lorde wrote in *There Is No Hierarchy of Oppression*, "I have learned that oppression and the intolerance of difference come in all shapes and sizes and colors and sexualities; and that among those of us who share the goals of liberation and a workable future for our children, there can be no hierarchies of oppression."[3]

Feminism is the vision and practice of a truly just society. It is about believing in our worth as women and girls. It is about the opportunity to dream and to see those dreams realized. It is a movement to have our stories told, our experiences recognized, our bodies protected, our lives valued, and our voices counted in all levels of decision-making and leadership.

BEING THE CHANGE WE WANT TO SEE

Alix Olson, a fabulous feminist spoken word artist whom I met years ago at a conference in Los Angeles, California, has a great collection of poetry about social justice and activism. In one of my favorite poems, *Warriors*, she says,

> . . . *cause if this is a movement we're making, we have got to get moving. In this crazy maze we've been handed, we've got to quit losing ourselves.*
> *We gotta use our big fat mouths to talk, We gotta use our big thick thighs to walk.*
> *We got to follow those who choose a different way to knock.*[4]

And she is right, because we are not just the future. The fight is today, and we have a stake in it. Every day, decisions are made that impact every level of our lives. We need to be part of the decision-making process. We need to believe in our individual and collective strength, to respect the connections we share—that what one does impacts another.

We need to take on this fight together, addressing all issues of discrimination. Men need to join the feminist movement, be partners in this fight for equality—a fight whose success will also benefit them. We need to broaden our understanding and definition of gender and allow people to define themselves. We need to ensure that we all are at the table, sharing our analysis and strategizing for our futures. We need to break the barriers of race, age, gender, sexuality and sexual orientation, physical ability, and all other identities that keep us separate. We must fight sexism, racism, ageism, homophobia, transphobia—all the isms to recognize that, collectively, we are stronger and that, while we experience discrimination uniquely and individually, there is a commonality to oppression. It is with this commonality that we can come together and fight so that we all experience a life of quality and equality. We must believe that we are worth fighting for—because we are. It's our fight. It's our rights. The torch of feminism is in our hands. It is in this vein that I reject the notion that being a girl is less than. I reject that only certain bodies can be girls. And I assert that doing things "like a girl" is powerful. So, say it with me . . .

Play like a girl. Act like a girl. Eat like a girl. Think like a girl. Organize like a girl. Write like a girl. Vote like a girl. Throw like a girl. Laugh like a girl. Move like a girl. Dream like a girl. Invent like a girl. Dance like a girl. Heal like a girl. Study like a girl. Run like a girl. Resist like a girl. Raise money like a girl. Celebrate like a girl. Dress like a girl. Invest like a girl. Argue like a girl. Raise hell like a girl. Speak like a girl. Stand up like a girl. Strategize like a girl. Speak out like a girl. Love like a girl. Yell like a girl. Do it like a girl. Act up like a girl. Lead like a girl. *Fight like a girl!*

ACKNOWLEDGMENTS

Writing this second edition was not without its challenges—personally and politically. I became a mother since my first edition was released. Writing with children is a whole different reality. It is beautiful chaos. Molly and Lola, I will always work to create a better world for you. Teaching you to fight like a girl is one of the greatest joys of my life.

To Jonathan: What a journey we have been on! Thank you for supporting and partnering with me.

To my mom: an incredible woman in her own right but who also modeled the kind of mom I hope to be. I have always had a deep love and appreciation for you, but even more now that I am mothering. Beyond mothering, you are brilliant and I so love our discussions.

To my dad: Thank you for challenging me to always be my best. And for always being there.

To my sisters, Aimee and Amanda, I love you more.

To the rest of the men in my family—Paul, Michael, Aidan, Adam, and Jasper, may you always be men who partner for justice.

To my editor, Ilene Kalish, and the staff at NYU Press: thank you for your patience as I worked through political devastations during the writing of this edition. Thank you for your support and efforts in bringing this book to print.

To the amazing women of Women's Health Specialists, A Feminist Women's Health Center: Thank you for helping me be a better advocate and a stronger ally. You impact my life daily and I'm so grateful for you all. And thank you for the work you tirelessly do in our communities.

To my colleagues: I learn from you every day. There is a camaraderie in our work that I so appreciate.

To my friends: Thank you for enduring passionate rants as I process current events. Thank you for advice, calling me out when needed, and for loving me.

I was remiss in the first edition to not acknowledge the Valdez family and the impact they had on me very early in my activist life. I continue to hold you all in my heart.

To my students: I often tell anyone who will listen that I have my dream job. To work with you, learn with you, and strive for justice and equity alongside you is more rewarding to me than you will ever know. Thank you for sharing your ideas and your lives with me.

To activists throughout the globe: Thank you for getting up every day and fighting for justice. Thank you for speaking your truth, sharing your stories, and visioning a better world.

I am who I am because of the many teachers, activists, advocates, practitioners, and visionaries who have come into and through my life. As I wrote in the first edition, my interactions with these folks have shaped who I am and what I think, to such an extent that I sometimes wonder where my ideas and knowledge distinguish themselves from those that belong to others. A collective consciousness has been shared with me, and for that I am immensely grateful.

APPENDIX A

Timeline and Checklist for Action

Note to the Reader: I hope that the ideas in this and the following appendices will assist you in fighting like a girl.

6 WEEKS PRIOR TO EVENT
Choose a site, date, and time.
Apply for any needed permits and make room reservations.
Contact potential speakers and performers.

5 WEEKS PRIOR TO EVENT
Create a flyer listing the date, site, time, and purpose of the event and contact information.
Mail flyer to supportive groups.
Begin posting flyers in public locations (e.g., coffee houses, laundromats, bookstores, college campuses).
Post information on your social media sites. Set up an events page.

4 WEEKS PRIOR TO EVENT
Contact local media calendar listings departments and send event notices.
Continue spreading information on the event.

3 WEEKS PRIOR TO EVENT
Confirm speakers and guests.
Make arrangements for necessary equipment.
Mail and/or e-mail event information to local supporters and members.

2 WEEKS PRIOR TO EVENT
Send press advisories and public service announcements to local media.

Plan visuals for the event, such as signs, banners, and stage backdrops.

Plan volunteer roster for event.

1 WEEK PRIOR TO EVENT

Contact group membership to inform about the event. Get commitments to attend.

Send reminder e-mails/texts.

Post updates to social media sites.

Send press releases to local media.

Poster-blitz community.

Make any visuals for event as previously planned.

3–5 DAYS PRIOR TO EVENT

Make final adjustments to program.

Get biographical data on speakers for introductions.

Hold volunteer trainings (especially for peacekeepers and facilitators).

1–2 DAYS PRIOR TO EVENT

Make follow-up calls to media.

Confirm equipment arrangements, including delivery and set-up time and costs.

Make reminder contact (e-mail/call/text) with volunteers, speakers, and performers.

DAY OF EVENT

Assemble volunteers on-site at least 1 1/2 hours in advance. Hang banners and signs.

Check equipment.

Greet performers and speakers, and confirm time limits and program with them.

Start on time, and stick to the program.

AFTER EVENT

Clean up event area.

Return rented or borrowed equipment.

Meet with organizers and de-brief.

Access and share news coverage and stories.

Write thank-you notes to speakers and helpers.

(Timeline and Checklist reprinted with permission from CA NOW's *Action for Justice Training Manual*, 2003; updated for second edition.)

APPENDIX B

Building an Activist Kit

An activist kit is something to take with you to events or to leave in your car or bag for last-minute outreach opportunities. A few things to consider putting in your kit:

1. Flyers for upcoming events and meetings (make sure to always include your contact information and/or QR code)
2. Sign-up list for volunteers and/or people who wish to be contacted about upcoming meetings or events
3. Clipboard
4. Pens
5. Information cards and flyers about your organization or effort, with contact and meeting information
6. Rubber bands (use rubber bands to keep flyers from flying away in outdoor settings)
7. Wrapped candy to give to visitors to your table (it's amazing how a bit of sweets can draw people in)

APPENDIX C

How to Write a Press Release

1. Use letterhead and type the release (do not handwrite . . . ever!).
2. Label the top NEWS RELEASE, PSA (public service announcement), CALENDAR LISTING, PRESS ADVISORY, or PRESS CONFERENCE, as appropriate. When you use all caps, you are signifying to the reporters that this is for their information, and not part of the text to be printed.
3. Provide one or two contact names and phone numbers (ALL CAPS).
4. Date it in this way—For Immediate Release MONTH, DATE, YEAR. Use today's date or the date the organization will receive the release. If you're sending in a calendar listing, you may wish to add an END DATE or EFFECTIVE UNTIL.
5. Write a headline for your press release. Make it catchy, and use a present-tense verb for action or interest. Note: reporters rarely use your headline, but it is still important to provide one.
6. Double-space the body of your story, and leave wide margins on both sides. The editor uses this space for rewriting or marking special printing instructions. If you must go beyond one page, number each page and end each page with MORE until the end, where you should write END at the bottom of the page.
7. Get your press release off to a good start—be interesting and intriguing. Include all pertinent information—who, what, when, where—in the first paragraph, often in the first sentence, or the lead, and the only sentence allowed to be so long.

8. Provide information in order of importance, or top down, which is why you have the pertinent information in the lead sentence. This way you catch all the readers who will not read the entire press release. Editors often cut from the bottom up without rereading or rewriting.

9. Use short sentences (except for the lead sentence) and multiple paragraphs. Ignore what you learned in English class! News paragraphs are kept short so that they can be cut to fit the space available.

10. Quote the statements of others. Such quotations add human interest and can assert your position.

11. Keep the verbs in simple tenses; present, simple past, or simple future. This makes for a quicker, more lively read. Use active, not passive, verbs.

12. Contractions may be used in quotations, but never in copy writing. You may quote "it's" and "can't" and "she's," but, otherwise, write, "it is" and "cannot" and "she is."

13. Use only one side of the page.

14. If you do not have a contact name, address the envelope to "News Desk" or "Assignment Desk" or "Calendar Editor," as appropriate.

15. Proofread!

(Guidelines adapted with permission from CA NOW's *Public Relations/ Media Guidelines for NOW Chapters,* **April 1999).**

APPENDIX D

Guidelines to a Good Media Interview

1. *First and foremost, interviews are not conversations.* You are speaking to the public, not the reporter. The reporter represents the public and is there to get information to relay to the public, and they will probably ask difficult or leading questions. Don't feel that you have to give detailed answers to every question or that you have to answer every question. Remember, you can say "no comment" to questions that you do not know how to answer or that are unrelated to the issue at hand.

2. *Don't be hostile or evasive.* Maintain your professionalism even when confronted with hostile interviewers. Don't fall into the trap of saying anything that will hurt your cause; stay focused, and remember why you are doing the interview.

3. *Prepare, prepare, prepare.* Have friends or fellow activists create practice questions to help prepare you for the interview. Think of at least one question you are least prepared for, or least want to address, and be ready to handle it in case it comes up.

4. *Set your own agenda.* Create talking points on the topic, outlining what you will say. Repeat them several times during the interview.

5. *Give good quotations.* Create sound bites, or concise quotations, for your issue(s). A sound bite does not need to be more than a sentence or two. Make it catchy; make it memorable. Be clever and original, but not melodramatic. If you can express yourself well and catch the attention of the reporter, you will most likely not only end up in print, but also earn a relationship with the reporter for future stories.

6. *Remember, there is no such thing as "off the record."* Be aware that, as soon as you grant an interview, anything that you say may end up in print. Many reporters will respect a request to go "off the record," but be careful. Remember that you are not having a conversation with a friend; you are both doing a job.

7. *As an interviewee, you have rights.*

   a. *You have the right to be comfortable.* You can set the time, location, and length of an interview, particularly if the reporter has requested the interview. Depending on how important the interview is to you, you may need to be flexible. Negotiate.

   b. *You have the right to request the topics to be discussed.* You have the right to know the purpose of the interview and to request an overview of the questions to be asked. Asking for specific questions is not usually appropriate; most reporters will not give this information, nor will editors allow interview subjects that kind of control over the story.

   c. *You have the right to ask questions of the reporter.* Reporters are supposed to be objective, but this is not usually the case. Ask a question to get the sense of the reporter's position on the issue or agenda under discussion. If you sense that the reporter is in opposition to you on the issue, stick to your main message and stay professional.

   d. *You have the right to make a follow-up call to the reporter to clarify any statements that you feel may have been misunderstood.* However, you do not get final approval of the story. The reporter is not your publicist. While you may ask for quotations to be read back to you, a reporter may not appreciate a request to have them confirmed and is not obligated to change them if you disagree with how you are quoted. It is best not to ask unless the story is particularly controversial or you have a reason to believe that the reporter misunderstood you during the interview.

e. *You have the right to confirm spelling of names and titles.* This is always a good thing to do, as you want the public to have accurate information about you and/or your organization.

f. *You have the right to share contact information to be relayed to the public.* Reporters usually want this information, anyhow, but it is always a good idea to confirm this information with the reporter, especially website references. You want those who hear or read the story to know how to get involved with your work.

(Guidelines adapted with permission from CA NOW's *Public Relations/ Media Guidelines for NOW Chapters,* April 1999).

APPENDIX E

Guidelines to Creating and Earning Effective Media

1. Remember, there are many kinds of media—print, TV, radio, and Internet—and each can be effective for getting your message across.
2. Know your local press, and create a media list; compile a comprehensive listing of your local print, radio, television, and blog news contacts. Be sure to include a contact name, title, address, phone number, fax number, and e-mail address.
3. Identify your allies—who are the feminist reporters? Which reporters write stories on the issues that concern you? Identifying your allies can help get your event covered or your stories told.
4. Take time to make personal contacts with people in the media—send an introductory letter/e-mail when first setting up your contacts, and include information about the issues you focus on, as well as your contact information.
5. Remember that reporters sometimes have a hidden agenda, or something that they want you to say. Approach every media interview with caution, and be wary of responding to stories or issues that trivialize your cause. If you don't have sufficient information to answer a question, decline to comment ("no comment"), rather than being pressured into answering something you do not know enough about or trying to meet the interviewer's deadline or agenda. Remember, there is no "off the record" when you are talking to reporters; they are not your friends. They have a job to do, and so do you—so stick to your message.

6. When working in a group, designate a media spokesperson(s). Make it clear to the group that these are the only people authorized to speak to the press and refer the press to these folks. Spokespeople need to be articulate and charismatic speakers. They need to be well informed on the issue and able to answer reporters' questions concisely, with "sound bites" that have been predetermined. Have a brainstorming session with your group prior to the event or in connection with the issue about which you will be interviewed to come up with ideas, points, and effective responses. Practice with one another.

7. Keep your message simple. Identify three key points or themes that are concise and to the point. Repeat these themes in your press release and during your interview. Saying less is more; keep to your points even when you feel you're being repetitive.

8. Write a news press release or media advisory. A release informs the media about your event or position on an issue. An advisory informs the media about an action or event and informs them about the date, time, location, and purpose. Mail, fax, or e-mail the advisory or release a few days before the event, and follow up with phone calls. The morning of the event, make reminder phone calls.

9. Come up with sound bites, which are thirty-second statements about your event or the issue you are working on. Practice your sound bites on your colleagues or fellow activists. Make them catchy, make them interesting, make them powerful—you want to catch the interest of the interviewer and your audience, not bore them.

10. Create a social media campaign. Designate someone to focus on Twitter, Instagram, Facebook, Snapchat, and any other relevant sites. Post updates throughout the event or campaign.

11. Does your event or group have a YouTube channel? Consider setting one up. Post clips from events, short interviews from members about the issue, and explain key points of your campaign. Make sure to share the channel on your website and/or social media sites.

12. Target your audience. Identify whom you are trying to reach, taking into consideration your choice of medium and the time of coverage.

13. Target the media. Explore the media "angles" to your story. Who is most likely to cover your event or issue? If you are working on pay equity, try the business reporters or one from the lifestyle section. If you are working on a reproductive rights, try the health reporters, legal writers, or national reporters. Shop around for reporters who have a good understanding of the issue, and make your press release relevant to their work (this increases your chances of getting coverage).

14. When doing a press conference or inviting the press to cover an event, remember to make your media visual. Create a backdrop for your speakers. Location is important for this. If talking about a legislative issue, hold your event or press conference in front of the capitol; if dealing with a legal issue, stand before a courthouse. Make signs or banners with clear messages (not too many words). Choose the right time—check press schedules and conflicting events, avoid Fridays and the 10 A.M. news rush, and don't schedule past 2 P.M. Create press packets with information about the event or issue and the participating organizations, with contact information.

15. Be timely and relevant, be accessible, be prepared, be reliable, and be consistent.

   a. Timeliness = Relevance. This makes a difference in whether you get your message printed or broadcast.

   b. Accessibility. If a story breaks, be available to comment. This is a great opportunity to get into the press and also helps to establish your relationship with the press.

   c. Preparedness. Never succumb to pressure to respond. Be prepared before you respond. Tell the reporter that you will call right back so that you can gather your thoughts and decide on your comment.

    d. Reliability. Be accurate in your facts and statistics.

    e. Literacy (related to reliability). Correct grammar, sentence structure, and punctuation in writing and body language while speaking create your credibility.

    f. Consistency. Sending out news releases or PSAs regularly is impressive and earns you respect and credibility.

16. Don't be afraid to ask for corrections when you are misquoted or your statements are taken out of context.

17. Follow up with the reporter. Send a thank-you note for good coverage, and take the opportunity to confirm your contact information for future stories. This is about maintaining and supporting your working relationship. A little effort can keep the relationship strong for years to come.

(Guidelines adapted with permission from CA NOW's *Public Relations/ Media Guidelines for NOW Chapters,* April 1999; updated for second edition.)

NOTES

PREFACE

1 There were three key grape boycotts in the history of the UFW, the first beginning in 1967. The boycott that I joined in 1987 was a part of the third boycott, which began in 1984 and continued until 2000, seven years after Chavez's death. Chavez's intention through this boycott was to call attention to the use of dangerous pesticides—a concern that continues today.

2 According to the National Center for Farmworkers' Health, farm workers seldom have access to disability compensation, occupational rehabilitation, or workers' compensation and are seldom able to prove claims for Social Security despite a lifetime of work. Additionally, the Environmental Protection Agency estimates that 300,000 farm workers are poisoned by pesticides every year (www.ncfh.org).

THE "F-WORD": AN INTRODUCTION

1 Title IX is the 1972 federal law that prohibits gender discrimination in education. Title IX states: "no person in the United States shall, on the basis of sex, be excluded from participation in, be denied the benefits of, or be subjected to discrimination under any educational program or activity receiving federal financial assistance."

2 Discrimination and oppression based upon physical ability.

3 Discrimination and oppression based upon body size.

4 Rosen, 2000, p. 160.

5 Ibid.

6 Rape, Abuse, Incest National Network, www.rainn.org, accessed March 8, 2018.

7 Center for Disease Control, *National Data on Intimate Partner Violence, Sexual Violence, and Stalking*, 2014.

8 U.S. EEOC, 2015.

9 Hill and Kearl, 2011.

10 Center for American Women and Politics, 2019.

11 Catalyst, "Statistical Overview of Women in the Workplace," 2016.

12 IWPR, 2015.

13 National Women's Law Center, "The Wage Gap: the Who, How, Why, and What to Do," 2018.

14 Ibid.

15 Guttmacher Institute, 2006; Gold et al., 1990.

16 NARAL, "Talking Points About Freedom of Choice: 10 Important Facts About Abortion," March 26, 2002 (citing Warren M. Hern, *Abortion Practices* [Philadelphia: Lippincott, 1984], pp. 23–24).

CHAPTER 1. FIGHT LIKE A GIRL

1 Count taken by march organizers.
2 The Steps to Taking Action are in large part taken from California NOW's *Action for Justice: Making a Difference for Women and Girls Activist Training Manual,* 2003.
3 American Press Institute, March 17, 2014.
4 Theresa Vargas, "Two radio stations refuse to air Oneida Nation ads on Redskins name," *Washington Post,* October 18, 2013.

CHAPTER 2. CATCH A WAVE

1 Freedman, 2002.
2 Rosen, 2000; Schlafly, 1972.
3 Hernández and Leong, 2004.
4 Chesler, 1997, p. 43.
5 Just to share a few of these realities: globally, at least one in three women and girls has been beaten or sexually abused in her lifetime (World Health Organization, 2018); at least 200 million women and girls are victims of female circumcision or other forms of genital mutilation (UNICEF, 2016); more than 700 million girls were forcibly married before the age of eighteen (UNICEF, 2014); honor killings take the lives of thousands of young women every year, mainly in North Africa, western Asia, and parts of South Asia (UNFPA, 2000); In the European Union, 18 percent of women experience stalking by the time they are fifteen years old (European Union Agency for Fundamental Rights, 2014).
6 Fraser, 2001, p. 57.
7 Ibid.
8 Dauer, 2001, pp. 65–66.
9 For more up-to-date information on CEDAW, visit the United Nations Human Rights Office of the High Commissioner, https://www.ohchr.org/EN/HRBodies/CEDAW/Pages/CEDAWIndex.aspx.
10 Ashiah Scharaga, "Practicing Feminism: Sacramento area students rally for social change," *Sacramento Bee,* August 29, 2015.

CHAPTER 3. A MOVEMENT FOR EVERYONE

1 Findlen, 2001, p. 71.
2 hooks, 2000, p. 55.
3 McIntosh, 1988, p. 1.
4 Kivel, 2002; Kivel, "The Benefit of Being White" exercise, http://paulkivel.com/resource/the-benefit-of-being-white/, accessed December 12, 2018.

5   Kivel, 2002, pp. 97–98.
6   McIntosh, 1988, p.1.
7   Malcolm X, 1964.
8   Rousso, 2002.
9   Bureau of Labor Statistics, U.S. Department of Labor, December 2017.
10 Jan and Stoddard, 1999.
11 NWLC, September 2017.
12 Vaid, 1999, p. 88.
13 Severson, 1998, p. 12–13.
14 Bornstein, 1998, p. 31.
15 More information on NOMAS is available at www.nomas.org.

CHAPTER 4. AT THE TABLE

1   Hymowitz and Weissman, 1987, p. 36.
2   I have heard Nancy Pelosi in person recount this experience, which gave me
    chills. This quotation is from "Nancy Pelosi's Aha! Moment," an article she wrote
    for *O, The Oprah Magazine* in April 2004.
3   Center for American Women and Politics, "Women in Elective Office 2019 Fact
    Sheet," 2019; Center for American Women and Politics, "Women of Color in
    Elective Office 2019 Factsheet," 2019.
4   Ibid.
5   Ibid.
6   U.S. Census Bureau, 2017.
7   UN-Women, "Facts and Figures: Leadership and Political Participation," citing
    Single House or Lower House Inter-Parliamentary Union, "Women in national
    parliaments, as of 1 June 2017."
8   Portions of this section are part of CA NOW's *21st Century Women in the Workplace
    Taskforce Report* (2003), written by Rachel Allen, Helen Grieco, and myself.
9   Girls Incorporated, 1992.
10 Gould, 2015.
11 Bureau of Labor Statistics, *Labor Force Statistics from the Current Population
    Survey, Household Data Annual Averages, 11. Employed persons by detailed
    occupation, sex, race, and Hispanic or Latino ethnicity,* 2017.
12 Bureau of Labor Statistics, *Occupational Employement and Wages,* 2016.
13 Bureau of Labor Statistics, *Occupational Outlook Handbook,* 2016.
14 Warner and Corley, 2017; Catalyst, "Women in S&P 500 Companies."
15 Warner and Corley, 2017; Catalyst, "Women in S&P 500 Companies by Race/
    Ethnicity."
16 Johns, 2013.
17 Meyerson and Fletcher, 2000, pp. 126–36.
18 Ibid.
19 Ibid.

20 Lauzen, 2017.

21 Lauzen, 2018.

22 Ibid.

23 Ibid.

24 Baumgardner and Richards, 2000, p. 99.

25 Masci, 2014.

26 Additional information on this organization is available at www.we-are-church.org.

27 American Association of University Women (AAUW), 2017.

28 Title IX does not usually extend to military or religious schools, fraternities or sororities.

29 For more information on these cases or on Title IX, visit www.aauw.org.

30 AAUW, 2011b.

31 AAUW Public Policy and Government Relations Department, January 2001; California Women's Law Center Policy Brief, 2000; Women's Sports Foundation, 1998; Zimmerman and Reavill, 1998; Page et al., 1998; Sabo and Oglesby, 1995.

32 Lopiano, 2001.

33 National Coalition for Women and Girls in Education, "Title IX at 45 Report," 2017.

34 NWLC, 2001.

35 National Coalition for Women and Girls in Education, "Title IX at 45 Report," 2017.

36 Ibid.

37 Women's Sports Foundation, 2017.

38 Ibid.

39 Murray, 2002; National Coalition for Women and Girls in Education, "Title IX at 45 Report," 2017.

40 National Coalition for Women and Girls in Education, "Title IX at 45 Report," 2017.

41 Women's Sports Foundation, 2015.

42 Ibid.

43 AAUW, 2011a.

44 AAUW, 2015.

45 National Science Foundation, 2016.

46 National Center for Education Statistics, IPEDS Data Center, 2016.

47 Ibid.

48 Edin and Shaefer, 2015, p. 167.

49 Jaffe, 2016, p. 194.

CHAPTER 5. GOOD ENOUGH

1 Chernik, 2001.

2 Clance, 1985.

3 ANRED, 2004; Thompson, 1998; NEDA, 2013.

4 Adams, 2000.

5 Steele, 2001, p. 152.

6 Ibid., p. 143.

7 Bordo, 1993, p. 164.

8 Honey, 1984, p. 113.

9 Ibid., p. 119.

10 Strodder, 2000, p. 55.

11 Bordo, 1993, p. 102.

12 Haubegger, 1994, p. 48.

13 Stelter, 2011.

14 Koblin, 2016.

15 Ibid.

16 Ibid.

17 Kilbourne, 2010.

18 Ibid.

19 Klein, 2002.

20 Ibid., p. 30.

21 NEDA, 2002; Smolak, 1996.

22 LaRosa, 2017.

23 Hales et al., 2017, p. 1.

24 Research conducted by Ann Kearney-Cooke, physician-scholar with the Partnership for Women's Health at Columbia University and funded by *Seventeen* magazine and Procter & Gamble; Hunker, 2000.

25 Roni Caryn Rabin, "More teenage girls seeking genital cosmetic surgery," *New York Times*, April 25, 2016.

26 J. L. Bercaw-Pratt, X. M. Santos, J. Sanchez, L. Ayensu-Coker, D. R. Nebgen, and J. E. Dietrich, "The incidence, attitudes and practices of the removal of pubic hair as a body modification," *Journal of Pediatric and Adolescent Gynecology*, Vol. 25, No. 1 (2012).

27 Ibid.

28 American Society of Plastic Surgeons, 2017.

29 Ibid.

30 American Society for Metabolic and Bariatric Surgery, "Estimate of Bariatric Surgery Numbers, 2011–2015."

31 American Society for Metabolic and Bariatric Surgery, "Studies Weigh in on Safety and Effectiveness of Newer Bariatric and Metabolic Surgery Procedure," June 2012.

32 Bonnie Ward, "Why do obese men get bariatric surgery far less than women?," *UC San Diego Health System Newsroom*, April 29, 2015.

33 Taren et al., 2001.

34 Bureau of Transportation Statistics, "National Household Travel Survey, 2001–2002," accessed October 19, 2016.

35 Society for Health and Physical Educators, formerly National Association for Sport and Physical Education (NASPE), "2016 Shape of the Nation," 2016.

36 Coleman-Jensen et al., 2018, p. 1.

37 USDA, 2009.

38 NAAFA, "Weight discrimination laws," 2016.

39 Ibid.

40 NAAFA, "Making a case for legislation to end size discrimination."

41 Ibid.

42 Ibid.

43 Baker, 2014.

44 Wolpert, 2007; Ferdman, 2015; Fain, 2016.

45 Wolpert, 2007.

46 Taylor, 2018, p. 116.

47 Feminist Majority, "Feminist Against Sweatshops," 2014.

48 Davis, 2015; Stark and Whisnant, 2004.

49 Coalition to Abolish Slavery and Trafficking, accessed 11/22/2016; Clarren, 2006.

50 Greenhouse, 1999; Carlsen, 1999; Miller, 1999; Clarren, 2006.

51 Clarren, 2006.

52 Feminist Majority, "Feminist Against Sweatshops," 2014.

53 iSeal, "A Shared Approach to Living Wage: A Joint Statement," accessed November 22, 2016. For more information, visit www.isealalliance.org.

54 Ibid.

55 Carey Nadeau, "New Data: Calculating the Living Wage for U.S. States, Counties and Metro Areas," *Living Wage Calculator*, August 19, 2016, accessed October 24, 2016.

56 Ibid.

57 Global Exchange, "Sweatfree FAQs," accessed October 26, 2016. For more information, visit https://globalexchange.org/.

58 National Labor Committee (reports), "Disney's Children's Books Made with Blood, Sweat and Tears of Young Workers in China," August 18, 2005; "Chi Fung Factory, Apopa, El Salvador: Nike, NBA, Jordan, Adidas, Wal-Mart, VF Corporation," 2005; "Update: Maternity Leave in Bangladesh," January 13, 2005.

59 Charles Davis, "California's Garment Workers Reveal: Sweatshops Aren't Just a Problem Overseas," *Take Part*, September 10, 2015, accessed October 25, 2016.

60 *The Seattle Syndrome*, directed by Steve Bradshaw, 2000.

61 Ibid.

62 Ibid.

63 Kristina Bravo, "These Big-Name Fashion Brands Just Agreed to Pay Their Workers More," *Take Part*, September 21, 2014, accessed October 24, 2016.

64 Fraser, 1997, p. 283.

CHAPTER 6. KNOCK 'EM UP . . . KNOCK 'EM DOWN

1 Most women with a tipped uterus don't experience any problems. Some women, however, experience pain during sexual intercourse or menstruation.

2 Whiteman, 2015.

3 Whiteman, 2015; Black, 2005; Cloutier-Steele, 2003; West and Dranov, 2002.

4 Westervelt, 2015; Johnson et al., 2014; Schiebinger, 2003; Carnes, 1999.

5 For more information about the Feminist Women's Health Centers, visit www. fwhc.org and www.womenshealthspecialists.org, or read *A New View of a Woman's Body* (Feminist Health Press, 1991) and *A Woman's Book of Choices* (Chalker and Downer, 1992).

6 Martin, 1992, p. 93.

7 Ibid., p. 84.

8 Guttmacher Institute, *Sex and HIV Education: State Laws and Policies*, 2017.

9 Guttmacher Institute, *American Teens' Sources of Sexual Health Education, Factsheet*, 2016.

10 Guttmacher Institute, *Sex and HIV Education: State Laws and Policies*, 2017.

11 Guttmacher Institute, *Sex Education: Needs, Programs and Policies*, 2003; Kaiser Family Foundation, 2000; Kirby, 1999.

12 Guttmacher Institute, *Sex Education: Needs, Programs and Policies*, 2003.

13 Ibid., p. 13; Darroch et al., 2001.

14 Guttmacher Institute, *Sex Education: Needs, Programs and Policies*, 2003, p. 14; Darroch et al., 2001; Boonstra, 2002, pp. 7–10.

15 Jones and Jerman, 2016.

16 Women's Health Specialists: A Feminist Women's Health Center, at www. womenshealthspecialists.org, and the Federation of Feminist Women's Health Centers, at www.fwhc.org.

17 Guttmacher Institute, 2018, p. 1; Guttmacher Institute, *Facts in Brief: Sexuality Education*, 2002; Finer et al., 2005.

18 Gentilviso, 2012.

19 Guttmacher, 2018, p. 1; Finer, 2016.

20 National Abortion Federation, *Women Who Have Abortions Fact Sheet*, 2003; Guttmacher Institute, *Facts in Brief: Sexuality Education*, 2002.

21 Guttmacher, 2018, p. 1; Jones, 2018; Jones et al., 2012.

22 NARAL Pro-Choice America, "Talking Points About Freedom of Choice: 10 Important Facts About Abortion," March 26, 2002 (citing Warren M. Hern, *Abortion Practice* [Philadelphia: Lippincott, 1984], pp. 23–24).

23 National Abortion Federation, *Safety of Abortion*.

24 Ibid.

25 World Health Organization, 2016.

26 Guttmacher Institute, *Facts in Brief: Sexuality Education*, 2002.

27 Guttmacher Institute, 2018; Jones, 2016.

28 Ibid.

29 NARAL Pro-Choice America, 2017; Donohoe, 2007; National Abortion Federation, 1996, 2003.

30 Breyer, 2018.

31 Becerra, 2017.

32 Luker, 1984, pp. 12–13.

33 Barker-Benfield, 2000.

34 Ehrenreich and English, 1970.

35 Ibid., p. 21.

36 Barker-Benfield, 2000, p. 61.

37 Luker, 1984, p. 15.

38 Ibid., pp. 14–15.

39 Ross and Solinger, 2017, p. 23.

40 Luker, p. 15.

41 Ibid.

42 Ibid., pp. 15–16.

43 Miller, 1993, p. 63.

44 Ibid., pp. 12–13.

45 National Abortion Federation, *Bans on Specific Abortion Methods Used After the First Trimester, State Laws and Policies*, 2017.

46 Guttmacher Institute, *An Overview of Abortion Laws, State Laws and Policies*, 2017.

47 National Abortion Federation, *NAF Violence and Disruption Statistics*, 2016.

48 Kann, 2017.

49 Roberts, 1997, pp. 90–91.

50 Ibid., p. 95.

51 Ibid., p. 96.

52 SisterSong, "What is Reproductive Justice?"

53 Ibid.

54 Ross and Solinger, 2017, p. 74.

55 Kaiser Family Foundation, 2016.

CHAPTER 7. FIGHTING BACK

1 "High School Girls Pummel Man Who Exposed Himself," Reuters, October 31, 2003.

 2 NCADV, 2015.

 3 Centers for Disease Control (CDC), The National Intimate Partner and Sexual Violence Survey *Facts Everyone Know about Intimate Partner Violence, Sexual Violence, and Stalking*, 2014.

 4 Centers for Disease Control (CDC), National Center for Injury Prevention and Control, *Division of Violence Prevention: Sexual Violence Facts at a Glance*, 2012.

5   Centers for Disease Control (CDC), *National Data on Intimate Partner Violence, Sexual Violence, and Stalking*, 2011.

6   Alanna Vagianos, "1 in 3 Women Has Been Sexually Harassed At Work, According to Study," *Huffington Post*, February 19, 2015.

7   Hill and Kearl, 2011.

8   Centers for Disease Control (CDC), *Intimate Partner Violence: Factsheet*, 2004; Tjaden and Thoennes, 2000a; Centers for Disease Control (CDC), *National Data on Intimate Partner Violence, Sexual Violence, and Stalking*, 2011.

9   Centers for Disease Control (CDC), *National Data on Intimate Partner Violence, Sexual Violence, and Stalking*, 2011, 2011.

10 Centers for Disease Control (CDC), The National Intimate Partner and Sexual Violence Survey, *Facts Everyone Know about Intimate Partner Violence, Sexual Violence, and Stalking*, 2014; National Coalition of Anti-Violence Programs (NCAVP), 2016, p. 14.

11 The types of intimate partner violence are widely published and are available from a number of domestic violence centers that provide resource information and from state-based alliances.

12 I was first introduced to this chart through a presentation from a domestic violence–prevention educator at Women Escaping a Violent Environment (WEAVE) in Sacramento, California.

13 Black et al., 2011.

14 Centers for Disease Control (CDC), The National Intimate Partner and Sexual Violence Survey, *Facts Everyone Know about Intimate Partner Violence, Sexual Violence, and Stalking*, 2014.

15 Truman and Morgan, 2014.

16 Gazmararian et al., 2000; ACOG, 2012.

17 Cooper and Smith, 2011.

18 NCADV, 2015.

19 Ibid.

20 NCIPC, "Dating Violence Fact Sheet."

21 2016 UNODC TIP Report; Equality NOW, accessed March 12, 2018.

22 NCMEC, 2017.

23 Clawson et al., 2009.

24 Sinozich and Langton, 2014.

25 Tjaden and Thoennes, 2000; Sinozich and Langton, 2014.

26 National Advisory Council on Violence Against Women, 2001; NIJ, 2010.

27 U.S. Code 920.

28 Sanday, 1990, p. 9.

29 Ibid., p. 13.

30 Ibid., p. 4.

31 Porter, 2010.

32 Freedman, 2002, pp. 279–280.

33 Bergen, 1999, and Imbornoni, "Timeline of Key Events in the American Women's Rights Movement," available at www.infoplease.com/spot/womenstimeline1 .html#1961.

34 Tanenbaum, 2000, p. 7.

35 Ibid., p. 9.

36 Department of Justice, Office of Justice Programs, Bureau of Justice Statistics, *National Crime Victimization Survey, 2010–2014*, 2015.

37 *New York Times* magazine, "Rape Hype," June 13, 1993.

38 Sut Jhally, *Date Rape Backlash*, 1994 (videocassette).

39 Stableford, 2013; Wemple, 2013.

40 Ben Armbruster, "Fox Pundit Says Women in the Military Should 'Expect' to be Raped," *Think Progress*, February 13, 2012, accessed December 15, 2016.

41 Doyle Murphy, "'Boys will be boys,' Montana prosecutor tells 5-year-old rape victim's mom: report," *New York Daily News*, February 16, 2014, accessed December 15, 2016.

42 Aaron Blake, "Todd Akin, GOP Senate candidate: 'Legitimate rape' rarely causes pregnancy," *Washington Post*, August 19, 2012, accessed December 15, 2016.

43 Ashley Fantz, "Outrage over 6-month sentence for Brock Turner in Stanford rape case," *CNN*, June 7, 2016, accessed December 15, 2016.

44 *New York Times*, "Transcript: Donald Trump's Taped Comments About Women," October 8, 2016.

45 National Alliance to End Sexual Violence, *2013 Rape Crisis Center Survey*.

46 Bekiempis, 2015.

47 Ibid.

48 For more information about Jackson Katz and his work, visit his website at www. jacksonkatz.com.

49 Katz and Earp, 2013, available at http://www.mediaed.org/.

50 One of the most offensive video games designed for a male audience; a player (depicted as a male) can have sex with a prostitute (shown by a bouncing car) to restore his health. While paying the prostitute decreases the player's funds, he can beat her to death and get his money back. Supposedly restricted to players seventeen years and older, the game is frequently available to younger players who are often well aware of its premise. To take action, contact Rockstar Games and its owner, Take-Two Interactive Software, Inc., as well as the maker of PlayStation 2, Sony Computer Entertainment, Inc.

51 Katz and Earp, 1999b, p. 23.

52 For more information, visit www.whiteribbon.ca/about_us.

53 Black et al., 2011.

54 Porter, 2010.

55 National Women's Law Center, "Sexual Harassment in the Workplace," Factsheet, November 2016.

56 Ibid.
57 Ibid.
58 Ibid.
59 Berman, 2013.
60 Ibid.
61 Baksh, 2016.
62 Ibid.
63 AAUW, 2011.
64 Ibid.
65 UNICEF, "Female Genital Mutilation/Cutting: A global concern," 2016. See more at http://www.unwomen.org/en/what-we-do/ending-violence-against-women/facts-and-figures#notes.
66 Hvistendahl, 2011; UNFPA, 2016.
67 Guilmoto, 2012.
68 UNICEF, "Ending Child Marriage: Progress and Prospects," 2014, pp. 2, 4. See more at http://www.unwomen.org/en/what-we-do/ending-violence-against-women/facts-and-figures#notes.
69 United Nations General Assembly, A/HRC/23/47/Add.1, "Report of the Special Rapporteur on extrajudicial, summary or arbitrary executions," Christof Heyns, Mission to India, April 26, 2013.
70 Amnesty International, 2011.
71 *BBC News*, "Pakistan honour killings on the rise, report reveals," April 1, 2016.
72 United Nations, Secretary-General annual report, 2013; 2012; United Nations, 1996.
73 United Nations Economic and Social Council, Commission on Human Rights, E/CN.4/1996/68, "Question of the violation of human rights and fundamental freedoms in any part of the world, with particular reference to colonial and other dependent territories: Report on the situation of human rights in Rwanda submitted by Mr. René Degni-Ségui, Special Rapporteur of the Commission on Human Rights, under paragraph 20 of resolution S-3/1 of 25 May 1994," January 29, 1996.
74 European Union Agency for Fundamental Rights, *Violence against women: an EU-wide survey, Annex 3*, 2014, p. 184–188. See more at: http://www.unwomen.org/en/what-we-do/ending-violence-against-women/facts-and-figures#notes.
75 UNODC, *Global Report on Trafficking in Persons*, 2014, p. 5, 11. See more at: http://www.unwomen.org/en/what-we-do/ending-violence-against-women/facts-and-figures#notes.
76 International Labour Organization (ILO), 2017. Accessed on December 13, 2018.
77 United Nations, 2000.
78 Lederer, in Mankiller et al., *The Reader's Companion to U.S. Women's History*, 1998.
79 For additional information, visit www.clotheslineproject.org.
80 NCAVP, 2013.

CHAPTER 8. LEADING THE WAY

1 Labaton and Lundy Martin, 2004, p. 289.

2 Chesler, 1997, p. 45.

3 Byrd et al., 2011, p. 219.

4 Olson, 2001. For more of Alix's poetry, visit www.alixolson.com.

BIBLIOGRAPHY

Adams, Jane Meredith. "Mommy, Am I Fat?" WebMD Feature, June 12, 2000. www.wemd.com/content/article/1111739_50367#.

Agosín, Marjorie, ed. *Women, Gender and Human Rights: A Global Perspective.* New Brunswick, NJ: Rutgers University Press, 2001.

American Association of University Women (AAUW). *Crossing the Line: Sexual Harassment at School.* AAUW, 2011a.

American Association of University Women (AAUW). *Separated by Sex: Title IX and Single-Sex Education.* AAUW Public Policy and Government Relations Department, October 2011b.

American Association of University Women (AAUW). *Affirmative Action.* AAUW, 2006.

American Association of University Women (AAUW). *Solving the Equation: The Variables for Women's Success in Engineering and Computing.* AAUW, 2015.

American Association of University Women (AAUW). *Quick Facts: Title IX.* June 2017.

American College of Obstetricians and Gynecologists (ACOG), Committee of Health Care for Underserved Women. "Committee Opinion: Intimate Partner Violence, Number 518." ACOG: February 2012.

American Press Institute. "How Americans Get Their News." March 17, 2014.

American Society of Plastic Surgeons. "2003 gender distribution cosmetic procedures." American Society of Plastic Surgeons, Department of Public Relations, media@plasticsurgery.org or www.plasticsurgery.org.

American Society of Plastic Surgeons. "Gastric bypass surgery popularity leads to jump in plastic surgery procedures, according to ASPS statistics." ASPS Press Release, March 10, 2004.

American Society of Plastic Surgeons. "People choosing cosmetic plastic surgery triples since 1992" (electronic version). PR Newswire, April 19, 2002. http://findarticles.com/cf_0/m4PRN/2002_April_19/85897203/.

American Society of Plastic Surgeons. "2017 Cosmetic Surgery Gender Distribution." American Society of Plastic Surgeons, Department of Public Relations, 2017. www.plasticsurgery.org.

Amnesty International. *Annual Report: Mexico 2011.* Amnesty International, 2011.

Annenberg Public Policy Center. "The glass ceiling persists: 3rd annual APPC report on women leaders in communications companies." Annenberg Public Policy Center, Washington, DC, December 19, 2003.

Anorexia Nervosa and Related Eating Disorders (ANRED). "Statistics: How many people have eating disorders?" *ANRED*, January 2004.

Ash, Lucy. "India's dowry death." *BBC News UK Edition*, July 16, 2003.

Associated Press. "CDC overstated risks of being overweight." *MSNBC*, April 19, 2005. http://www.msnbc.msn.com/id/7561422/.

Associated Press. "Gastric bypass coverage dropped by insurer." *CNN*, March 3, 2004. http://www.cnn.com/2004/HEALTH/03/03/gastric.bypass.ap.

Bachman, R., and L. E. Saltzman. "Violence against women: Estimates for the redesigned survey." Bureau of Justice Statistics, Special Report, U.S. Department of Justice, August 1995.

Bacon, Linda. *Body Respect: What Conventional Health Books Get Wrong, Leave Out, and Just Plain Fail to Understand about Weight.* Dallas, TX: BenBella Books, 2014.

Bacon, Linda. *Health At Every Size: The Surprising Truth About Your Weight.* Dallas, TX: BenBella Books, 2010.

Baker, Jes. "6 Things I Understand About the Fat Acceptance Movement." *Huffington Post*, April 24, 2014. Accessed March 5, 2018.

Baksh, Kurina. "Workplace Discrimination: The LGBT Workforce." *Huffington Post*, June 22, 2016.

Barker-Benfield, G. J. *The Horrors of the Half-Known Life: Male Attitudes Toward Women and Sexuality in Nineteenth-Century America.* New York: Routledge, 2000.

Baumgardner, Jennifer, and Amy Richards. *Manifesta: Young Women, Feminism, and the Future.* New York: Farrar, Straus and Giroux, 2000.

Becerra, Xavier. Statement: "Attorney General Becerra Vows to Defend California's Reproductive FACT Act in the United States Supreme Court." November 13, 2017. Accessed March 12, 2018. https://oag.ca.gov/news/press-releases/attorney-general-becerra-vows-defend-california%E2%80%99s-reproductive-fact-act-united.

Bekiempis, Victoria. "When Campus Rapists Don't Think They're Rapists." *Newsweek*, January 9, 2015.

Bergen, Racquel Kennedy. "Marital rape." Applied Research Forum National Electronic Network on Violence Against Women, March 1999.

Berman, Jillian. "Workplace sexual harassment poll finds large share of workers suffer, don't report." *Huffington Post*, August 27, 2013.

Black, Alexis. "Unnecessary surgery exposed! Why 60% of all surgeries are medically unjustified and how surgeons exploit patients to generate profits." *Newstarget*, October 7, 2005.

Black, M. C., K. C. Basile, M. J. Breiding, S. G. Smith, M. L. Walters, M. T. Merrick, J. Chen, and M. R. Stevens. *The National Intimate Partner and Sexual Violence Survey (NISVS): 2010 Summary Report.* Atlanta, GA: National Center for Injury Prevention and Control, Centers for Disease Control and Prevention, 2011.

Boonstra, H. "Teen pregnancy: Trends and lessons learned." *The Guttmacher Report on Public Policy*, Vol. 5, No. 1 (2002).

Bordo, Susan. *Unbearable Weight: Feminism, Western Culture, and the Body*. Berkeley: University of California Press, 1993.

Bornstein, Kate. *My Gender Workbook*. New York: Routledge, 1998.

Bradshaw, Steve (dir.). *The Seattle Syndrome*. Bull Frog Films, 2000.

Breyer, J. "National Institute of Family and Life Advocates, DBA NIFLA, Et Al., Petitioners v. Xavier Becerra, Attorney General of California, Et Al, On Writ of Certiorari to the United States Court of Appeals for the Ninth Circuit." U.S. Supreme Court, June 26, 2018.

Brumberg, Joan Jacobs. *The Body Project: An Intimate History of American Girls*. New York: Random House, 1997.

Bureau of Labor Statistics. *Labor Force Statistics from the Current Population Survey, Household Data Annual Averages, 11. Employed persons by detailed occupation, sex, race, and Hispanic or Latino ethnicity*, 2017.

Bureau of Labor Statistics. *Occupational Employment and Wages*, May 2016.

Bureau of Labor Statistics. *Occupational Outlook Handbook*, 2016.

Bureau of Labor Statistics, U.S. Department of Labor. "Table A-6. Employment status of the civilian population by sex, age, and disability status, not seasonally adjusted," December 2017. Last modified January 5, 2018.

Business Wire. "Diet Drug—Fen-Phen Litigation Settlement." May 13, 1999. http://www.findarticles.com/p/articles/mi_mOEIN/is_1999_may_13/ai_54625436.

Byrd, Rudolph, Johnnetta Betsch Cole, and Beverly Guy-Sheftall. *I Am Your Sister: Collected and Unpublished Writings of Audre Lorde*. Oxford: Oxford University Press, 2011.

California Women's Law Center Policy Brief. "Sex discrimination and athletics." Policy Brief, 2000.

Carlsen, William. "Sweatshop conditions alleged on U.S. island retailers sued for selling 'Made in USA' garments." *San Francisco Chronicle*, January 14, 1999.

Carnes, Molly, M.D. "Health care in the U.S.: Is there evidence for systematic gender bias?" *Wisconsin Medical Journal*, December 1999: 15–19, 25.

Carter, Allie. "1/3 of US women have abortions—87% of US counties have no provider." ACLU, July 19, 2010. Accessed April 21, 2017.

Catalyst. "Statistical Overview of Women in the Workplace," April 6, 2016. http://www.catalyst.org/knowledge/statistical-overview-women-workforce.

Catalyst, "Women in S&P 500 Companies." Accessed February 23, 2018. http://www.catalyst.org/knowledge/women-sp-500-companies.

Catalyst, "Women in S&P 500 Companies by Race/Ethnicity." Accessed February 23, 2018. http://www.catalyst.org/knowledge/women-sp-500-companies-raceethnicity.

CBS SportsLine. "U.S. intercollegiate study: Men make up majority of women's sports coaches," June 12, 1998. http://www.caaws.ca/whas_New/June/coaches_study_Jn13.htm.

Center for American Women and Politics. "Women in elective office 2018 fact sheet." 2018.

Center for American Women and Politics. "Women in the U.S. Congress 2019 Fact Sheet." New Brunswick, NJ: Eagleton Institute of Politics, Rutgers University, 2019.

Center for American Women and Politics. "Women of Color in Elective Office 2006 Fact Sheet." New Brunswick, NJ: Eagleton Institute of Politics, Rutgers University, 2006.

Centers for Disease Control (CDC), The National Intimate Partner and Sexual Violence Survey. *Facts Everyone Should Know about Intimate Partner Violence, Sexual Violence, and Stalking*, 2014.

Chalker, Rebecca, and Carol Downer. *A Woman's Book of Choices: Abortion, Menstrual Extraction, RU-486*. New York: Four Walls, Eight Windows, 1992.

Chernik, Abra Fortune. "The body politic." In Barbara Findlen (ed.), *Listen Up: Voices from the Next Feminist Generation* (pp. 103–111). Seattle: Seal Press, 2001.

Chesler, Phyllis. *Letters to a Young Feminist*. New York: Four Walls, Eight Windows, 1997.

Clance, Pauline Rose. *The Impostor Phenomenon: Overcoming the Fear That Haunts Your Success*. Atlanta, GA: Peachtree, 1985.

Clarren, Rebecca. "Paradise Lost: Greed, Sex Slavery, Forced Abortions and Right-Wing Moralists." *Ms. Magazine*, Spring 2006.

Clawson, Heather J., Nicole Dutch, Amy Solomon, and Lisa Goldblatt Grace. "Human Trafficking Into and Within the United States: A Review of the Literature." Study of HHS Programs Serving Human Trafficking Victims, 2009. Accessed March 12, 2018. http://aspe.hhs.gov/hsp/07/humantrafficking/LitRev/.

Cloutier-Steele, Lise. *Misinformed Consent: Women's Stories About Unnecessary Hysterectomy*. Chester, NJ: Next Decade, 2003.

Coalition to Abolish Slavery and Trafficking. www.castla.org.

Coleman-Jensen, Alisha, Matthew P. Rabbitt, Christian A. Gregory, and Anita Singh. *Household Food Security in the United States in 2017*. United States Department of Agriculture, September 2018.

Cooper, Alexia and Erica Smith, BJS Statisticians. *Homicide Trends in the United States, 1980–2008*. U.S. Department of Justice, Office of Justice Programs, Bureau of Justice Statistics, November 2011.

Croteau, David, and William Hoynes. *Media Society: Industries, Images and Audiences*. Thousand Oaks, CA: Pine Forge Press, 2000.

Curphey, Shauna. "Number of stay-at-home dads rising." *Women's eNews*, July 4, 2003.

Curtis, John W. *Faculty Salary and Faculty Distribution Fact Sheet 2003–04*. Washington, DC: American Association of University Professors, 2003–04.

Dancy, Denise. "Dating violence in adolescence." *National Center for State Courts' Family Violence Forum*, Vol. 2, No. 4 (Winter 2003).

Dao, James. "Legislators push for state action on gay marriage." *New York Times*, February 27, 2004. www.nytimes.com.

Darroch, J. E., D. J. Landry, and S. Singh. "Changing emphasis in sexuality education in U.S. public secondary schools, 1988–1999." *Family Planning Perspectives*, Vol. 32, No. 5 (2000): 204–211, 265.

Darroch, Jacqueline E., Jennifer J. Frost, and Susheela Singh. *Teenage Sexual and Reproductive Behavior in Developed Countries: Can More Progress Be Made?* Occasional Report, New York, Alan Guttmacher Institute, No. 3, 2001.

Dauer, S. "Indivisible or invisible: Women's human rights in the public and private sphere." In M. Agosín (ed.), *Women, Gender and Human Rights: A Global Perspective* (pp. 65–82). New Brunswick, NJ: Rutgers University Press, 2001.

Davis, Charles. "Slavery, Wage Theft, and LA's Global Labor Problem: Activists and organizers expose a thin line between human "trafficking" and other forms of exploitation." *Daily Good*, September 17, 2015.

Department of Justice, Office of Justice Programs, Bureau of Justice Statistics. *National Crime Victimization Survey, 2010–2014*, 2015.

Diamant, A. L., C. Wold, K. Spritzer, and L. Gelberg. "Health behaviors, health status and access to and use of health care: A population-based study of lesbian, bisexual and heterosexual women." *Archives of Family Medicine*, Vol. 9, No. 10 (2000): 1043–1051.

Donohoe, Martin. *Parental Notification and Consent Laws for Teen Abortions: Overview and 2006 Ballot Measures.* MEDSCAPE Ob/Gyn & Women's Health, February 9, 2007.

Drogin, Richard. "Statistical analysis of gender patterns in Wal-Mart workforce." Prepared for expert testimony on behalf of Drogin, Kakigi and Associates. Berkeley, CA: February 2003.

Edin, Kathryn, and H. Luke Shaefer. *$2.00 A Day: Living on Almost Nothing in America.* New York: First Mariner Books, 2015.

Ehrenreich, Barbara. *Nickel and Dimed: On (Not) Getting By in America.* New York: Metropolitan Books, 2001.

Ehrenreich, Barbara, and Deirdre English. *Witches, Midwives and Nurses: A History of Women Healers.* New York: Feminist Press, 1970.

European Union Agency for Fundamental Rights. *Violence Against Women: An EU-Wide Survey.* European Union Agency for Fundamental Rights, 2014.

Fain, Jean. "A Neuroscientist Tackles 'Why Diets Make Us Fat.'" *NPR*, June 7, 2016. Accessed March 5, 2018.

Feminist Majority. "Feminist Against Sweatshops." 2014.

Ferdman, Roberto A. "Why diets don't actually work, according to a researcher who has studied them for decades." *Washington Post*, May 4, 2015. Accessed March 5, 2018.

Findlen, Barbara, ed. *Listen Up: Voices from the Next Feminist Generation.* Seattle: Seal Press, 2001.

Finer, L. B., et al. "Reasons U.S. women have abortions: quantitative and qualitative perspectives." *Perspectives on Sexual and Reproductive Health*, Vol. 37, No. 3 (2005): 110–118.

Finer L.B. and Zolna MR, "Declines in unintended pregnancy in the United States, 2008–2011." *New England Journal of Medicine*, 2016, 374(9):843–852, doi:10.1056/NEJMsa1506575.

Foshee, V. A., G. F. Linder, K. E. Bauman, S. A. Langwick, X. B. Arriaga, J. L. Heath, P. M. McMahon, and S. Bangdiwala. "The safe dates project: Theoretical basis, evaluation design, and selected baseline findings." Youth Violence Prevention: Description and baseline data from 13 evaluation projects (K. Powell, D. Hawkins, eds.), *American Journal of Preventive Medicine*, Supplement, Vol. 12, No. 5 (1996): 39–47. Cited at www.cdc.gov/ncipc/factsheets/datviol.htm.

Fraser, Arvonne S. "Becoming human: The origins and development of women's human rights." In Marjorie Agosín (ed.), *Women, Gender, and Human Rights: A Global Perspective* (pp. 16–64). New Brunswick, NJ: Rutgers University Press, 2001.

Fraser, Laura. *Losing It: American's Obsession with Weight and the Industry That Feeds on It.* New York: Dutton, 1997.

Freedman, Estelle. *No Turning Back: The History of Feminism and the Future of Women.* New York: Ballantine, 2002.

Garland-Thomson, Rosemarie. "Re-shaping, re-thinking, re-defining: Feminist disability studies." Barbara Waxman Fiduccia Papers on Women and Girls with Disabilities. Washington, DC: Center for Women Policy Studies, 2001.

Gazmararian, J. A., R. Petersen, A. M. Spitz, M. M. Goodwin, L. E. Saltzman, and J. S. Marks. "Violence and reproductive health; current knowledge and future research directions." *Maternal and Child Health Journal*, Vol. 4, No. 2 (2000): 79–84. Cited at www.cdc.gov/ncipc/factsheets/ipvfacts.htm.

Gentilviso, Chris. "Todd Akin on Abortion: 'Legitimate Rape' Victims Have 'Ways to Try to Shut That Whole Thing Down.'" *Huffington Post*, August 18, 2012.

Girls Incorporated. *Past the Pink and Blue Predicament: Freeing the Next Generation from Sex Stereotypes.* Indianapolis: Girls Incorporated National Resources Center, 1992.

Gold, Rachel Benson. "Implications for Family Planning of Post-Welfare Reform Insurance Trends." *The Guttmacher Report on Public Policy.* New York and Washington, DC: The Alan Guttmacher Institute, December 1999.

Gold, R. B., S. K. Henshaw, and L. D. Lindberg. *Abortion and Women's Health: A Turning Point for America?* New York: Alan Guttmacher Institute, 1990.

Gould, Elise. "Child care workers aren't paid enough to make ends meet." Economic Policy Institute, November 5, 2015.

Gray, H. M., and V. Foshee. "Adolescent dating violence: Differences between one-sided and mutually violent profiles." *Journal of Interpersonal Violence*, Vol. 12, No. 1 (1997): 126–141. Cited at www.cdc.gov/ncipc/factsheets/datviol.htm.

Greenfield, Lawrence A. "Sex offenses and offenders: An analysis of data on rape and sexual assault." Bureau of Justice Statistics, Office of Justice Programs, U.S. Department of Justice, Washington, DC, 1997.

Greenhouse, Steven. "18 major retailers and apparel makers are accused of using sweatshops." *New York Times*, January 14, 1999.

Guilmoto, Christophe. *Sex Imbalances at Birth: Current trends, consequences and policy implications.* UNFPA Asia and Pacific Regional Office, 2012.

Guttmacher Institute. *American Teens' Sources of Sexual Health Education, Factsheet.* April 2016. Accessed April 9, 2017.

Guttmacher Institute. *An Overview of Abortion Laws, State Laws and Policies.* April 15, 2017. Accessed April 25, 2017.

Guttmacher Institute. Factsheet: Induced Abortion in the United States. New York: Guttmacher Institute, January 2018.

Guttmacher Institute. *Facts in Brief: Facts on Induced Abortion in the United States.* New York and Washington, DC: Guttmacher Institute, May 4, 2006.

Guttmacher Institute. *Facts in Brief: Sexuality Education.* AGI: New York and Washington, DC, 2002.

Guttmacher Institute. *Induced Abortion in the United States, Factsheet.* January 2017.

Guttmacher Institute. *Sex and HIV Education: State Laws and Policies.* April 1, 2017. Accessed April 9, 2017.

Guttmacher Institute. *Sex Education: Needs, Programs and Policies.* New York and Washington, DC: Guttmacher Institute, September 2003.

Hales, C. M., M. D. Carroll, C. D. Fryar, and C. L. Ogden. "Prevalence of Obesity among Adults and Youth: United States, 2015–2016." NCHS Data Brief, No. 288. Hyattsville, MD: National Center for Health Statistics, 2017.

Haubegger, Christy. "I'm not fat, I'm Latina." *Essence,* Vol. 25, No. 8 (December 1994).

Heery, William J. "Corporate mentoring: Shattering the glass ceiling." *Harrington Group Newsletter,* Vol. 3, Issue 7 (August 9, 2002).

Herman, Edward, and Noam Chomsky. *Manufacturing Consent: The Political Economy of the Mass Media.* New York: Pantheon Books, 2002.

Hernández, Daisy, and Pandora L. Leong. "Feminism's future young feminists of color take the mic." *In These Times,* April 21, 2004.

Hesse-Biber, Sharlene. *Am I Thin Enough Yet?: The Cult of Thinness and the Commercialization of Identity.* New York: Oxford University Press, 1996.

Hewlitt, Sylvia Ann. *Creating a Life: Professional Women and the Quest for Children.* New York: Talk Miramax Books, 2002.

Hill, Catherine, PhD., and Holly Kearl, MA. *Crossing the Line: Sexual Harassment at School.* American Association of University Women, 2011.

Honey, Maureen. *Creating Rosie the Riveter: Class, Gender, and Propaganda during World War II.* Amherst: University of Massachusetts Press, 1984.

hooks, bell. *Feminism Is for Everybody: Passionate Politics.* Cambridge, MA: South End Press, 2000.

Hunker, Paula Gray. "Pressure to Be Perfect (Teenagers and Plastic Surgery)." *Insight on the News,* March 13, 2000.

Hvistendahl, M. *Unnatural Selection: Choosing Boys over Girls, and the Consequences of a World Full of Men.* New York: Public Affairs Publishing, 2011.

Hymowitz, Carol, and Michaele Weissman. *A History of Women in America.* New York: Bantam Books, 1978.

Imbornoni, Ann-Marie. *Timeline of Key Events in the American Women's Rights Movement*. www.infoplease.com/spot/womenstimeline1.html#1961.

Institute for Women's Policy Research (IWPR). "The union advantage for women," August 2015.

International Labour Organization (ILO). *Global Estimates of Modern Slavery: Forced Labour and Forced Marriage*. Geneva: International Labour Office (ILO), 2017.

International Women's Democracy Center. *Fact Sheet: Women's Political Participation*, 2002.

International Women's Democracy Center. *Women in Politics: A Timeline*, 2002.

Isidore, Chris. "Less pay for more popular play." *CNN Money*, June 23, 2003.

Jaffe, Sarah. *Necessary Trouble: Americans in Revolt*. New York: Nation Books, 2016.

Jan, S., and S. Stoddard. *Chart Book on Women and Disability in the United States. An InfoUse Report*. Washington, DC: U.S. National Institute on Disability and Rehabilitation Research, 1999.

Jhally, Sut. *Date Rape Backlash*. Media Education Foundation, 1994 (videocassette).

Johns, Merida L. "Breaking the glass ceiling: structural, cultural, and organizational barriers preventing women from achieving senior and executive positions." *Perspectives in Health Information Management* Vol. 10, Winter (2013): 1e. https://www.ncbi.nlm.nih.gov/pmc/articles/PMC3544145/

Johnson, Paula, Therese Fitzgerald, Alina Salganicoff, Susan Wood, and Jill Goldstein. *Sex-Specific Medical Research: Why Women's Health Can't Wait*. Brigham and Women's Hospital, 2014.

Jones, R. K., L. Frohwirth, and A. M. Moore. "More than poverty: disruptive events among women having abortions in the USA." *Journal of Family Planning and Reproductive Health Care*, Vol. 39, No. 1 (2012): 36–43.

Jones, Rachel, and Jenna Jerman. *Abortion Incidence and Service Availability in the United States 2014*. Guttmacher Institute, 2016. Accessed April 21, 2017.

Jones, R. K. "Reported contraceptive use in the month of becoming pregnant among U.S. abortion patients in 2000 and 2014." *Contraception* (2018). doi:10.1016/j.contraception.2017.12.018.

Kaiser Family Foundation. *Sex Education in America: A View from Inside the Nation's Classrooms*. Menlo Park: Kaiser Family Foundation, 2000.

Kaiser Family Foundation. *Women's Health Insurance Coverage Fact Sheet*, October 2016.

Kann, Sharon. "Fox's *The Five* Moves to Prime Time, Calls for Anti-Abortion Violence." *Media Matters for America* blog, April 25, 2017. Accessed April 25, 2017.

Katz, Jackson, and Jeremy Earp. *Tough Guise: Violence, Media, and the Crisis in Masculinity*. Media Education Foundation, 1999a.

Katz, Jackson, and Jeremy Earp. *Tough Guise: Violence, Media, and the Crisis in Masculinity Study Guide*. Media Education Foundation, 1999b.

Katz, Jackson, and Jeremy Earp. *Tough Guise 2: Violence, Manhood and American Culture*. Media Education Foundation, 2013.

Kilbourne, Jean. *Killing Us Softly 4: Advertising's Image of Women*. Northampton, MA: Media Education Foundation, 2010.

Killermann, Sam. *The Social Justice Advocate's Handbook: A Guide to Gender*. Austin, TX: Impetus Books, 2013.

Kilpatrick, D. G., C. N. Edmunds, and A. Seymour. "Rape in America: A report to the nation." Arlington, VA: National Victim Center, 1992.

King, Gilbert. *Women, Child—For Sale: The New Slave Trade in the 21st Century*. New York: Penguin, 2004.

Kingsbury, Kathleen. "Few laws help gays in cases of domestic violence." *Columbia News Service*, July 21, 2004.

Kirby, Douglas. "Sexuality and sex education at home and school." *Adolescent Medicine: State of the Art Reviews*, Vol. 10, No. 2 (1999): 195–209.

Kivel, Paul. *Uprooting Racism: How White People Can Work for Racial Justice*. Gabriola Island, BC, Canada: New Society Publishers, 2002.

Kivel, Paul. "The Benefit of Being White" exercise. Accessed December 12, 2018. www.paulkivel.com.

Klein, Naomi. *No Logo*. New York: Picador USA, 2002.

Koblin, John. "How Much Do We Love TV? Let Us Count the Ways." *New York Times*, June 30, 2016.

Labaton, Vivien, and Dawn Lundy Martin (eds.). *The Fire This Time: Young Activists and the New Feminism*. New York: Anchor Books, 2004.

LaRosa, John. "U.S. Weight Loss Market Worth $66 Billion." *Market Data Research*, May 4, 2017. Accessed March 1, 2018.

Lauer, Nancy Cook. "Studies show women's role in media shrinking." *Women's eNews*, May 21, 2002.

Lauzen, Martha M. "It's a Man's (Celluloid) World 2017: Portrayals of Female Characters in the 100 Top Films of 2017." The Center for the Study of Women in Television and Film, San Diego State University, San Diego, CA, 2018.

Lauzen, Martha M. "The Celluloid Ceiling: Behind-the-Scenes Employment of Women on the Top 100, 250, and 500 Films of 2016." The Center for the Study of Women in Television and Film, San Diego State University, San Diego, CA, 2017.

Loder, Asjylyn. "Date rape drugs still available, despite crackdown." *Women's eNews*, January 16, 2004.

Loder, Asjylyn. "Statistics suggest more rape victims speak up." *Women's eNews*, September 4, 2003.

Lopiano, Donna. "Dropping men's sports—the Division I football/basketball arms race is the culprit in the cutting of men's Olympic sports: The Foundation's position." *Women's Sports Foundation*, May 9, 2001.

Luker, Kristen. *Abortion and the Politics of Motherhood*. Berkeley: University of California Press, 1984.

Makespeace, J. M. "Gender differences in courtship violence victimization." *Family Relations*, Vol. 35 (1986): 383–388. Cited at www.cdc.gov/ncipc/factsheets/datviol.htm.

Malcolm X. "Malcolm X's Speech at the Founding Rally of the Organization of Afro-American Unity," 1964. Accessed December 12, 2018. https://blackpast. org/1964-malcolm-x-s-speech-founding-rally-organization-afro-american-unity.

Mankiller, Wilma, Gwendolyn Mink, Marysa Navarro, Barbara Smith, and Gloria Steinem (eds.). *The Reader's Companion to U.S. Women's History*. New York: Houghton Mifflin, 1998.

Marshall, Carolyn. "More than 50 gay couples are married in San Francisco." *New York Times*, February 13, 2004. www.nytimes.com.

Martin, Emily. *The Woman in the Body: A Cultural Analysis of Reproduction*. Boston: Beacon Press, 1992.

Masci, David. "The divide over ordaining women." Pew Research Center, September 9, 2014.

Mathis, Nancy. "Health and environment: Global statistics on women's health are chilling." *Women's eNews*, June 7, 2001.

McIntosh, Peggy. "White Privilege and Male Privilege: A Personal Account of Coming to See Correspondences Through Work in Women's Studies." Working Paper, Wellesley College, 1988.

Meyerson, Debra E., and Joyce K. Fletcher. "A modest manifesto for shattering the glass ceiling." *Harvard Business Review*, Vol. 78, No. 1 (January–February 2000): 126–36.

Miller, Michael. "Major U.S. retailers sued in sweatshop law case." *Los Angeles Times*, January 14, 1999.

Miller, Patricia. *The Worst of Times: Illegal Abortion—Survivors, Practitioners, Coroners, Cops, and Children of Women Who Died Talk About Its Horrors*. New York: Harper Perennial, 1993.

Moore, Michael. *Stupid White Men . . . and Other Sorry Excuses for the State of the Nation*. New York: Regan Books, 2001.

Moskowitz, Daniel B. "The skinny on diet drug settlement." *Business and Health*, October 2000: 23.

Murray, Sarah. "Posting up in the pink ghetto." *Women's Sports Foundation*, April 10, 2002.

NARAL Pro-Choice America. "Mandatory Parental-Involvement Laws Threaten Young Women's Safety," January 1, 2017. Accessed April 28, 2017.

National Abortion Federation. *Bans on Specific Abortion Methods Used After the First Trimester, State Laws and Policies*, April 1, 2017. Accessed April 25, 2017.

National Abortion Federation. *NAF Violence and Disruption Statistics*, 2016.

National Abortion Federation. *Safety of Abortion*. Accessed April 21, 2017.

National Abortion Federation. *Teenage Women, Abortion and the Law Fact Sheet*, 1996, revised 2003.

National Abortion Federation. *Women Who Have Abortions Fact Sheet*, 2003.

National Advisory Council on Violence Against Women. *Toolkit to End Violence Against Women*, November 2001.

National Association for Sport and Physical Education (NASPE). "Shape of the Nation Executive Summary," October 2001.

National Association to Advance Fat Acceptance (NAAFA). "Making a case for legislation to end size discrimination." Accessed March 5, 2018.

National Association to Advance Fat Acceptance (NAAFA). "Weight discrimination laws," 2016. Accessed March 5, 2018.

National Center for Education Statistics, IPEDS Data Center. "Full-Time Instructional Staff, by Faculty and Tenure Status, Academic Rank, Race/Ethnicity, and Gender (Degree-Granting Institutions): Fall 2015," *Fall Staff 2015 Survey*, 2016.

National Center for Injury Prevention and Council (NCIPC). "Dating Violence Fact Sheet." Accessed December 11, 2003. http://www.cdc.gov/ncipc/factsheets/datviol. htm.

National Center for Injury Prevention and Control (NCIPC). "National Data on Intimate Partner Violence, Sexual Violence, and Stalking." Accessed August 17, 2016. http://www.cdc.gov/violenceprevention/pdf/nisvs-fact-sheet-2014.pdf.

National Center for Missing and Exploited Children (NCMEC). *2017 Child Sex Trafficking Report*. Accessed March 12, 2018.

National Coalition for Women and Girls in Education. "Title IX at 45 Report," 2017.

National Coalition of Anti-Violence Programs (NCVAP). *Lesbian, Gay, Bisexual, Transgender, Queer, and HIV-Affected Intimate Partner Violence in 2012*. New York City Gay and Lesbian Anti-Violence Project, Inc., 2013.

National Coalition of Anti-Violence Programs (NCAVP). *Lesbian, Gay, Bisexual, Transgender, Queer, and HIV-Affected Hate Violence in 2016*. New York: Emily Waters, 2016.

National Eating Disorders Association (NEDA). "Statistics: Eating disorders and the precursors." Seattle: 2002.

National Institute of Justice (NIJ). "Report of Sexual Violence Incidents." Washington, DC: Office of Justice Programs, October 2010.

National Science Foundation. *Science and Engineering Indicators*, 2016.

National Women's Law Center (NWLC). "GAO report shows schools added athletic opportunities for women by raising revenue, not cutting men's teams," March 8, 2001 (press release).

National Women's Law Center (NWLC). "Sexual Harassment in the Workplace," Factsheet, November 2016.

National Women's Law Center (NWLC). "Women and Health Insurance." Washington, DC: April 2003.

National Women's Law Center (NWLC). "Workplace Justice: The Wage Gap: The Who, How, Why, and What To Do," Factsheet, October 2018.

NCADV. *Domestic violence national statistics*, 2015. www.ncadv.org.

Olson, Alix. "Warriors." *Built Like That*, 2002 (CD).

Orenstein, Peggy. *Flux: Women on Sex, Work, Love, Kids and Life in a Half-changed World*. New York: Doubleday, 2000.

Page, R. M., J. Hammermeister, A. Scanlan, and L. Gilbert. "Is school sports participation a protective factor against adolescent health risk behavior?" *Journal of Health Education*, Vol. 29, No. 3 (1998): 186–192.

Paulozzi, L. J., L. A. Saltzman, M. J. Thompson, and P. Holmgren. "Surveillance for homicide among intimate partners—United States, 1981–1998." *CDC Surveillance Summaries* Vol. 50 (SS-3) (2001): 1–16. Cited at www.cdc.gov/ncipc/factsheets/ipvfacts.htm.

PBS *Frontline. Merchants of Cool*, 2001 (videocassette).

Penn, Michael, and Rahel Nardos. *Overcoming Violence Against Women and Girls: The International Campaign to Eradicate a Worldwide Problem*. New York: Rowman and Littlefield, 2003.

Pipher, Mary. *Hunger Pains: The Modern Woman's Tragic Quest for Thinness*. New York: Ballantine Books, 1995.

Pipher, Mary. *Reviving Ophelia: Saving the Selves of Adolescent Girls*. New York: Grosset/Putnam Books, 1994.

Porter, Tony. "A Call to Men." Transcript. TED Talks, December 2010.

Reuters. "Obesity in U.S. carries hefty price tag." *MSNBC*, June 27, 2005. http://www.msnbc.msn.com/id/8376790/.

River, F., and J. Erlich. *Community Organizing in a Diverse Society*. Boston: Allyn and Bacon, 1998.

Roberts, Dorothy. *Killing the Black Body: Race, Reproduction and the Meaning of Liberty*. New York: Vintage Books, 1997.

Rosen, Ruth. *The World Split Open: How the Modern Women's Movement Changed America*. New York: Penguin Putnam, 2000.

Ross, Loretta, and Rickie Solinger. *Reproductive Justice: An Introduction*. Berkeley: University of California Press, 2017.

Rousso, Harilyn. "Briefing on girls and young women with disabilities." Center for Women Policy Studies, September 19, 2002.

Rousso, Harilyn. "Strong proud sisters: Girls and young women with disabilities." Center for Women Policy Studies, Barbara Waxman Fiduccia Papers on Women and Girls with Disabilities, 2001.

Ryan, Harriet. "Ending rape kits wait puts price on justice." *CNN*, April 25, 2003. http://www.cnn.com/2003/LAW/04/25/ctv.rape.kit.

Sabo, D., and C. Oglesby. "Ending sexual harassment in sport: A commitment whose time has come." *Women in Sport and Physical Activity Journal*, Vol. 4, No. 2 (1995): 84–104.

Sanday, Peggy Reeves. *Fraternity Gang Rape*. New York: NYU Press, 1990.

Schiebinger, Londa. "Women's health and clinical trials." *Journal of Clinical Investigation*, Vol. 112 (2003): 973–977.

Schlafly, Phyllis. "The right to be a woman." *The Phyllis Schlafly Report* 6 (November 1972).

Schmidt, Charles. "Obesity a weighty issue for children." *Environmental Health Perspectives*, October 2003.

Schmitt, Eric. "Female GIs report rapes, assaults by fellow troops." *San Francisco Chronicle*, February 26, 2004.

Severson, Kristen. "Identity politics and progress: Don't fence me in (or Out)." *Off Our Backs*, Vol. 28, No. 4 (April 1998): 12–13.

Sinozich, Sofi, and Lynn Langton. *Rape and Sexual Assault Victimization Among College-Age Females, 1995–2013*. Department of Justice, December 2014.

SisterSong, "What is Reproductive Justice?" Accessed April 25, 2017. sistersong.net.

Smolak, L. *National Eating Disorders Association/Next Door Neighbors Puppet Guide Book*, 1996.

Stableford, Dylan. "*CNN* criticized for Steubenville verdict coverage." *Yahoo News*, March 18, 2013. Accessed December 15, 2016.

Stark, Christine, and Rebecca Whisnant, eds. *Not for Sale: Feminists Resisting Prostitution and Pornography*. Australia: Spinifex Press, 2004.

Steele, Valerie. *The Corset: A Cultural History*. New Haven: Yale University Press, 2001.

Stelter, Brian. "Ownership of TV Sets Falls in U.S." *New York Times*, May 3, 2011.

Strodder, Chris. *Swingin' Chicks of the 60s*. San Rafael, CA: Cedco, 2000.

Sweatshop Watch. *California Garment Industry: Pyramid of Power and Profit*, 2002.

Sweatshop Watch. *Sweatshop Watch newsletter*, Vol. 7, No. 2 (Summer 2001).

Tanenbaum, Leora. *Slut! Growing up Female with a Bad Reputation*. New York: Perennial, 2000.

Taren, Douglas, Cynthia A. Thomson, Nancy Alexander Koff, Paul R. Gordon, Mary J. Marian, Tamsen L. Bassford, John V. Fulginiti, and Cheryl K. Ritenbaugh. "Effect of an integrated nutrition curriculum on medical education, student clinical performance, and student perception of medical-nutrition training." *American Journal of Clinical Nutrition*, Vol. 73, No. 6 (June 2001): 1107–1112.

Taylor, Sonya Renee. *The Body is not an Apology: The Power of Radical Self-Love*. Oakland, CA: Berrett-Koehler Publishers, 2018.

Thompson, Becky W. "Eating disorders." *The Reader's Companion to U.S. Women's History*. New York: Houghton Mifflin, 1998.

Tjaden P., and N. Thoennes. "Full report of the prevalence, incidence, and consequences of violence against women: findings from the national violence against women survey." Report NCJ 183781. Washington, DC: National Institute of Justice and the Centers for Diseases Control and Prevention, 2000.

Truman, Jennifer, and Rachel Morgan. *Nonfatal Domestic Violence, 2003–2012*. Washington, DC: U.S. Department of Justice, Office of Justice Statistics, Bureau of Justice Statistics, April 2014.

United Nations. "Human rights: Women and violence fact sheet." United Nations Department of Public Information (DPI/1772/HR), February 1996.

United Nations. "Review and appraisal of the implementation of the Beijing Platform for Action: Report of the Secretary-General." United Nations Department of Public Information (E/CN.6/2000/PC/2), May 2000.

United Nations, Division for the Advancement of Women. "Online Updates for the Convention on the Elimination of All Forms of Discrimination Against Women (CEDAW)," June 2006. www.un.org/womenwatch.

United Nations Children's Fund (UNICEF). "Ending Child Marriage: Progress and prospects." New York: UNICEF, 2014.

United Nations Children's Fund (UNICEF). *Female Genital Mutilation/Cutting: A Global Concern.* New York: UNICEF, 2016.

United Nations Population Fund (UNFPA). "Ending violence against women and girls." State of the World Population, 2000.

United Nations Population Fund (UNFPA). "Gender-biased sex selection," July 29, 2016.

U.S. Census Bureau. *Profile of General Demographic Characteristics: 2000.* Washington, DC: U.S. Census Bureau, 2000.

U.S. Census Bureau. *Statistical Abstract of the United States: 2001. The National Data Book.* Washington, DC: U.S. Census Bureau, 2001.

U.S. Census Bureau. *Quick Facts.* Washington, DC: U.S. Census Bureau, July 2, 2017.

U.S. Department of Agriculture (USDA). *Access to Affordable and Nutritious Food: Measuring and Understanding Food Deserts and Their Consequences,* June 2009. Accessed March 5, 2018.

U.S. Department of Education. *Trends in Educational Equity of Girls and Women,* June 2000.

U.S. Department of Labor, Bureau of Labor Statistics. *November 2004 National Occupational Employment and Wage Estimates, Building and Grounds Cleaning and Maintenance Occupations.* Accessed May 19, 2006. www.bls.gov/oes/current/oes_37bu.htm.

U.S. Department of Labor, Bureau of Labor Statistics. *Occupational Outlook Handbook, 2006–07 Edition, Automotive Service Technicians and Mechanics.* Accessed May 19, 2006. http://www.bls.gov/oco/ocos181.htm.

U.S. Department of Labor, Bureau of Labor Statistics. *Occupational Outlook Handbook, 2006–07 Edition, Child Care Workers.* Accessed May 19, 2006. http://www.bls.gov/oco/ocos170.htm.

U.S. Department of Labor, Bureau of Labor Statistics, Women's Bureau. "20 leading occupations of employed women full-time wage and salary workers, 2004 annual averages." Washington, DC: 2004.

U.S. Equal Employment Opportunity Commission (EEOC). "Testimony of Fatima Goss Graves, Vice President for Education and Employment National Women's Law

Center," January 14, 2015. Accessed August 17, 2016. https://www.eeoc.gov/eeoc/meetings/1-14-15/graves.cfm.

Vaid, Urvashi. "Linking arms and movements: Lesbian rights summit of the National Organization for Women, April 23–25 in Washington, DC, 1999." *Advocate*, June 8, 1999, p. 88.

Valdivieso, Veronica. "DNA warrants: A panacea for old, cold rape cases?" *Georgetown Law Journal*, Vol. 90 (2002): 1009–1053.

Wagner, Sally Roesch. *Sisters in Spirit: Iroquois Influence on Early Feminists*. Summertown, TN: Native Voices, 2001.

Warner, Judith, and Danielle Corley. "The Women's Leadership Gap." Center for American Progress, May 21, 2017.

Waxman, Henry. *The Content of Federally Funded Abstinence-Only Education Programs*. U.S. House of Representatives Committee on Government Reform; Minority Staff, Special Investigations Division, December 2004.

Wemple, Erik. "*CNN* is getting hammered for Steubenville coverage." *Washington Post*, March 18, 2013. Accessed December 15, 2016.

West, Stanley, and Paula Dranov. *The Hysterectomy Hoax: The Truth About Why Many Hysterectomies Are Unnecessary and How to Avoid Them*. Chester, NJ: Next Decade, 2002.

Westervelt, Amy. "The medical research gender gap: how excluding women from clinical trials is hurting our health." *Guardian*, April 30, 2015. Accessed April 9, 2017.

White, Emily. *Fast Girls: Teenage Tribes and the Myth of the Slut*. New York: Scribner, 2002.

Whiteman, Honor. "Almost 1 in 5 hysterectomies are 'unnecessary,' study finds." *Medical News Today*, January 11, 2015. Accessed April 9, 2017.

Wolpert, Stuart. "Dieting does not work, UCLA researchers report." *UCLA Newsroom*, April 3, 2007. Accessed March 5, 2018.

Women's Sports Foundation. "Pay Inequity in Athletics." East Meadow, NY: Women's Sports Foundation, July 20, 2015.

Women's Sports Foundation. "Sport and Teen Pregnancy." East Meadow, NY: Women's Sports Foundation, 1998.

Women's Sports Foundation. "The Women's Sports Foundation Report Brief: Her Life Depends On It III & Collegiate Coaching and Athletic Administration." East Meadow, NY: Women's Sports Foundation, November 2017.

Women's Sports Foundation. "Title IX and race in intercollegiate sport." East Meadow, NY: Women's Sports Foundation, 2003.

Woodworth, Terrance. "DEA Congressional Testimony before the House Commerce Committee Subcommittee on Oversight and Investigation," March 11, 1999.

World Health Organization. "Female Genital Mutilation: Integrating the Prevention and the Management of the Health Complications into the Curricula of Nursing and Midwifery." *Policy Guidelines for Nurses and Midwives*. New York: World Health Organization, 2001.

World Health Organization. *Maternal Death Fact Sheet,* updated November 2016.

World Health Organization. "Sexual violence fact sheet." New York: World Health Organization, 2002.

World Health Organization. *WHO: Addressing Violence Against Women: Key Achievements and Priorities.* New York: World Health Organization, 2018.

Zimmerman, Jean, and Gil Reavill. *Raising Our Athletic Daughters: How Sports Can Build Self-Esteem and Save Girls' Lives.* New York: Main Street Books, 1998.

INDEX

Abortion: access, 44, 193; anti-choice activity, 192, 194, 205, 209, 214–215; courts, 193–194, 210–213; demographics, 198–199; fake clinics/crisis pregnancy centers, 202–204; global gag rule (Mexico City Policy), 194–195; *Gonzales v. Carhart*, 209, 213; history, 204–208; language, 208–209, 214–215; legality, 207–208; myths of, 198; *National Institute of Family and Life Advocates v. Becerra*, 203–204, 213; *Planned Parenthood v. American Coalition of Life Activists*, 194; politics of, 196, 215; Reproductive Fact Act, 203; *Roe v Wade*, 41, 53, 182, 207–209, 211–212; safety of abortion, 200, 208; womanhood vs. "fetushood," 194, 208–210; violence and harassment, 193–194, 214–215; why women have abortions, 197–198; young women and abortion, 201–202. *See also* Reproductive health

Activism, ix–x, 17–22, anti-violence, 257–261; building an activist kit, 283; definition of, 18; in daily life, 29–31; guidelines, 22; how to be an ally, 22–23; March for Women's Lives, 21, 46; and self-care, 31; steps to taking action, 23–26; timeline and checklist, 279–281; types of actions to take, 17, 19–22; Women's March, 21–22, 47, 74–75, 195

Adams, Abigail, 35, 114, 270

Anorexia. *See* Eating disorders

Anthony, Susan B., 36, 37, 50, 116

Aptheker, Bettina, x, 149

Asexual, definition of, 7

Bacon, Linda, *Health at Every Size*, 165

Baldwin, Tammy, 120

Baumgardner, Jennifer, 46, 127

Black Lives Matter, 68, 79, 87, 110; founders Patrisse Cullors, Alicia Garza, Opal Tometi, 46, 87, 273

Body Dysmorphic Disorder. *See* Eating disorders

Body Image: activism, 174–175; advertising and media influence, 157–158; changing the image, 156, 164–166, 173–174; corsets, 152; dieting, 158–160, 165; history of, 152–154; Hollywood, 154, 156; plastic surgery, 152, 160–162; power, 152, 155; race/racism, 152–153; radical self love, 166; sports and Title IX, 154; weight loss surgery, 162; young women, 160–161

Bornstein, Kate, 103

Bulimia. *See* Eating disorders

CEDAW, 64–65, 68, 122, 141, 148, 258, 261, 296n9; definition of, 65

Chesler, Phyllis, 61–62, 274

Clinton, Hillary Rodham, 11, 47, 122, 269

Consciousness raising, 75

Daughters of Bilitis, 39, 271; Del Martin and Phyllis Lyon, 39, 94, 271

Davids, Sharice, 87, 273

ABOUT THE AUTHOR

Megan Seely is a feminist and activist. She was the youngest person ever elected president of the California National Organization for Women and served two terms, from 2001 to 2005. She serves on the Board of Directors for the Feminist Women's Health Centers in Northern California. An activist from a very young age, she has been involved in community organizing, protests, marches, street theater, hunger strikes, rallies, and campaigns on the local, state, and national levels. She is Professor of Sociology, Women and Gender Studies, and Social Justice Studies. She is raising two daughters, lives, and teaches in northern California. You can follow her on Twitter @meganseely.